Living Control Systems Publishing
Menlo Park, CA
www.livingcontrolsystems.com

The Death of Jeffrey Stapleton

of Jeffrey

Stapleton

Exploring the Way
Lawyers Think

Hugh Gibbons

Living Control Systems Publishing
Menlo Park, CA

First used in 1990 as course literature at Franklin Pierce Law Center, now the New Hampshire School of Law, University of New Hampshire. This 2013 edition revised and expanded.

Line drawings by Jean Bidwell
Cover photo by Adam Hunger/Reuters

Library of Congress Control Number: 2012941603

Publishers Cataloging in Publication
Gibbons, Hugh 1939 –
      The death of Jeffrey Stapleton :
      Exploring the way lawyers think
      xiv, 218 p. : ill. ; 28 cm.

      978-1-938090-08-0 (softcover, perfect binding)
      978-1-938090-09-7 (hardcover, case binding)

      1. Legal Theory. 2. Law.
      3. Control theory. I. Title.
      II. Title: Exploring the way lawyers think

BC151.G52 2013

This book

The Death of Jeffrey Stapleton
Exploring the Way Lawyers Think

is available as a free PDF download from the publisher's website, www.livingcontrolsystems.com, as well as the free online libraries www.archive.org and www.z-lib.org, which will help ensure that this book and others on the subject of *Perceptual Control Theory, PCT,* will be available to students for many decades to come.

File name: ExploringHowLawyersThinkGibbons2013.pdf

The file is password protected. Changes are not allowed. Printing at high resolution and content copying are allowed. Before you print, check the modest price from your favorite Internet bookstore.

For related books and papers, search *Perceptual Control Theory*

For drop ship volume orders, mix and match, contact the publisher.

For biographical information about Hugh Gibbons, see the publisher's website.

Minor updates and this note added in 2020.

Contents

Publisher's note

What makes this work unique are the explanations embodied in Part II, all based on a new concept of how all living organisms work. Here is some background.

A revolution in the engineering sciences

In 1927, Harold Stephen Black, an American electrical engineer, revolutionized the field of applied electronics by inventing the negative feedback amplifier, a control device. To some, his invention is considered the most important breakthrough of the twentieth century in the field of electronics, since it has a wide area of application.[1]

Today, we are surrounded by control devices, doing work humans used to perform. One application most everyone is familiar with is the cruise control in your car. Here, instead of the driver monitoring the speed of the car and stepping on the gas as needed, a negative feedback control circuit senses the speed, compares it to the speed set by the driver, then steps on the gas, as needed.

While engineers understand how control works and now build capable robots, most lay people and psychologists, while they may have a very general sense that we control, do not yet understand this very simple phenomenon.

A revolution under way in psychology and social sciences

Understanding the process of control provides an explanation for the way living organisms behave, what behavior is, how it works, and what it accomplishes. This idea has been developed by William T. Powers in great detail for 60 years. Powers' work, which applies the theory of control to the field of psychology, is now called Perceptual Control Theory, PCT. It lays a foundation for psychology to become a natural science rather than merely an art.

This has profound implications for litigation where psychology is involved.

The insight PCT offers can be applied in many different fields to great advantage. One field is law. Others are represented in Recommended Reading, page 211.

What does this have to do with a book on how lawyers think?

Lawyers recognize that intention is very important. People are responsible for their actions because their actions are purposeful. PCT explains how purpose works. Purposeful behavior is control.

---

1 For more, see http://en.wikipedia.org/wiki/Harold_Stephen_Black.

Hugh Gibbons was teaching law and economics in Evanston, Illinois in 1973 when Aldine published William T. Powers' seminal work *Behavior: The Control of Perception*.[2] Because Powers had contacts in Evanston, Gibbons learned of this work right away. He read it and realized that it refutes contemporary psychology and its methods—which have been of very limited use for understanding law or for resolving legal conflicts.[3]

Working alone, Gibbons' first interpretation of PCT and its application to law came in 1984: *Justifying Law: An Explanation of the Deep Structure of American Law*, Law and Philosophy, Vol. 3, No. 2, pp. 165-279.

Gibbons proceeded to develop course literature to teach new students how to understand law using the principles of PCT. This took the form of *The Death of Jeffrey Stapleton*, with the final version ready by 1990. As you can see in this work, PCT explains motivation in a way that makes sense to lawyers.

But professor Gibbons did not stop there. Through the 1990s and early 2000s he kept thinking about PCT and the basics of law. He proceeded to develop *Rights and Wrongs: The Tangled Twins of American Law* (2001). A multimedia program on CD-ROM, this has been converted to a series of videos, posted at biologyoflaw.org under STORY.

Gibbons followed up with *The Biological Basis of Human Rights*, presented at the 4th Annual Scholarship Conference of the Society for Evolutionary Analysis in Law, 2002. Published by the Boston University Public Interest Law Journal, Vol 13, Number 1 (Fall 2003).

Finally, before he retired in 2005, Gibbons created the website *BiologyOfLaw*. Once abandoned, this has now been substantially restored: www.biologyoflaw.org.

Papers mentioned above are available at that site. Enjoy!

Dag Forssell
Hayward, CA

2 See p. 214 for Powers' seminal work, *Behavior: The Control of Perception*
3 The experimental method widely used in psychology was borrowed without change from the method used in the physical sciences. In physics and engineering the study of inanimate objects and processes with linear cause-effect relationships between two variables are the rule and the method appropriate. Without change, this experimental method fails to provide for the fact that organisms are living (animate) control systems where circular, interactive relationships between multiple variables are the rule. As a result, a huge body of observations in psychology (much now embedded in our culture) reflect the properties of various experimental setups, not the organisms purportedly studied.

Preface

Introduction to the 2013 edition

Law is the institution that is based upon the assumption that human beings are responsible for their own behavior and the effect of their behavior on others. Perceptual Control Theory, PCT, is the science that explains what behavior is and how it works. The relationship between law and PCT is that simple.

In this volume I will use a tragedy—the death of a musical prodigy at the hands of a reckless driver—to explore the way our minds work when we "think legally." All of us think legally many times each day, often so automatically that we are largely unaware of it: Who was responsible for the breakup of a family, the collapse of a corporation, the failure to investigate a crime? When is it permissible to use force, to lie to achieve our ends, to take credit for another's work, to download something from the internet without permission? These questions roll through our minds with little effort, and the answers to them shape how we think about our behavior.

To get a sense of our thinking, I will slow it down, hopefully not to the point of tedium. From four decades of teaching law to students from a great many other countries, as well as my own, I'm quite confident that our thinking will be very similar regardless of where we've come from. When we've resolved the case, I will turn to PCT for a theoretical account of our thinking, which I will present in words and diagrams.

Let me give a quick illustration. One of the classic mysteries of law is the fact that it requires jurors and judges to make an assessment of the inner state of the defendant's mind: How on earth is one person ever to know what's going on in another's mind? Every interesting legal question requires us to do that. Consider the firefighter who is crushed by a person falling out of a building. The firefighter's estate might bring suit against the estate of the falling man, which instantly raises a question about why the man fell. Did he leap to his death to commit suicide, failing to check out the area where his body would land? Or was the building on fire and he leaped out in a desperate attempt to avoid the heat? Or was he thrown off the roof of the building by someone who intended him ill? Or was there a longstanding conflict between him and the firefighter?

The answer to those questions will let the jury determine the mental state of the defendant. The jury will have no way to determine it with certainty, but certainty is not required. They will debate the issue, reevaluate the evidence, and finally get "comfortable" with one assessment of the defendant's inner state or another. In a truly difficult case, there may not be enough evidence to allow them to get comfortable with any assessment, but those are rare.

Perceptual Control Theory gives us a framework for explaining where purposive behavior comes from (for example, from a desire to enter a world in which there is no fire at one's back), thereby explaining the way that law works. PCT explains a lot more, from the mechanics of controlling an automobile to understanding what happens to a person whose purposive powers have disintegrated due to an addiction. Here, we will satisfy ourselves with an understanding of the way we think through a legal problem.

Hugh Gibbons, J.D.
Professor of Law Emeritus
New Hampshire School of Law,
University of New Hampshire

PART I

ANALYZING THE CASE

CHAPTER ONE

Jeffrey's death

A tall, slender woman enters our office with a piece of paper clutched in her hand. Wordlessly, she hands us the paper, which is part of the front page of the local newspaper.

LEXINGTON. August 9.

Jeffrey Stapleton, famed seven-year-old piano prodigy, was pronounced Dead on Arrival yesterday at Lexington Hospital at 3:00PM.

From her appearance, this woman has a problem. Her name is Margaret Stapleton. It would appear that she is the mother of Jeffrey Stapleton. She has a problem, but it is not at all clear that from what we know at this instant that it is a legal problem. Thousands of people die each day. Some of those deaths are a welcome relief, some are tragedies. Very few of them generate legal problems. Standing alone, Jeffrey's death has no legal significance. Before we know whether or not there is a legal problem, we need to read further in the story.

Dr. Michelle Wesley stated that Stapleton appears to have succumbed to a viral infection contracted on a recent concert tour of Asia.

Dr. Wesley's statement clearly creates a *medical* question: How is it that a healthy seven-year-old dies as a result of a viral infection? But is there a *legal* problem lurking here somewhere?

What does it take to create a legal problem? Viruses create medical problems. It takes people to create legal problems. Might there be a person lurking in this story, perhaps a doctor who failed to treat Jeffrey's disease correctly? If so, we would have the beginning of a legal problem.

We need not look further in that direction, however, for we have misread the newspaper article. This is what the article actually says:

> Dr. Michelle Wesley stated that Stapleton succumbed
> to a massive head injury which apparently resulted from
> an impact with an automobile.

Now we do have a legal problem, for we have another person in the story—the driver of the car—who was the cause of the tragedy. Why is it that the death of one person, caused by another, creates a *legal* problem? What is it about viruses that makes them a problem for doctors, while car drivers are a problem for lawyers?

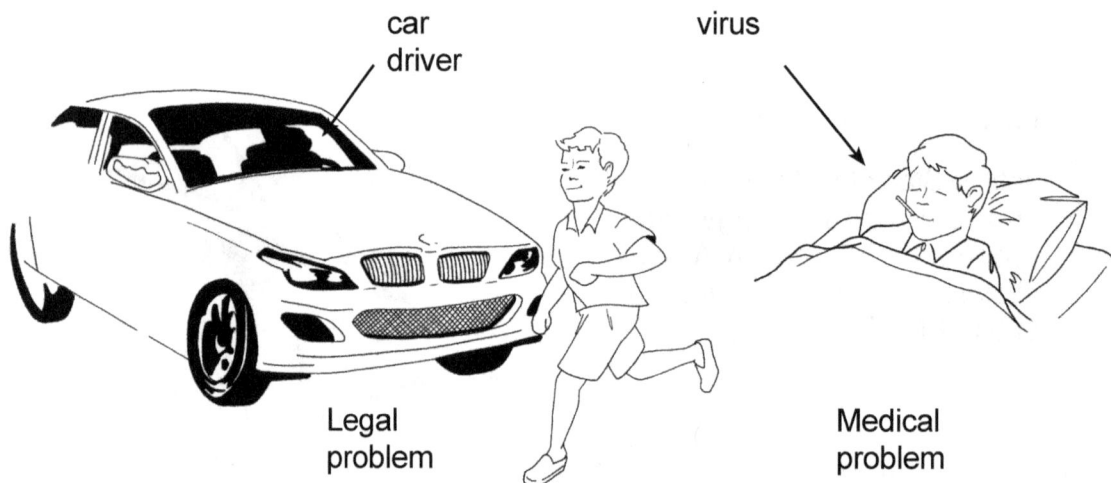

Figure 1.1   The difference between a medical and a legal problem.

Viruses don't make choices. They aren't *responsible* for the disease they cause, for they don't choose to cause disease any more than a boulder rolling down hill chooses to destroy that which is in its path. Boulders and viruses simply obey the laws of physics.

People do make choices. That fact is the fulcrum of law, the reason that there is law. Law exists to guide and limit the choices that we make. The driver of the car that hit Jeffrey made some choices. If those choices are in any way the cause of Jeffrey's death, the driver must explain himself. If, on the other hand, the brakes of the car failed unpredictably, it will be the automobile manufacturer who will be held to account.

A legal problem is a state of mind that arises from the perception that the actions of one person have caused misfortune to another. The "state of mind" that I refer to is the state that your mind should be in at this moment relative to Jeffrey Stapleton. Jeffrey's death was apparently caused by the driver of a car. That demands an explanation.

Detecting conflict

Before we look more deeply into Jeffrey's case, I want to look more deeply into your present state of mind, which should be in a state of *tension*. Where did the accident happen? Who was driving the car? Was Jeffrey in plain sight when he was hit? What were the driving conditions?

If you cannot feel that tension, reread the newspaper account and write out a list of questions about the case that you would like to have answered. Those questions are the conscious outcroppings of the tension to which I refer. Until those questions are answered, the tension of the case will remain. They will drive your thought, forcing you to keep searching until you have resolved the tension in your mind.

Tension is the engine that drives legal thought. But what gets legal thought started? No one, not even a lawyer, could stand being in a state of mental tension about everything. What does it take to get the legal thought process going?

Human beings appear to have a conflict detector. I first became conscious of the existence of such a detector while watching an early Super Bowl game with a group of friends. A running back broke into the open. The free safety, coming at him from across field, launched himself head first into the running back in a move that is today called "spearing." The running back crumpled as if hit by a sledgehammer, to the general delight of the group watching the game. One member of the group, a lawyer, was outraged by it. She felt that the act was ... what? ... "too much," "outrageous," "unfair." She had trouble explaining exactly what she meant, but she clearly felt that the free safety had acted outside the rules of the game and had done something that he should account for.

At the time, I wondered what the lawyer was thinking. Didn't she ever relax? But then it struck me that she had some kind of detector, some kind of mental process that enabled her to see what for the rest of us was hidden in the excitement of the game. As she talked to us about the event, we began to feel what she felt.

I imagine that the conflict detector acts something like this:

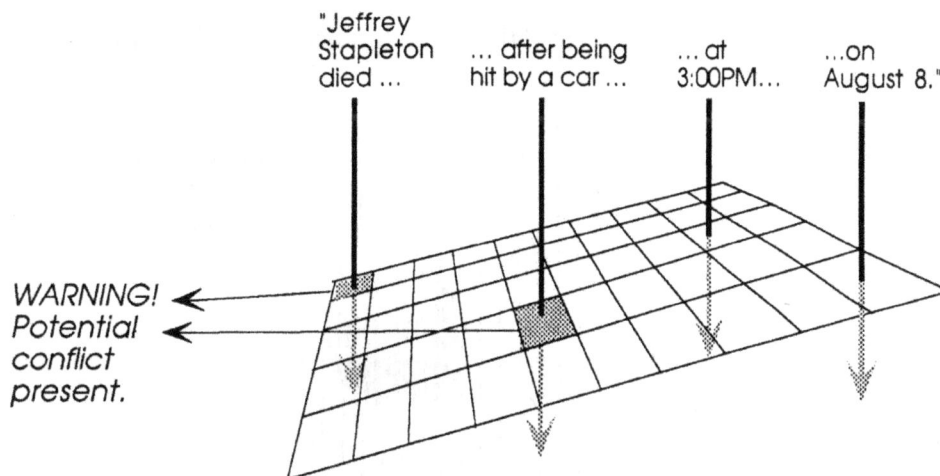

Figure 1.2   The conflict detector.

Perceptions, like the sight of the Super Bowl game or the facts of Jeffrey's case, are subconsciously passed through some kind of detector. Most perceptions pass through it without effect, like the date and time of Jeffrey's death in the example illustrated in Figure 1.2. They are of no significance. But the fact that Jeffrey died, in conjunction with the fact that it was caused by an automobile, cause the detector to go off.

There is nothing particularly legal about the conflict detector. It seems to be a part of a general ability possessed by humans and other animals to detect threats. An eight month old infant, who is just learning to crawl, will not crawl off the edge of a table. The infant has an ability to recognize edges and height, and it somehow has the sense to spot the two as a danger and to avoid it. An infant can also detect conflict in the voices and actions of the people around it. A nasty argument in the family will quicken the infant's pulse just as quickly as it raises the pulse rate of the ones who are arguing.

The ability to detect conflict seems to be an innate sense, though in reaching that conclusion I am perhaps too strongly influenced by my cats. When they were only weeks old, both of them could spot a dog at an amazing distance and take evasive action. One would simply hide, which is understandable. The other was more interesting, for he was able to tell instantly whether the dog was a threat or not. Many times my heart was in my mouth as I watched a dog spot my cat trotting across the yard and take off after him, only to pull up short and go through the contortions that dogs go through when they want to be friends. Let a truly aggressive dog come near the house, however, and this cat disappeared from sight, even before the dog was out of its owner's car.

This cat somehow has an advanced ability to detect future conflict. Were he a lawyer, he would clearly have no trouble determining that the circumstances surrounding Jeffrey Stapleton's death merit further inquiry.

Identifying legally significant conflicts

The lawyer's sense of conflict must be honed to a sharp edge, for the lawyer is concerned with only a small percentage of the actual conflicts in a society. Most conflict, thankfully, is not legally significant.

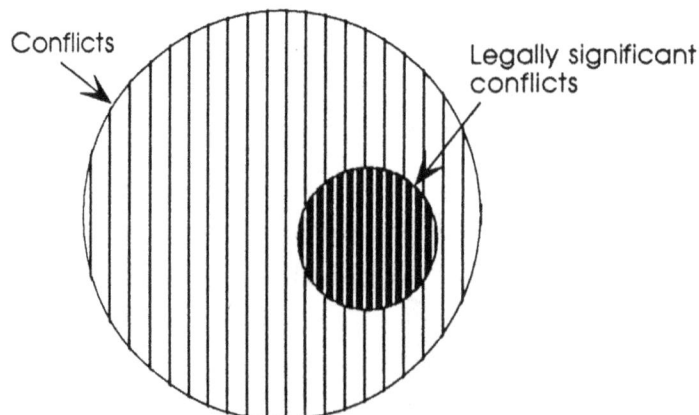

Figure 1.3   Courts will entertain only a small portion of
              the conflicts that occur in society.

The law distinguishes the conflicts that it will consider from those that it will not consider by defining the set of conflicts that are *actionable*. The term "actionable" refers to a "cause of action:" A conflict is actionable if a court will entertain a cause of action by one party to the conflict. A "cause of action," in everyday parlance, is a law suit in *civil court* in which one party seeks to recover money damages from another. The law will entertain a lawsuit for only a small percentage of the conflicts that happen every day.

A prime class of conflicts that are not actionable are conflicts over ideas, such as the bitter disputes that sometimes take place between academics or members of different religious groups. Those conflicts can get very serious, dominating or even destroying the lives of the combatants. Yet courts will not listen to them, unless they result in acts of physical violence or in an untruth that destroys someone's reputation. Why is it that if your reputation is destroyed by a truthful statement the law will not allow your action against the one who made the statement, but if it is destroyed by an untruth, it will?

Distinguishing legally significant conflicts from those that are not actionable is crucial to the success of the lawyer. A lawyer who spends time pursuing conflicts that are not actionable is unlikely to make a living. The next step in our exploration of Jeff Stapleton's case is to determine whether his case is actionable.

Before we do that, however, I want to ask what happens if the lawyer has a clear conflict that courts do not consider actionable. Recall the example above of the lawyer who felt that the safety who speared the running back in the Super Bowl had done something that should be actionable in a court of law. No court at that time recognized a cause of action for anything that happened during a football game. That situation could be represented in this way:

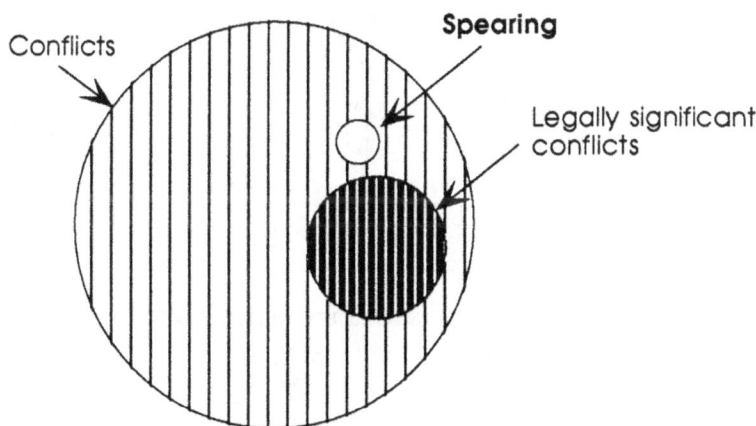

Figure 1.4 Spearing lay outside of the set of conflicts that a court would consider.

While spearing lay outside of those conflicts that a court would recognize, the lawyer felt that it was similar enough to cases that courts do recognize that. if she had the running back as a client, it would be worth bringing a law suit in an attempt to get the court to consider it. Courts are creative in that way. They will consider cases that they had previously rejected, if the lawyer can convince the court that the case is covered by principles that the court has previously recognized.

Courts have long recognized a cause of action for *battery* by a person who is intentionally injured by another. If my friend could convince the court that spearing is a battery, the court might expand the terrain of conflicts that it would listen to. But football is a willing act—the players subject themselves to being battered. A court will not entertain an action in battery by a person who subjects himself to battery. Case closed? Not for this lawyer, for she felt that spearing lay outside of the type of battering that football players willingly subject themselves to, since spearing is contrary to the rules of the game. Courts had been reluctant to enter onto the playing field to make fine distinctions between behavior that was legitimate in the game and that which is gratuitously injurious.

Later events proved that that situation was not permanent. Courts will now consider cases arising out of injuries in sporting events. That can be visualized in this way:

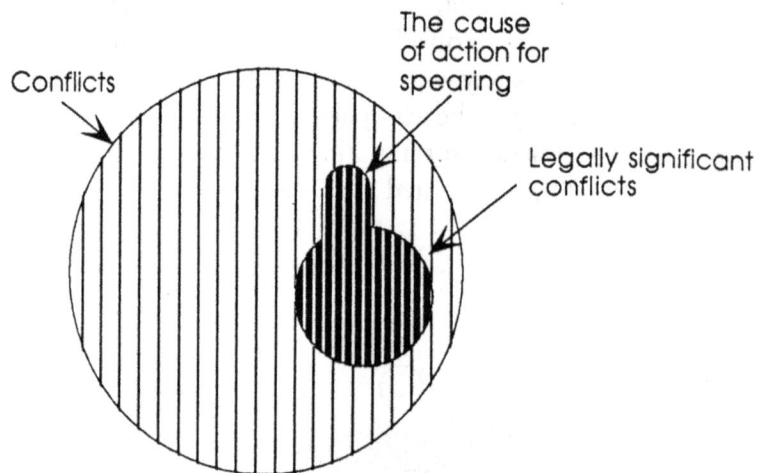

Figure 1.5   A court may entertain a case that it had never before considered, thereby expanding the terrain of legally significant conflicts.

That is one way in which the law expands. The period since World War II has been one of rapid expansion in the terrain of conflicts that the law will examine. Where once, for example, a woman who was the victim of sexual harassment had simply to bear it, today she may invoke a court to resolve that conflict. The same is now true for behavior during sporting events that goes beyond the accepted standards of the game.

Pursuing a case that is not presently actionable in law requires great determination, for the law is a conservative institution that undertakes change grudgingly. As we pursue Jeffrey Stapleton's case, we will hope to discover that it is covered by existing law. We will be looking for facts that place it squarely within the territory of legally significant conflicts. If we are unable to do that, but we feel that an injustice has nonetheless been done, we will be forced to ask ourselves whether we have the determination to nonetheless pursue the case in law. That is a situation that we would rather not be in, so we will try hard to place his case within the existing law.

CHAPTER TWO

Building the case

This is a copy of the accident report filed by Officer Kathleen McGinty of the Lexington Police Department that we got after assuring Margaret Stapleton that we would look into the case.

TOWN OF LEXINGTON
REPORT OF MOTOR VEHICLE ACCIDENT

DATE OF ACCIDENT	DAY OF THE WEEK	HOUR	NAME OF INVESTIGATING OFFICER	NUMBER OF VEHICLES INVOLVED
8 Aug. 90	Tuesday	2:35PM	Kathleen McGinty	1

VEHICLE 1

NAME OF OPERATOR				DRIVERS LICENSE NUMBER
Not known (hit and run)				Not known

NAME OF OWNER	MAKE	YEAR	COLOR	REGISTRATION NUMBER
John Newland	Ford	1986	Gray	LK1072

ADDRESS OF OWNER	DAMAGE TO VEHICLE
1284 Beacon Hill Rd., Lexington	Slight damage to right front fender

INJURED 1

NAME OF INJURED			SEVERITY OF INJURY
Jeffrey Stapleton			Expired

ADDRESS OF INJURED	SEX	AGE	STATUS
1800 Bridge St., Apt. 10, Ashville	M	7	Pedestrian

CAUSE OF DEATH	TREATING PHYSICIAN
Massive subdural hematoma	Dr. Michelle Wesley

Point of impact, 20' west of State, 14' from curb.

N

State Street

Purley Street

Vehicle 1 eastbound in lane struck Injured 1, who was apparently sitting in the roadway next to a parked car on the south side of the street, with its right front fender. Skid marks indicate that driver saw Injured 1 and swerved to avoid him 35' before impact with right side of front fender. Driver left the scene of the accident and has not been identified. Vehicle 1 reported stolen by owner at 4:45PM. Vehicle 1 recovered by Brewster police, 10:15PM, 8 August.

The report indicates that Jeffrey was sitting in the road when he was hit by a stolen car driven by an unidentified hit and run driver,. That is not a promising start to the case. If we cannot find the driver of the car, Jeffrey's death may prove to be a conflict that has no resolution. Before we give up, however, we must see what we can make of the accident report. As we do that, we must reflect upon what it is that is going on in our minds as we do it, for, as mundane as it appears to be, the process of finding the "facts" of a case is very complex.

Facts

A "fact" is a statement about the world—it may be a verbal statement or a picture or a numerical representation—that can, at least in principle, be empirically verified. The accident report is full of facts. The name of the investigating officer, for example, is stated to be "Kathleen McGinty." We could verify that easily enough by making an appointment with Kathleen McGinty and asking her if she truly was the investigating officer in this case.

Most of the statements in the report are simple *reports* of a relationship or event. A report is a representation that is made without interpretation. The registration number of the vehicle, for example, is given as "LK1072." That number should be in one-to-one correspondence with the number on the license plate of the car that hit Jeffrey.

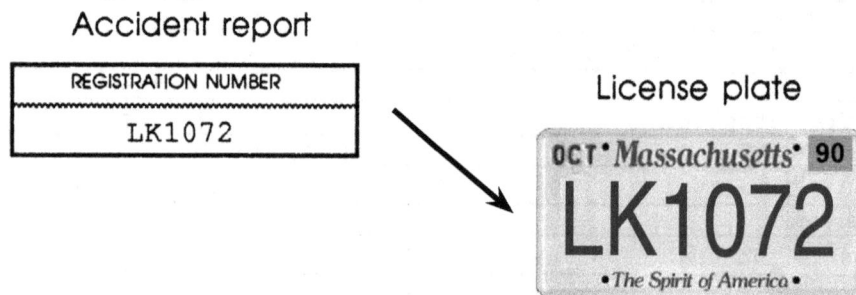

Figure 2.1   The correspondence between a "fact" and
              the reality that the fact corresponds to.

The statement is true if an examination of the car reveals a license plate with the corresponding number and the state's records indicate that the car and the license plate go together. That examination is an "empirical" validation of the fact. To count as an empirical validation, the relationship between the reality and the statement about the reality must be observable by anyone who cares to look. If only Officer McGinty, for instance, saw the number as "LK1072," while everyone else saw 1K1072," her report would not pass empirical muster. It would be false, no matter how fervently she believes it.

It is important to notice that even the barest fact requires an exercise in human judgment.

The empirical test of Officer McGinty's report of the license number rests upon the observations that others make about the relationship between the license plate and her statement of the number. The test of its truth, in other words, lies in what *others* think is true, based upon their observations. If, in their judgment, her number is inaccurate, it *is* inaccurate.

I make such heavy going of this because an attitude of radical skepticism about facts is essential to legal thinking. In everyday life we take most of the statements that we hear to be true, without conscious reflection. To question them all would be unbearably tedious. But that may breed a confusion between what exists and what some person thinks exists. From the accident report we can determine that Officer McGinty *thinks* that the license number of the car was LK1072, but we are seriously confused if we think that her statement *makes* it true.

A lawyer must question every statement, for all statements are ultimately based upon the judgment of a person. That judgment may be wrong, or it may be corrupt. Officer McGinty may have falsified the license number of the car to cover up for a friend who was the driver of the car. If it is important to the case, the lawyer will question the accuracy of any fact, however obviously true and however irritating that questioning may be to the one who made the statement.

Most of the statements made in the accident report are, like the auto registration number, naked reports—statements that bear a direct correspondence to the reality that they describe. These are the "hard facts" of the case, the statements whose truth can be directly tested by empirical observation. We should, for example, be able to confirm by direct observation that John Newland is the registered owner of the car, that he reported it stolen at 4:45 PM on the day of the accident, and that he lives at 1284 Beacon Hill Road in Lexington.

Although the accident report does not contain any statements that are obviously nonsensical, there are a few that raise interesting questions. How is it, for example, that Jeffrey Stapleton, who lived in the town of Ashville, wound up on a street in Lexington? Unless his home in Ashville and the location of the accident are very close to each other, it is unlikely that he got there under his own steam. How did he get there? A call to Officer McGinty yields the following:

> Ashville is 65 miles from Lexington. Jeffrey was driven to Lexington by his mother, Margaret, who was visiting a friend, Emily Paul. Emily lives at 202 Purley Street, which is on the northwest corner of Purley and State Streets. Margaret was at the scene of the accident when Officer McGinty arrived and was taken to the Lexington Hospital, where she was sedated.

Those statements bear further inquiry, but first we will look further into the accident report.

Inferences

In the accident report Officer McGinty described how John Newland's 1986 Ford struck Jeffrey. She was not present at the scene of the accident. How could she make such a statement? The car itself was not present at the scene of the accident. It was picked up as an abandoned car at 10:15 that night by the police in the town of Brewster. What suggests that this was the car that hit Jeffrey?

According to Officer McGinty, her version of the accident was based upon the following:

> After Jeffrey Stapleton was declared Dead on Arrival, Dr. Wesley removed some flecks of paint from his head and right shoulder. In her opinion, death had been caused by an impact with a car, an opinion that was supported by an examination of the scene of the accident, which showed skid marks leading up to Jeffrey's body.
>
> The color of the paint flecks was identified in the police lab and a report was issued to neighboring police departments to look for a gray car that showed evidence of a collision with a person.
>
> Newland's 1986 Ford was recovered from the Brewster police and its paint matched to the flecks of paint removed from Jeffrey.
>
> The Ford had a dent of about 130 square inches immediately behind the right front wheel well of the car, about 20 inches above the ground. Paint taken from the car at that point matched that found on Jeffrey's body.

Officer McGinty's reconstruction of the accident is based upon the hard facts that were available to her when she made the report. From the correspondence between the paint on the car and the flecks found on Jeffrey she inferred that this was the car that struck him.

Notice that the statement in the accident report that, "Vehicle 1 struck Jeffrey." is not a fact in the same sense as the hard facts that we considered above. It cannot be empirically verified in the same way that they could be. The problem lies in the word, "struck." No one was present when Jeffrey was hit, so there is no one to make a direct representation of what happened. Who "struck" whom is irretrievably lost in the past. To reconstruct it we must *infer* what happened.

Fact: The paint on Jeffrey's head matched
the paint on John Newland's 1986 Ford.

↓

Inference: John Newland's car struck Jeffrey

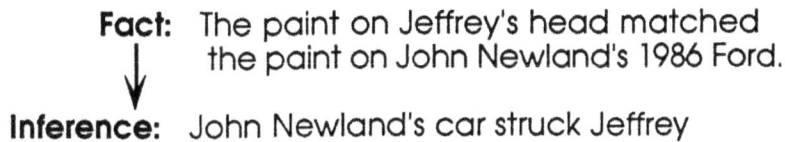

Figure 2.2   Drawing an inference from a fact.

We cannot test inferences against any particular reality, as we can with factual statements. We must test inferences against reason and experience, in the light of the *context* of the event. Here, Jeffrey's body was found in Purley Street, his head crushed by a heavy blow. Skid marks thirty-five feet long were found on the street to the left of his body. We suspect that he was hit by a car, so the inference is consistent with our suspicions.

Confirming the inference, it would be hard to imagine how the type of paint on the Newland car could have gotten onto Jeffrey in any other way. It is simply counterintuitive and contrary to our experience to think that someone scraped the paint from the car and sprinkled it on Jeffrey's head, or that Jeffrey was hit by another car with identical paint. Those possibilities are not utterly impossible, but they are so unlikely that, in the absence of facts that directly oppose the inference, we can disregard them.

What do we do with the uncertainty that arises from an inference? Notice that we have accepted the inference that Newland's car struck Jeffrey without an exhaustive search for alternative explanations. It may be that the scientific literature, if we read it, reveals numerous examples of chance migrations of automobile paint. We are not interested. Our job as lawyers is not to make a study of paint migration but to understand how Jeffrey died. We are after a *satisfying* explanation of the facts, one that reduces the tension that we feel from the unanswered questions that we have about the case.

This is not a very satisfying explanation of inferences, at least not to those who, like me, have been hoping to be able to teach a computer how to make an inference. Computers don't feel, and I have suggested that the test of an inference lies in the feeling of satisfaction—tension reduction—that it brings. Computers can determine whether an inference follows logically from its premises. We could, for example, program a computer to determine whether or not the following inference is true or not:

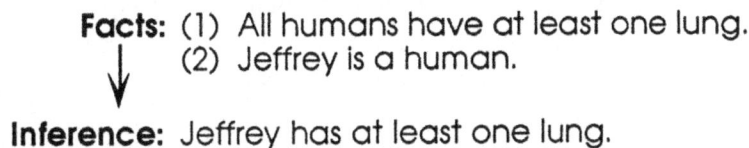

Facts: (1) All humans have at least one lung.
(2) Jeffrey is a human.

↓

Inference: Jeffrey has at least one lung.

Figure 2.3   An inference that a computer could make.

The inference that, "Jeffrey has at least one lung." follows logically from the two given facts. If they are true, the inference must be true. Were all inferences of that sort, we could train computers to make them and go on to more interesting things. In law, however, virtually none of the inferences that are significant are like that. It is extremely rare, for example, to be able to state a fact like, "All humans have at least one lung."

Facts in the real world are usually a mess, like the ones surrounding Jeffrey's death. Is it possible that the skid marks to the left of Jeffrey's body were there before his death and had nothing to do with it? Sure. Is it possible that someone crushed Jeffrey's skull, then doctored up the body and the car to make it look like an accident? Perhaps. Is it true that every time paint flecks from a car are found on a person. they got there because a car struck the person? No.

Were we limited to strictly logical inferences, legal thinking would be brought to a standstill. In law, we test inferences against the totality of our logical powers, reasoning ability, past experience, and perception of the context. We stop testing an inference when we feel "satisfied" with it. Satisfaction is an emotional process, not a logical one.[1]

Perhaps you can sense the emotional basis of inferences with an example. Here is the picture of Jeffrey Stapleton that appeared in Chapter 1.

From the picture, can you infer whether Jeffrey was right-handed or left-handed? Look at the hair line across his forehead. It is not regular. I detect a slight hint of a part on the left side. People who are right-handed usually part their hair on the left because they brush their hair with their right hand. I am not at all sure of that, but I am well enough satisfied with it that I will think of Jeffrey as being right-handed during the rest of this case. If his handedness becomes significant to the case, I might want to check my inference by looking for facts that confirm it. But until it becomes important, I will live with it. His right-handedness will become part of the way that I understand "Jeffrey Stapleton."

Are you as satisfied with that inference as I am? Perhaps your experience is different from mine—perhaps you are a right-hander who parts her hair on the right. Or perhaps you infer that, since he was only seven years old, Jeffrey's parents have been combing his hair and there is no way to tell which side he would part it on if he were combing it himself. Or perhaps you have very high standards for accepting an inference. The basis for my inference is problematic; it does not come close to being a sound logical deduction.

---

1   For an explanation of emotions, see *On Emotions and PCT: A Brief Overview*, p. 218, as well as the original chapter on emotion, restored in the revised and expanded edition of *Behavior: The Control of Perception*, page 214. Because this chapter was cut by the publisher of the 1973 edition, Gibbon's did not have the benefit of Powers' suggested explanation of emotions.

If you do not find my inference compelling, it has had no success in reducing the tension that you should have felt as the result of my question. You should still feel "up in the air" about it. I might represent the difference between you and me in this way:

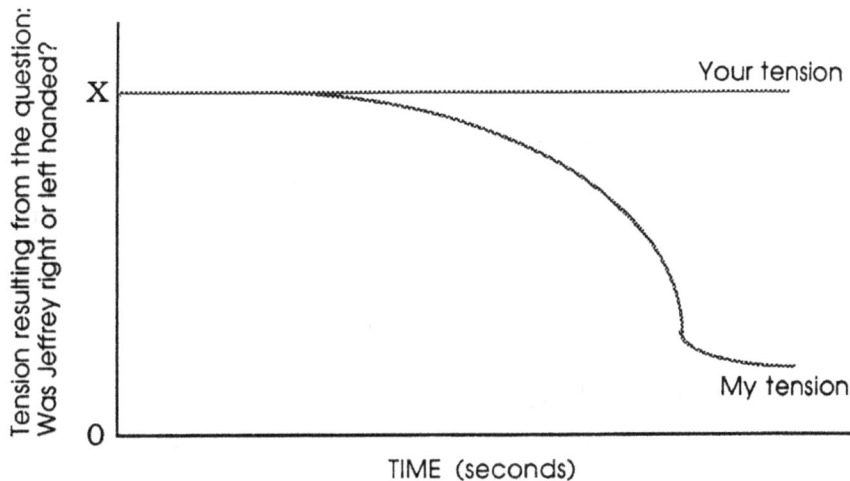

Figure 2.4   Differences in the level of satisfaction felt from an inference.

The question that I asked above ("From the picture, can you infer whether Jeffrey was right-handed or left-handed?") created some kind of a tension in each of us. That tension is what led us to look for an answer to the question. We differ in the amount of tension that the question created, but assume that it produced the same amount of tension in each of us—level "X" in Figure 2.4. In me, that tension led to a line of thought that in a few seconds produced the inference that he was right-handed, which reduced the tension that I felt, but did not eliminate it (my tension level in Figure 2.4 fell, but not to zero). I am comfortable thinking of him as right-handed, but that inference is not settled in my mind.

My explanation did not reduce your tension. It did not produce a feeling of satisfaction. Jeffrey's handedness is still a completely open question. Perhaps he was ambidextrous.

What makes lawyers think?

I have brought up the idea of mental tension in both of the first two chapters because it is an idea that I think is quite important to our understanding of the way that we think about law. It is relatively easy to think about the *structures* that we use in thinking, like the structure of a logical inference. It is very difficult to get any grip on the *dynamics* of thinking, on the flow of thought in our minds as we think.

We use a number of everyday words to refer to the dynamics of thinking. We say, for example, that a person is *curious* about something, meaning, I suppose, that he is thinking about something because he has a number of unanswered questions about it. If the questions are really gnawing at him, we say that he is *perplexed,* or *fascinated,* or *intrigued.* Each of those words suggest that there is more going on in the person's mind than reason or logic. The person who is perplexed is driven by a feeling that demands satisfaction. That person is in a state of "tension" and the tension will drive the person's thought until it is resolved.

I use the term "tension" to refer to the state of mind that demands further thought for a very personal reason. As I reflect upon my own mental state when I am pursuing a case or question, the feeling is exactly like the feeling I have when I sense tension in a piece of music. If you are familiar with musical tensions, you probably know what I mean. If you are not, it is worth a moment to think about it. (Notice that the last sentence was an attempt to place your mind in a state of tension about tensions, to make you curious enough about them that you will pay attention to the next paragraph.)

Music plays directly upon our emotions. One of the emotions that it produces is the feeling of tension, the feeling that something further *must* happen, a feeling of loose ends that must be resolved. It produces that feeling in several very mechanical ways, one of which is by a chord that is composed of two notes that are separated from each other by five notes, as shown in Figure 2.5.

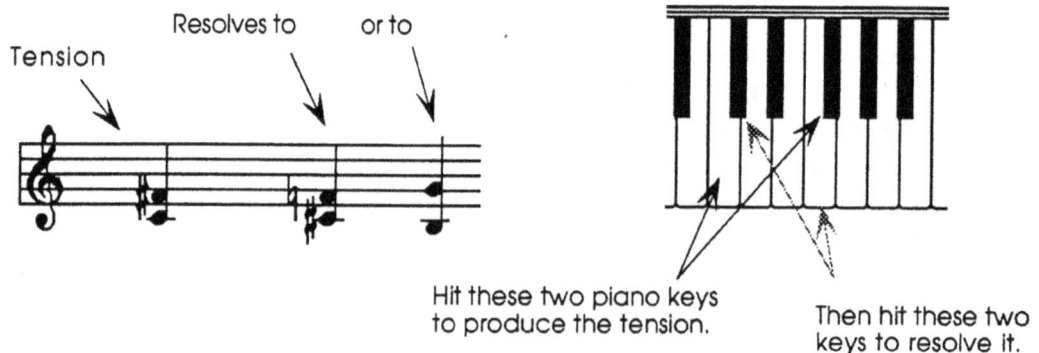

Figure 2.5   A musical tension and its resolution.

No one knows why this combination of notes produces the feeling of tension in people, or why the feeling is released by a chord composed of notes one note above or below the notes of the tension chord. If you are unfamiliar with this phenomenon, you might want to try it out on a keyboard, playing the notes indicated in Figure 2.5 and listening intently to your own mental state as you do so (if you are under enough tension, you will actually do that).

A musical tension produces a corresponding feeling of mental tension, as indicated in Figure 2.6.

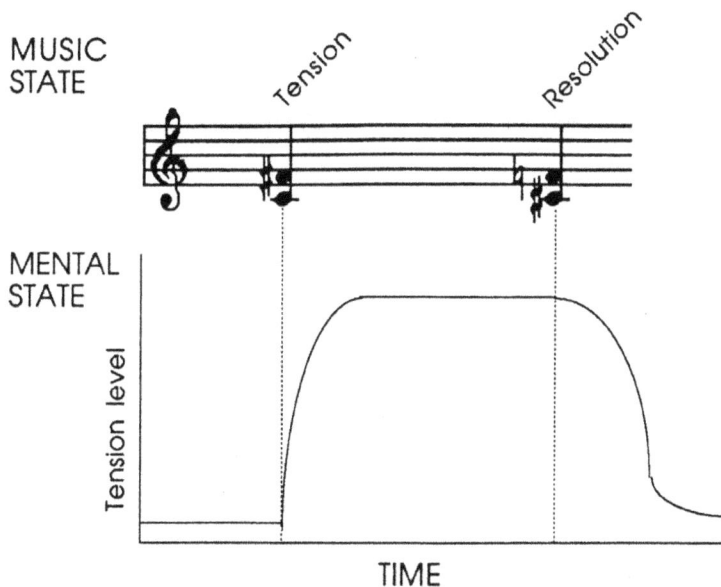

Figure 2.6   The correspondence between a musical tension and
the mental state that it produces.

The height of the tension curve—the intensity of the feeling of tension—varies from person to person. Some are very sensitive to it. others are hardly influenced by it. Some composers use musical tension as a trick, ending a song with a tension. I find that so irritating that I will often hum the notes that resolve the tension. My friends, only dimly aware of the tension, find that curious behavior on my part, from which I gather that my own mental state is very sensitive to musical tension. In terms of Figure 2.6, my mental tension curve is very much higher than that of some of my friends.

Music is, of course, only one of the many things that can produce tension. An interesting question may provoke us to inquire further. A distant sound, different from those that we are familiar with, may alert us. A perceived threat may disturb us. Approaching a toll booth and realizing that you have no money in your pocket may produce panic. A dangerous task, a confusing passage in a book, an unresolved mystery—all of these, and many more, may create tension.

People differ greatly in their sensitivity to sources of tension. Experienced performers, for example, are relaxed in front of an audience, while others feel so much tension from having to speak in public that they are reduced to gibbering idiots. Tension can become pathological, rising to a level that we call *anxiety,* which interferes with the person's performance. Tension itself is essential, for it animates thought and action. It is only when it runs out of hand in the form of anxiety that it is troublesome.

What does the idea of tension enable us to understand? For one thing, it may explain why you have read this far in this book, while others have long since abandoned it. We can safely assume that you are not a dullard, incapable of feeling intellectual tension. But how highly motivated are you? What did you do when you came across the accident report at the beginning of this chapter? If Jeffrey Stapleton's case actually interested you (that is, put you into a state of tension) you would have paused to read it, to squeeze it for every bit of light that it could shed on his case. Some will have given it hardly a glance. Why?

The idea of tension allows us to address something that is highly significant in legal thought: What causes a lawyer to *stop* thinking about a case? That is a far more important question than it might seem because it is impossible to ever have a complete understanding of even the simplest law case. Every lawyer must stop thinking about every case long before she has a full understanding of it. How does she decide when her understanding of the case is solid enough for her to safely stop?

We can see the problem that the lawyer faces by contrasting it with a domain like arithmetic that does not present the same problem. If I asked you, for example, to add the numbers 77 and 119, you would have a problem that had a clear solution: the solution will be a number with three digits. When you get a number with three digits by following a procedure that has produced good results in the past, you will be done with the problem.

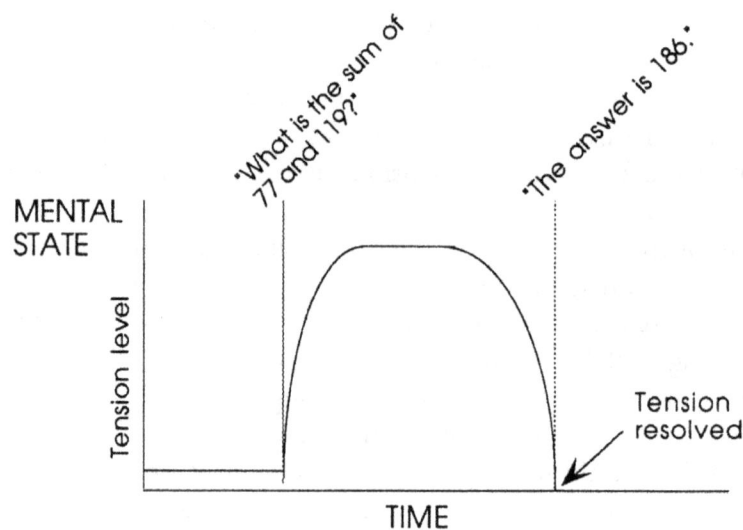

Figure 2.7   The tension levels involved in the solution to an arithmetic problem.

Arithmetic problems generate crisp, clear solutions that eliminate tension. Figure 2.7 pictures the mental state of a person solving an addition problem. His tension rises as the question is presented to him, then falls as he produces an answer. Since math problems have a clear, unambiguous correct answer, it is possible for the person's tension to fall to zero, to be completely resolved. Contrast that with the situation pictured in Figure 2.4, where my inference about Jeffrey's handedness left me with considerable unresolved tension. Legal questions rarely permit the kind of crisp, certain resolution that math problems do.

The attentive reader will have noticed, however, that the answer that resolved the tension in Figure 2.7—186—is not correct. The sum of 77 and 119 is, in fact, 196. The possibility that it was incorrect did not bother the person pictured in Figure 2.7. As soon as he came up with a plausible answer his tension dropped to zero; the problem was solved.

A different person, perhaps one who was by nature more cautious, or less confident in his adding skills, might not have stopped when he got the first answer. He would have asked himself whether he was comfortable with the number and proceeded to check it. That person's thought is pictured in Figure 2.8.

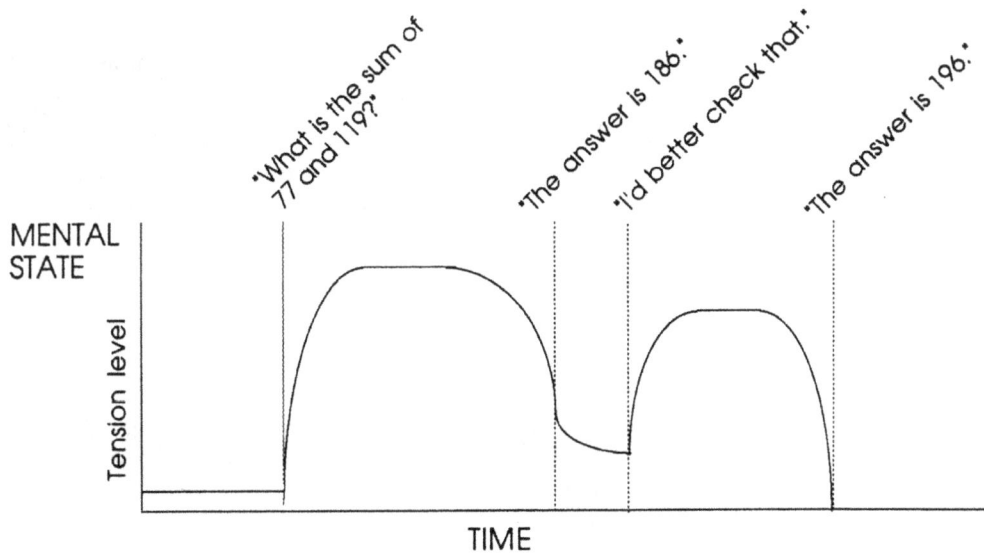

Figure 2.8   The tension levels produced by a person who checks his work.

When this person got his first answer, his tension level didn't drop to zero. He looked at the number. Something bothered him about it, increasing his tension and causing him to recalculate. Only when he recalculated and discovered the mistake had he, in his own mind, solved the problem. He felt satisfied with the answer.

The two people pictured in Figures 2.7 and 2.8 are different in the way they deal with tension. The one in Figure 2.8 is cautious; the one in Figure 2.7 is headstrong. Both must *decide* when the problem is solved, but they have different rules for doing it. Arithmetic has simple procedures for checking every calculation, yet we do not always check our own calculations.

Why not?

The problem faced by the lawyer is far more difficult, for there is no procedure for getting a "correct" answer to a legal problem. There is, in fact, no definition of what a correct answer to an interesting legal problem *is*. The reason for that is implicit in the nature of the legal "facts" and "inferences" that we considered earlier in this chapter. The facts and inferences that form the basic ingredients of legal analysis are themselves judgments. They contrast starkly with the numbers that are the basic ingredients of arithmetic. Numbers are constructs that bear no necessary relationship to anything. When I say, "What is the sum of 77 and 119?" you can provide an answer by applying the constructed rules of addition. The answer, 196, is true, in and of itself, without reference to any events in the world.

A legal "fact," by contrast, is a representation of some other reality. It is "true" only if different observers, acting under the rules of empiricism, would *agree* that it is an accurate representation of that reality (recall the example of the license plate earlier in this chapter). The fact is true only if any observer, correctly applying the rules of empiricism, would agree that it was true.

Consider the plight of the lawyer ... better, consider your own plight as you try to make sense out of Jeffrey Stapleton's case. From what you know thus far, can you demonstrate that the inference that, "John Newland's car struck Jeffrey." is true? I can't, and I am the one who is writing the book. The best I can say is that that I find that inference *satisfying*. It fits with the facts that I find *satisfying*. I will *take it to be true,* until I find facts that conflict with it.

I would diagram my own tension level on Jeffrey's case in this way:

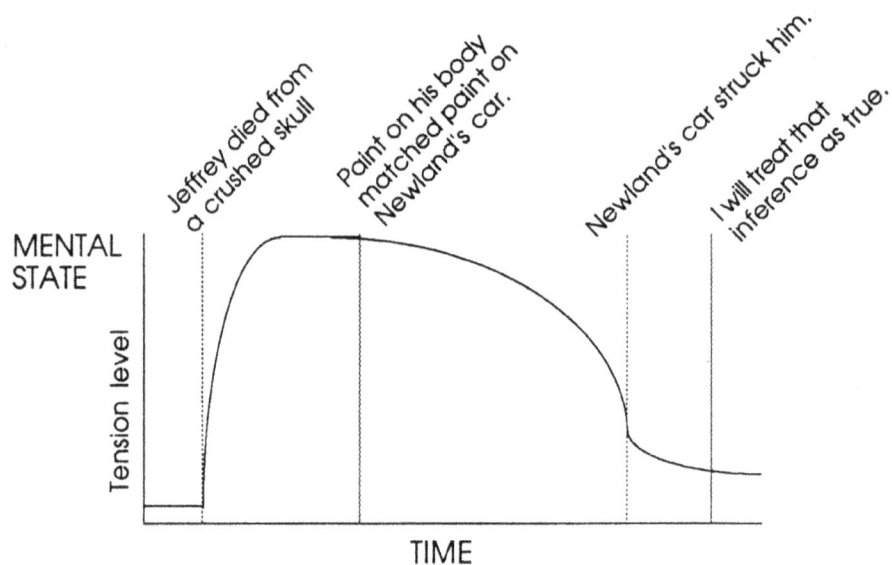

Figure 2.9   My tension levels at each stage in the analysis of Jeffrey's case.

I am not certain that Newland's car struck Jeffrey—my tension level on that point has not gone to zero. But I am comfortable enough with it that I will get on with the analysis of the case. Legal reasoning is *contingent* in that sense; it keeps going, though no successful resolution of each step in the analysis is possible. It generates countless loose ends, facts and inferences that the lawyer must constantly bear in mind, pulling them up for further thought as the analysis proceeds and conflicting information is generated.

The idea of tension gives us the beginning of an answer to the question asked in this section: What makes lawyers think? The short answer is that lawyers think for the same reason that everyone else does; their perceptions create tension in their minds, which they resolve by thinking. But there is something of a difference with lawyers; there is a special source of tension working on lawyers—their professional obligation to their clients. Law school inculcates, and other legal institutions continually reinforce, the duty of the lawyer to her client. The effect of that duty is to reduce the importance of the lawyer's innate mental liveliness and sense of curiosity in creating tension. I have known lawyers, dullards by any measure, who became titans of mental activity when working on a matter for a client. Tenaciously refusing to accept even the most obvious fact as true without close examination, resolutely testing every assumption and inference, untiringly pursuing a satisfying resolution to the case, their duty to their clients generated a tension in their thought that forced them to understand things that, without the client, were of no interest whatsoever. The constant, tedious recitation of the lawyer's duty to her client is a crucial source of motivation to many lawyers.

Inferences about another's mental state

Recall that at the end of the last chapter our task was to determine whether or not Jeffrey Stapleton's death was legally significant. Most tragedies are not legally significant; they just happen. The inference that John Newland's car struck Jeffrey, however, surely suggests that there is a legal problem lurking in this case. But that inference is not legally sufficient, for it makes no more sense to hold cars responsible for a person's death than to blame viruses for causing sickness. We need to link a person with Jeffrey's death.

The person we are after is staring us in the face: the driver of the Newland car. The police have been unable to find the driver, so we will not be able to refer to him by name. But we can refer to him as "the driver" and link him to Jeffrey's death. To do that will require more facts and inferences than we have made thus far.

Our own experience with cars suggests that virtually every moving car has a driver. Since the Newland car was clearly moving at the time it struck Jeffrey, we could infer that it was under the control of a driver at that time. The accident report, however, gives us a little more to go on, for it tells us that the car that hit him left 35 feet of skid marks on the street immediately to the west of Jeffrey's body. Since cars do not apply their own brakes, we can use that fact to support the inference that the Newland car was under the control—albeit, poorly under the control, if the skid marks are any indication—of a driver at the time that it struck Jeffrey.

Putting that inference together with our earlier inference establishes the basis for a legal problem because it puts a human being into the picture:

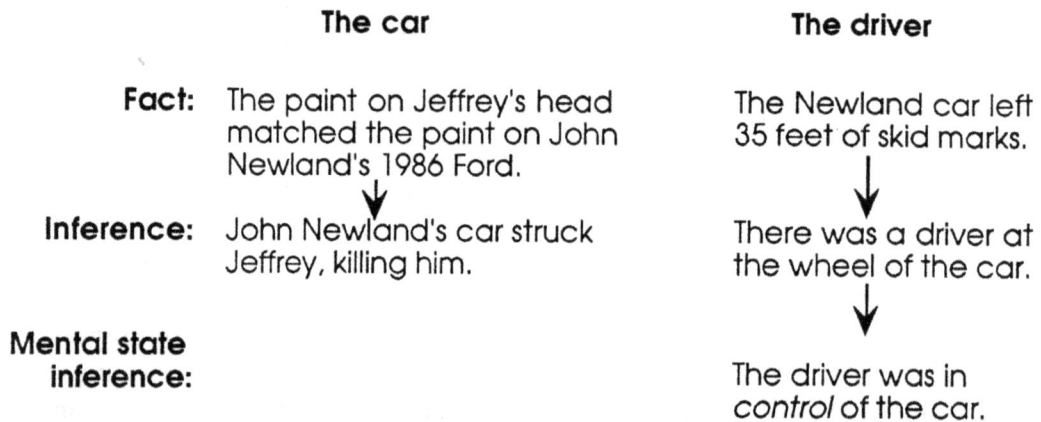

	The car	**The driver**
Fact:	The paint on Jeffrey's head matched the paint on John Newland's 1986 Ford.	The Newland car left 35 feet of skid marks.
	↓	↓
Inference:	John Newland's car struck Jeffrey, killing him.	There was a driver at the wheel of the car.
		↓
Mental state inference:		The driver was in *control* of the car.

Figure 2.10   The set of inferences pointing to the driver of the car.

These two chains of inference connect the driver of the car to Jeffrey's death. Notice, however. that to do that we have to make a new kind of inference: an inference about the driver's mental state.

From the fact that the car left skid marks (a fact that remains to be confirmed), we can infer that there was someone at the wheel of the car. That inference is, at least in principle, objectively verifiable: if someone was present at the time of the accident, he can confirm that there was someone at the wheel of the car. But that inference is not quite sufficient. To connect the driver of the car to Jeffrey's death we must draw an inference about the driver's mental state. That is what we do when we infer that the driver was in control of the car.

To say that a person controls a car is to imply that it is moving in response to a *desire* by that person (say, to drive on an errand) and that that person may change the speed and direction of the car at will The presence of the car is, then, a choice made by the driver for which the driver may be held responsible. If the driver could have altered the speed and direction of the car (which he could, if he was in control), then it follows that he is responsible for failing to do so if he perceived (another mental state inference) the risk that it presented to Jeffrey.

The mental state inference lies at the heart of legal thinking, for it is that mental state that creates the phenomenon of choice that distinguishes people from boulders and viruses. If we could say of boulders that they *knew* what they were doing when they headed off down the hill, that they *perceived* of the risks that they created for people downhill, and that they could *choose* to head in a different direction if they *wanted to,* we could subject boulders to the law. We cannot, of course, do that. As far as we can tell, boulders do not have a mental state; they do not "know" or "want" to do anything. People *do*.

It is possible that the driver of the car was as dumb as a boulder. We cannot see into his mind, or into anyone else's mind. When we make an inference about another's mental state we are drawing a conclusion that cannot be verified. Each person's mental state is irretrievably obscured from objective view. Every inference about it is subject to attack. The driver of the Newland car could claim, for example, that he was not in control of the car because: (1) the brakes or steering of the car malfunctioned and would not let him avoid Jeffrey; (2) a person sitting in the passenger seat was telling him where to go at gunpoint; (3) he had had an epileptic seizure or a heart attack moments before the car struck Jeffrey; or (4) the devil had control of him as he drove along the street. Any of those arguments might cause us to rethink the inference that he was in control of the car.

At this point, however, we have an inference that we feel comfortable with, and that inference tells us, finally, that Jeffrey's death raises a legal problem:

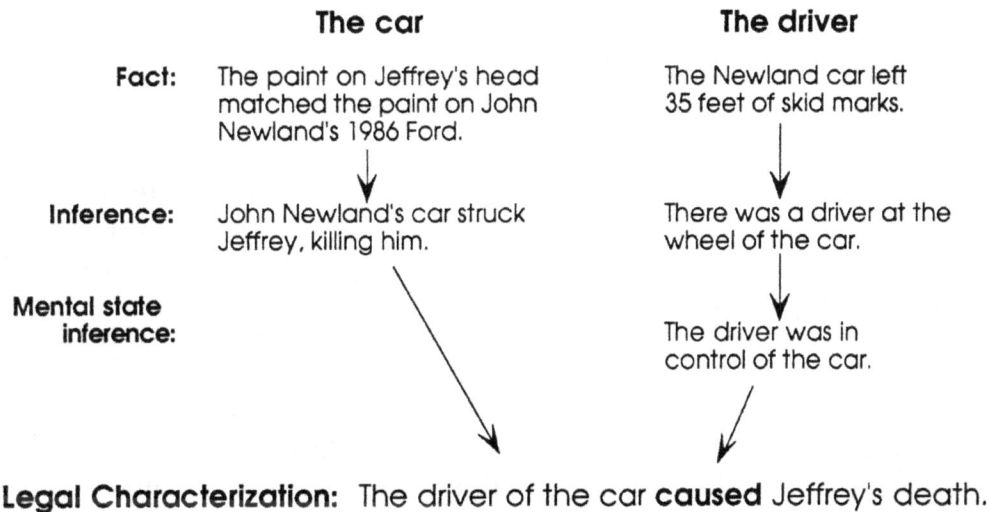

	The car	**The driver**
Fact:	The paint on Jeffrey's head matched the paint on John Newland's 1986 Ford.	The Newland car left 35 feet of skid marks.
Inference:	John Newland's car struck Jeffrey, killing him.	There was a driver at the wheel of the car.
Mental state inference:		The driver was in control of the car.

Legal Characterization: The driver of the car **caused** Jeffrey's death.

Figure 2.11   The facts and inferences supporting the legal characterization that the car caused Jeffrey's death.

I refer to the conclusion that Jeffrey's death was caused by the driver of the car a legal characterization." It is "legal" because it is in a form that the law can respond to. A court will entertain a cause of action on behalf of one whose death has been caused by another. The statement describes a conflict that the law will listen to.

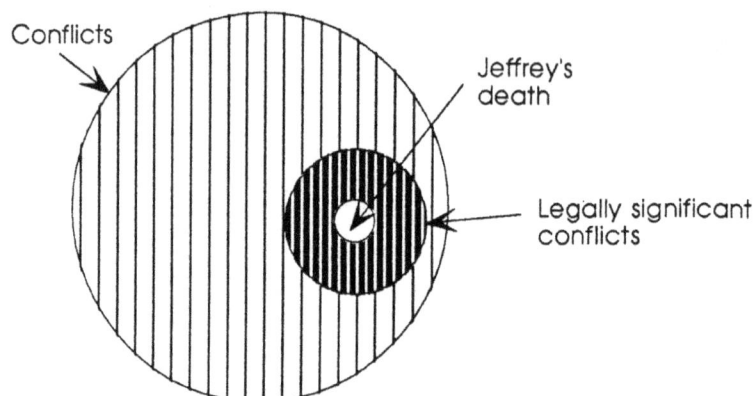

Figure 2.12   Jeffrey's death lies squarely in the middle of
the problems that a court will entertain.

It is a "characterization" because it does more than nakedly recite the facts and inferences upon which it is based. It states that the driver caused Jeffrey's death. We are pretty comfortable with the proposition that the car killed Jeffrey and that the driver was in control of the car at the time. But when we say that the driver "caused" Jeffrey's death, we add a great deal to the picture. Would we say that Jeffrey's parents caused his death, because if they had not produced Jeffrey he would not have been present to be hit by the car? Or that the farmers of America caused his death by supplying him with the food that kept him alive until the day of the accident?

There is a great deal wrapped up in the word "caused" in that statement. It clearly means far more than a physicist would mean by the same word. It is pregnant with overtones of moral responsibility.

While the conclusion that the driver caused Jeffrey's death is supported by the facts of the case as we know them, there is still some tension left in that proposition. For one thing, we have not connected the skid marks on the road to the Newland car. Those marks may have been there before the accident. But it does strain the imagination (that is, the tension level of this question is very low) to think that the location of the skid marks and of Jeffrey's body are coincidental, so we can get on with the analysis of the case. Further, if the Newland car did not leave the skid marks, that would suggest that the driver did not attempt to avoid Jeffrey, which would make the case against him worse. We can safely ignore this problem for the present.

There is also a bit of tension left in the inference that the car was under the control of the driver at the time that it hit Jeffrey. Because of the skid marks, it does not appear that the driver *intended* to hit Jeffrey. He or she apparently tried to avoid Jeffrey, but couldn't manage it. If the reason that he couldn't manage it is that the car's steering failed, the conclusion that he caused Jeffrey's death may be called into question. Perhaps we had better have a mechanic check out the car.

At this point we have a plausible legal problem. one that is lively enough to justify further inquiry.

CHAPTER THREE

Finding fault

To this point we have been concerned with determining what happened to Jeffrey Stapleton. That effort has been purely *descriptive*. We have simply been trying to develop a coherent sense of the events that led to his death. While there are numerous loose ends in the picture that we have been able to paint, it seems that there is reason to believe that someone may have been *at fault* in Jeffrey's death.

Our thinking now moves to a different level, for we cannot determine fault by thinking that is simply descriptive. All the facts in the world will not tell us whether we should attach moral fault, and legal responsibility, to the driver of the car. To do that we must employ another kind of thinking. The standard term for this kind of thought is "normative" thinking. It compares what happened against some kind of standard, or "norm," of proper behavior to determine whether or not the behavior conformed to the standard.

The difference between descriptive and normative thinking is the difference between the scientist and the lawyer. The scientist limits herself to descriptive thought, to describing and explaining that which is empirically verifiable. The lawyer is also concerned with describing and explaining what happened, as we saw in the last chapter. But that is just the beginning of the lawyer's task, for the lawyer must *justify* what happened.

The nature of normative thought is so slippery that we must be resolute—even tedious—in describing it. It is odd, in a sense, that normative thinking should be so obscure, for you, and every other human being, have been doing it since before you can remember. You have *blamed* people for what they did, felt *guilty* for things that you have done, held others *responsible* for their actions, and found *fault* with teachers, bosses, and car designers. To do that you had to employ normative thinking. You are, by now, very good at it, so good that you often do it without being aware that you are doing it.

In another sense, however, it is not at all odd that we are ignorant about normative thinking. We would be ignorant about descriptive thinking were it not for the generations of epistemologists, philosophers of science, and psychologists who have spent entire careers trying to understand it. The empirical method is a well-studied set of procedures for determining what counts as an observation and what explanations of observations are legitimate.

There is no corresponding body of study in law, no theory of the "normative method." Law students are instructed according to the case method, in which they are given problems and simply told to solve them. There is little incentive for them to understand how it is that they solve them. There is, in other words, little tension in the lawyer's mind about the *way* that he thinks.

The signal feature of normative thinking lies in evaluating something that happened against a concept of what *should* have happened.

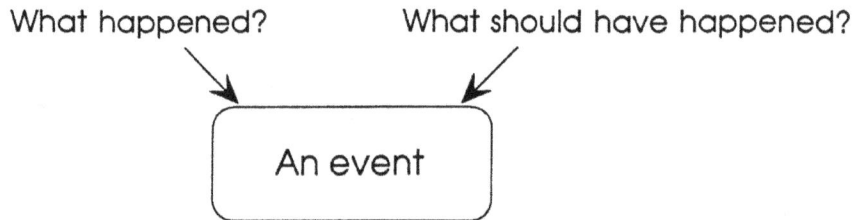

Figure 3.1   The binocular nature of normative thinking.

Normative thinking is binocular; it evaluates an event from two perspectives, then compares those perspectives. One perspective is sheerly descriptive: What happened? That is the perspective that we have taken on Jeffrey's case thus far.

The other perspective asks what *should* have happened. Let us pursue that question in Jeffrey's case. The starkest entry on the accident report is Officer McGinty's statement that Jeffrey "was apparently sitting in the roadway next to a parked car on the south side of the street." That was Officer McGinty's deduction from the location of the damage on the Newland car (i.e., on the side of the right front fender, behind the wheel well) and the impact to Jeffrey's head. It seems clear that Jeffrey should not have been sitting in the street. A seven-year-old should know better than that. The last sentence sets forth a norm: Seven-year-olds should know better than to sit in the street and should not do it.

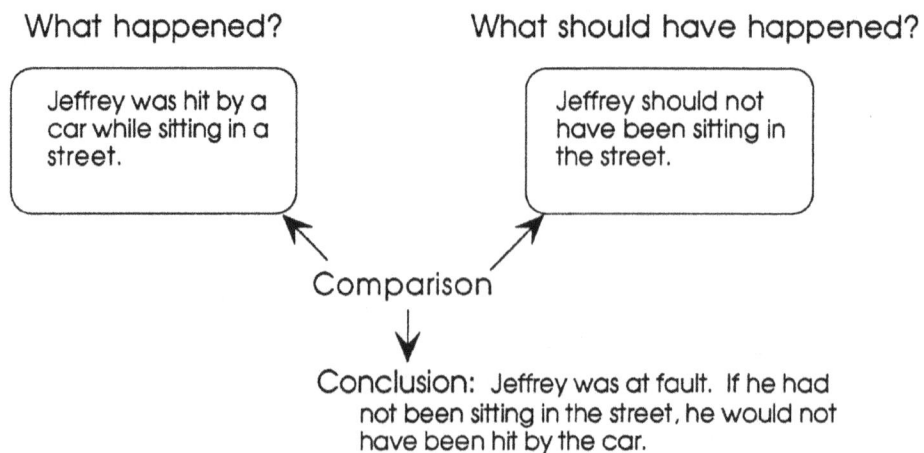

Figure 3.2   Reaching a normative conclusion.

When we compare the norm with what actually happened we see that the two do not overlap: Had Jeffrey been doing what he should have been doing, he would not have died. The obvious conclusion is that Jeffrey caused the injury to himself by his failure to observe proper behavior.

The source of legal norms

Norms are standards against which behavior is compared. Norms define behavior that is "normal" or expected. Behavior that is normal should not be confused with behavior that is "average." That is, norms describe *ideal* behavior, not behavior that is statistically average for a group. The average driver on an American highway, for example, drives considerably faster than the speed limit in most states. The speed limit sets out the norm. People who exceed it are "abnormal"—"speeders"—even though that makes most drivers abnormal.

Where do the norms that law applies come from? There are at any instant in a society countless millions of norms, many of which conflict. Some people harbor a norm that it is wrong to work on Sunday, others that it is wrong to wear long hair, to eat fatty food, to drive a car with an internal combustion engine, to smoke cigarettes, to speak ill of a dog. From the gigantic stew of norms that exist in a society, how does the law determine which ones it will enforce?

Great consequences follow from a decision in law to enforce a norm. If, for example, law were to adopt the norm that it is wrong to smoke cigarettes, thereby making it *illegal* to smoke them, the police power of the state would focus on smokers, subjecting them to arrest, fine, and incarceration. The dire consequences that follow from the legal enforcement of a norm require that they be justified, that law not quixotically pick a norm from here and one from there according to a whim of the moment.

Consider the effect of the norm in Figure 3.2 on Jeffrey's case. If a court adopted that norm, Jeffrey's case would be over before it began. The idea that a seven-year-old should know better than to sit in the road Is, I imagine, a norm that will not cause you great concern. But what is it rooted in? Would it be justified for a court to apply that norm to Jeffrey's case, thereby finding him to be the legal cause of his own death?

The norm in Figure 3.2 is rooted in history. In the countless cases in which judges and juries have considered the standards of proper behavior to apply to children. It is the consensus of those cases that a seven-year-old is capable of looking out for himself and therefore *must* look out for himself. The norm in this case *is a legal* norm, a norm that has been accepted and applied by courts of law.

From the stew of norms at work in society, the law has chosen to enforce a subset of them.

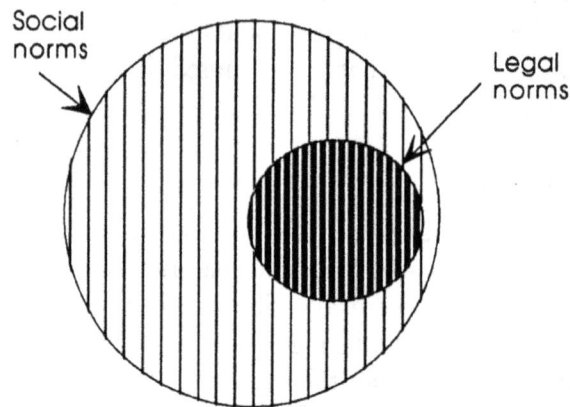

Figure 3.3   The relationship between legal and social norms.

If Figure 3.3 looks suspiciously like the diagrams that I used earlier to distinguish legally significant conflicts from the general set of social conflicts, that is no accident. They are, in fact, one and the same. Here's why. Let us say that I am out walking my dog one day and that she does something that really makes me mad, so I start berating her at the top of my lungs. A neighbor, hearing me, is injured by the notion that I am taking the beast to task and accuses me of abuse.

There will ensue a conflict between my neighbor and me, but it is not a conflict that a court will pay attention to. If my neighbor attempts to bring me to court for berating my dog, the court will dismiss the case, for the norm underlying my neighbor's position—"it is wrong to yell at a dog"—is not one that has been adopted (yet) by a court. But courts in some places have adopted the norm that it is wrong to mistreat a dog, so if the neighbor can show that my behavior amounts to mistreating my dog, I may be in trouble.

To determine whether or not a norm has been applied in the past the court will refer to the opinions written by judges in prior cases. The parties to a case will look for precedent to support their position. If I were sued by my neighbor for yelling at my dog, for example, my neighbor's lawyer would read prior cases involving the mistreatment of animals. If he found a case in which a person was guilty of mistreatment simply for yelling at an animal, he would argue to the court that it should listen to the case against me because there existed in law a norm that my behavior violated.

The historical justification for norms—if a norm has been used by a court in the past, it is justified to use it in the present—is not entirely satisfying. Courts can be wrong. There was, for example, a long period when courts enforced the norm that one person could own another person. That is today recognized as a horrible mistake. We expect a deeper justification for legal norms than that they have been applied in the past.

Principles of law

Courts do not choose what norms to apply the way diners choose what to eat at a pot luck dinner, choosing a bit from this pot and a bit from that pot over there. Legal norms must "make sense," must fit together. The norm that a seven-year-old should know better than to sit in a street, for example, also applies to eight-year-olds, nine-year-olds, and so on, all the way to adults. It would be bizarre to say that everyone but eleven-year-olds should know better than to sit in the street. That would not make sense.

The norm that applies to Jeffrey is a specific instance of a more general principle:

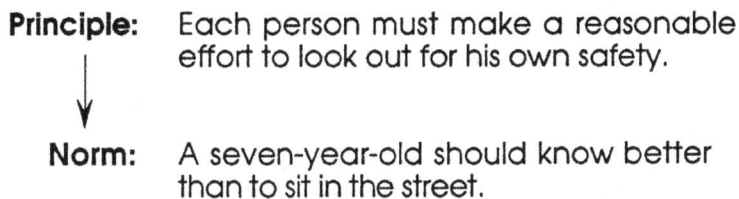

Principle: Each person must make a reasonable effort to look out for his own safety.

↓

Norm: A seven-year-old should know better than to sit in the street.

Figure 3.4   The relationship between a specific norm and the general principle that underlies it.

Notice that the principle is itself normative. It states that, "Each person *must....*" It creates a duty that applies to all: Everyone must look out for his own safety. It is not concerned with what *is,* but with what *should be.*

The principle establishes an obligation for a general class of people. The class covered by this principle is the most general—"Each person" means every person. The principle here applies to everyone. For that reason a principle cannot be applied to a particular case. To apply it, a specific norm must be derived for the situation of the case, like this:

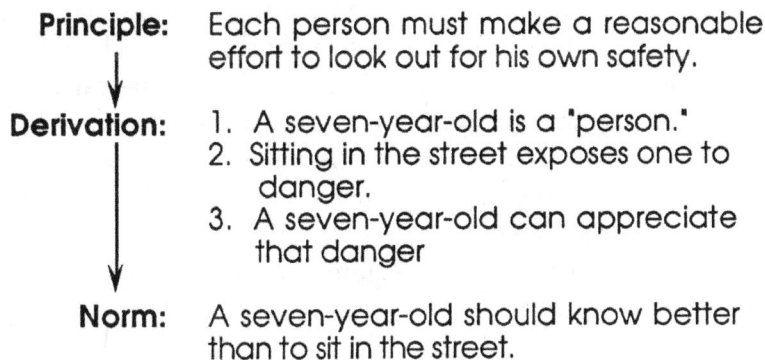

Principle: Each person must make a reasonable effort to look out for his own safety.

↓

Derivation: 1. A seven-year-old is a "person."
2. Sitting in the street exposes one to danger.
3. A seven-year-old can appreciate that danger

↓

Norm: A seven-year-old should know better than to sit in the street.

Figure 3.5   The derivation of a norm from a principle.

The rule of law

The norm applicable to a specific person is derived from the general principle. In this illustration, that derivation follows the rules of deductive logic. If each person must look out for his own safety, and if sitting in a street exposes one to danger (i.e., is inconsistent with looking out for one's own safety), and if a seven-year-old can appreciate that danger, it follows that a seven-year-old should know better than to sit in the street.

The norm provides us with a behavioral standard against which to evaluate the person's behavior. But it doesn't tell us what to do if the norm is violated. To do that we need a rule:

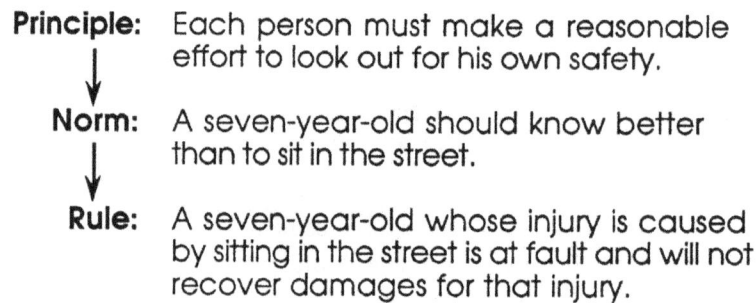

Principle: Each person must make a reasonable effort to look out for his own safety.

↓

Norm: A seven-year-old should know better than to sit in the street.

↓

Rule: A seven-year-old whose injury is caused by sitting in the street is at fault and will not recover damages for that injury.

Figure 3.6   The relationship between principles, norms and rules.

A rule of law sets out the legal consequences of a violation of a norm. It is the sharp end of law, the force that turns a norm into a statement that directs the use of power. Where a social norm results in social pressure applied by those who would enforce it, a legal norm animates the power of the state. From its violation follow consequences that the violator will not easily evade.

Those consequences look pretty bad for Jeffrey's case. If the rule in Figure 3.6 is applied to his case, it is over. According to what we know thus far, Jeffrey would not have been injured if he had not been sitting in the street. The rule says that if his injury was "caused" by sitting in the street, he will not recover damages. It took at least two people—Jeffrey and the driver of the car—to "cause" Jeffrey's injury. If either one of them had acted "correctly," the injury would not have happened. Each one of them is, therefore, a cause. Which means that Jeffrey caused the injury. Which means that his case is dead if we apply that rule.

The discovery of the rule of law in Figure 3.6 may resolve Jeffrey's case in our minds. We may close the case.

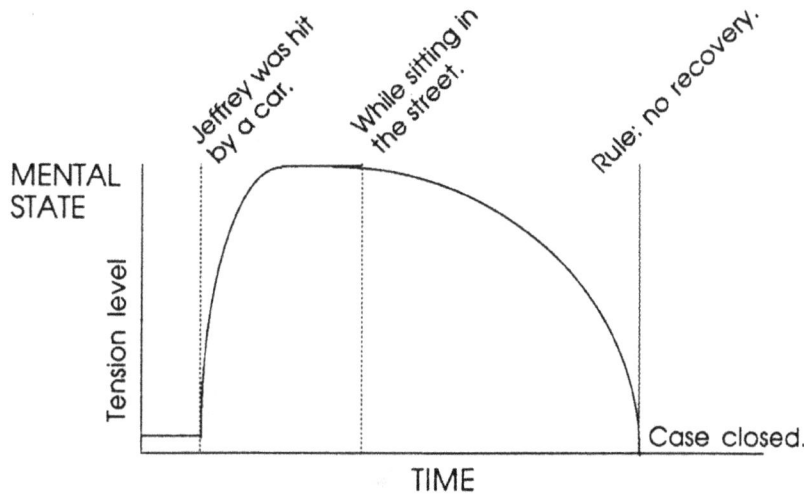

The figure shows a graph with a curve. The y-axis is labeled "MENTAL STATE" and "Tension level". The x-axis is labeled "TIME". Annotations along the curve read: "Jeffrey was hit by a car.", "While sitting in the street.", "Rule: no recovery.", and "Case closed."

Figure 3.7   The effect of the rule upon the consideration of the case.

Our understanding of the facts of the case and the rule applicable to the case may eliminate our tension about it. Were we lawyers who had been consulted by Jeffrey's parents, we might now call them on the telephone (it might be a bit embarrassing to talk to them in person) and tell them that the law would not allow any case in this situation.

If we did that, however, we would be like the mathematician in Figure 2.5, overly content with our first answer to a problem. Like a mathematician who checks her work, we are more resolute than that and will think back through the case looking for loose ends that are not resolved. We will find lots of loose ends, both in law and in fact. A look at Figure 3.6, for example, will reveal a concept that we have not fully considered: A person must make a "reasonable" effort to look out for his own safety. Could it be that Jeffrey had a good reason (good, that is, for a seven-year-old) for sitting in the street? Could it be that Officer McGinty was wrong in her inference that Jeffrey was sitting in the street? She warned us about her lack of certainty in that inference by saying that Jeffrey was "apparently" sitting in the roadway.

These questions should revive our interest in Jeffrey's case (note that that is a normative proposition; descriptively, you may long since have lost interest in Jeffrey's case).

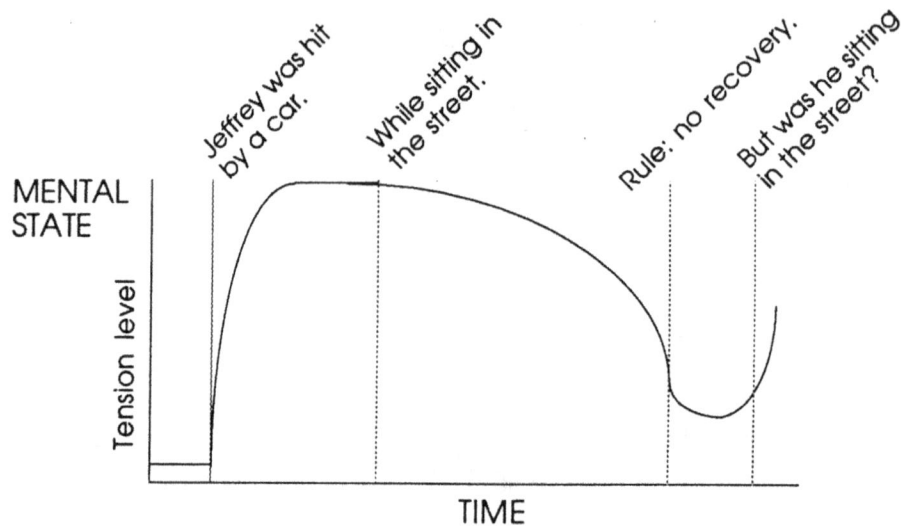

Figure 3.8   The effect of reconsidering the facts.

We might ask Officer McGinty for the basis for her statement.

> I was not able to find anyone who saw the accident happen. I said that he was "apparently" sitting in the roadway because when I put the damage to the car together with the injury to Jeffrey, it seemed to me that it could only have happened if he was sitting in the road.

If we are to penetrate this case further, we will have to do some investigating ourselves. The obvious approach is to look for an eyewitness, and the obvious place to look for an eyewitness is among those who live on the street. We begin our search at the house on the southwest corner of Purley and State, the house that is in front of the spot on Purley where Jeffrey was hit. An elderly man who lives in the house, a Mr. Montefiori, is at first reluctant to talk and seems evasive, which raises our suspicions and causes you to get a little pushy with him and causes me to turn on the charm. After a bit of that treatment, he tells us what happened.

> On the afternoon of October 8 I went out to the sidewalk to pick up my newspaper. I must have opened it up to look at the sports page. At any rate, It was pretty windy, so when I opened it up it blew out of my hand and scattered across the street. A kid who was playing on the sidewalk in front of the house across the street, saw what was happening and immediately dashed around picking up the paper.

Some of the paper was blowing around the street.

As he was picking it up a car coming down Purley saw him too late, hit its brakes, but hit him as he was bending down to pick up a paper. He didn't seem to hear the car coming.

I don't know how fast the car was going when it hit him, but it wasn't very fast. The car skidded as it came up to him, but never stopped. I didn't see the driver. When the police came, I pretended that I was not at home.

Jeffrey was not sitting in the street. He was bent over, picking up Montefiori's newspaper. He was, we might even say, on an errand of mercy, helping an old man recover a paper that was blowing in the wind, though that is a characterization of the facts that some might have trouble swallowing. How do these new facts stack up under the principle?

Spotting a question for the jury

The principle states that, "Each person must make a reasonable effort to look out for his own safety." Is it reasonable for a seven-year-old to be running in the street, picking up a newspaper under these circumstances? We might expect that an adult who was doing it would keep a sharp lookout for oncoming cars. We might <u>hope</u> that a seven-year-old would keep a sharp lookout, as well. But can we say that it is *unreasonable* for a seven-year-old to get so wrapped up in his mission of mercy that he failed to keep a sharp enough lookout?

That question calls for a *normative judgment*. There is nothing logical about that judgment. In fact, there is nothing that can be said about it at all. It is simply a decision that will be made "in the light of" the facts and the law of the case. What do you think? Was it reasonable for Jeffrey to chase the paper into the street? Was it reasonable for him to fail to see the car coming and to avoid it?

You and I might well differ on our answers to those questions. But, as lawyers, it doesn't much matter what we decide, for it is the jury that must ultimately make the decision. It is enough that we are sure that reasonable minds could differ on the question. In reaching its decision, the jury will be confronted with conflicting arguments of the following form:

What happened?

```
                    ┌──────────────────────┐
                    │ Jeffrey was hit while │
          ┌─────────│ chasing a newspaper   │─────────┐
          │         │ around the street.    │         │
          │         └──────────────────────┘         │
          ▼                                             ▼
What should have happened?              What should have happened?
— according to the **plaintiff**.        — according to the **defendant**.

┌────────────────────┐                  ┌────────────────────┐
│ It is not unreasonable │                │ Jeffrey should not │
│ for a seven-year-old   │                │ have been chasing  │
│ to do something        │                │ the paper.         │
│ impulsive, like chasing│                │                    │
│ a newspaper.           │                │ If he had not, or had │
│                        │                │ kept a better lookout,│
│ You can't blame him    │                │ he would not have  │
│ for that.              │                │ been hit by the car. │
└────────────────────┘                  └────────────────────┘
          │                                             │
          ▼                 **The jury's**              ▼
    Conclusion:              **normative**         Conclusion:
Jeffrey was not at fault. ◄── **decision.** ──►  Jeffrey was at fault.
```

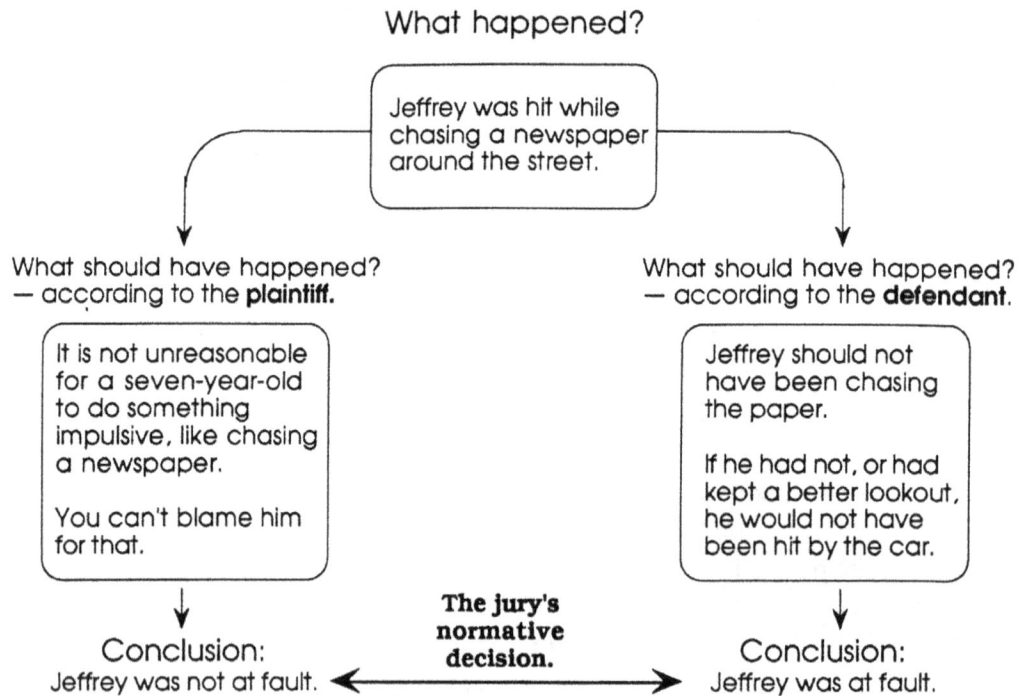

Figure 3.9   The structure of a question for the jury.

The jury's job is first to determine what actually happened. We assume that we will be able to bring Mr. Montefiori into court to show that Jeffrey was chasing his newspaper. If we cannot get him to testify, Jeffrey's case is far worse, for we will be left with only Officer McGinty's inference that Jeffrey was sitting in the street.

The jury's next job is to listen to the judge's interpretation of the law. Here the judge will tell the jury that Jeffrey had to use the level of reasonable care for his own safety that one would expect from a seven-year-old. The legal norm is perfectly general. Jeffrey will be held to the standard of behavior of a responsible seven-year-old.

Finally, the jury will have to decide whether or not Jeffrey's behavior conformed to that norm. They will be guided in that effort by the plaintiff's lawyer and the defendant's lawyer, who will give conflicting interpretations of what the standard required of Jeffrey and whether he conformed to it. The plaintiff's lawyer will emphasize the impulsiveness typical of seven-year-olds and the nature of Jeffrey's mission of mercy. The defendant's lawyer will argue that, impulsive or not, seven-year-olds know to pay attention when they enter a roadway and to look out for traffic, which Jeffrey apparently did not do.

As we look at Jeffrey's case, then, it appears that, while there is a serious question about his own fault, we have a plausible argument—that is, one that a jury might buy—that he should not be considered to have been at fault in this case. That argument rests upon Montefiori's testimony.

Attacking the rule of law

Instead of looking for facts that would blunt the rule that Jeffrey's case will be barred if he is at fault, we could have attacked the rule of law itself. Why should it be that a person is altogether barred from recovery when an injury is partially his own fault? Why should it be that the driver of the car should be one hundred percent free from responsibility, even though he was at least fifty percent at fault? Does that rule really follow from the principle?

The principle states that, "Each person must make a reasonable effort to look out for his own safety." How does it follow that if a person fails to make such a reasonable effort, he may have *no* recovery against another who is also at fault? It doesn't follow. It might make sense to reduce the person's recovery in proportion to his fault. But it hardly seems to make sense to let a wrongdoer off scot free because he hurt someone who was also at fault. Might such a rule not encourage drivers who see a kid in the street, who is not looking out for himself, to have a little sport with the kid, secure in the knowledge that if an injury occurs they will not be called to account for it?

When we are faced with a rule that does not seem to follow from a principle—that is, to "make sense"—we have an opportunity to prevail upon the court to change the rule. It may be that the rule is, however, supported by another principle. What might the other principle be in this case?

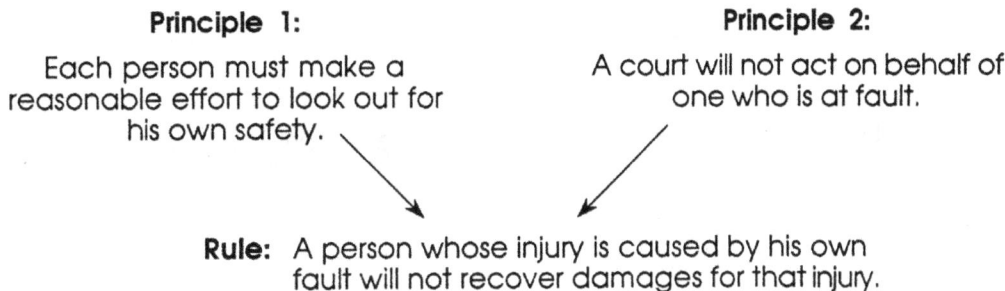

Principle 1:
Each person must make a reasonable effort to look out for his own safety.

Principle 2:
A court will not act on behalf of one who is at fault.

Rule: A person whose injury is caused by his own fault will not recover damages for that injury.

Figure 3.10   A rule resulting from the interaction of two principles.

The addition of Principle 2 would explain the rule that one who is at fault is barred from recovery. According to Principle 1, a person who fails to look out for his own safety is at fault. According to Principle 2, the court will not act on behalf of one who is at fault. From that it does follow that the person who is at fault should be unable to recover damages for an injury. If we argue to a court that it should change the rule, we will lose if it recognizes Principle 2. How can we tell whether or not it will? How does a court determine what principles to apply?

Where do principles of law come from?

The rule of law that we are considering here is one that has, in fact, disturbed courts for decades. It is called the rule of "contributory negligence." It provides that a victim will be completely barred from recovery for injury if the victim is in any way at fault. Courts have called the rule "harsh," pointing out that it bars a victim who is slightly negligent from recovery against people whose fault is far greater. Courts have created exceptions to the rule, fudging, as it were, on it when its effect has appeared unduly severe. And they have ignored the rule when applying it would be intolerable.

Many courts have overturned the rule, adopting a rule that allows people who are at fault to recover, but reduces the money that they receive in proportion to the magnitude of their fault. Why haven't all courts abolished the rule? If legal norms and rules follow deductively from principles, as pictured in Figure 3.6, how can it be that some courts have abolished the rule while others haven't?

If legal principles were laid out, written down somewhere for all to read, it would not figure that some courts have abolished the rule while others haven't. The rule would either follow from the published principles or it wouldn't. That is, indeed, the way that law works in those countries that follow the *civil law*, most notably France. The Civil Code sets out the highly general principles that guide the resolution of particular cases. The judge applies the principles to the case at hand, deducing the norms and rules applicable to the case from the principles.

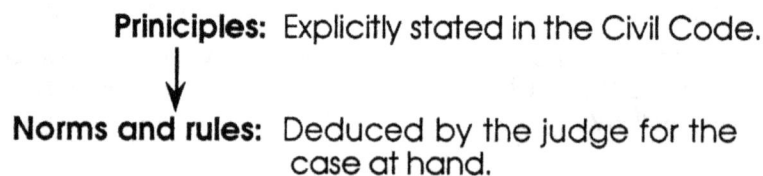

Priniciples: Explicitly stated in the Civil Code.

↓

Norms and rules: Deduced by the judge for the case at hand.

Figure 3.11   The source of law under the civil law.

If we wanted to attack the rule of contributory negligence in a civil law country, we would have at hand an explicit set of principles to look at. But where would we be if we found that the principles supporting the rule were those set out in Figure 3.10? Jeffrey's goose would be cooked, for it seems to me that the rule barring Jeffrey's recovery does indeed follow from those two principles. We could, of course, attack Principle 2, but civil code countries jealously protect their principles. A judge, even if she had the power to reinterpret Principle 2 for our case, would be very reluctant to tamper with it.

American law is not based upon an explicit set of principles. American legislatures have been reluctant to enunciate the kind of all-inclusive design for society that is required in order to fashion an explicit set of deep principles. Most American legislation is generated by a process of political deal-making. The parties to the deal usually do not agree on the principles that underlie a given piece of legislation.

A bill requiring a health inspection of rental properties, for example, may be backed by a tenant's group that wants to prove to its members that it is doing something for them, a landlord group that wants to raise the costs of its sleazy competitors by making them conform to the health standard, and the office of the Health Inspector, who wants a bigger budget. From such a deal principles do not emerge.

American judges are also reluctant to articulate general principles. Because they deal with individual cases, judges tend to have a mole's eye view of the law. Consider the judge who will handle Jeffrey's case, if the case gets that far. We will be asking him to overturn the rule of contributory negligence, a rule with a long, if troubled, history. It would take an act of enormous intellectual courage for the judge in our case to overturn it because that would implicitly change the principles upon which it is based, with untold ramifications in other cases. The judge in a particular case is hardly in a position to think through all of the ramifications of such a change. If he doesn't like the way a particular rule applies to a given case, it is far easier for him to fashion an exception to the rule than to overturn the rule as a whole.

If we have, then, a system of law in which the legislature is almost incapable of enunciating a principle and judges are reluctant to make any bigger step than the one they have to make to resolve the case before them, where do the principles of law come from under our system? Could it be that our law is, in fact, like a pot luck dinner, with norms picked a bit from this pot and a bit from that pot according to the way they please the judge or legislature at a particular moment? Could it be that our law looks like this:

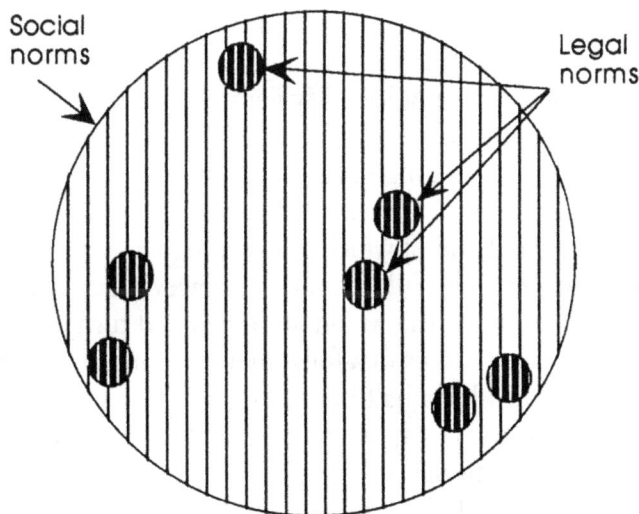

Figure 3.12   Pot luck law: picking a norm from here, a norm from there.

Could it be that there is no deep connection between the rules of law, that they are simply whatever the judge or legislature decides they should be at the moment? If that were true we might have quite an easy time attacking the rule of contributory negligence in Jeffrey's case. If the judge is free to choose the norms, we can simply prevail upon her to choose a different norm for Jeffrey. There will be no consequences, for the judge in the next case will simply pick whatever norms appeal to him at the time.

Judges are often tempted to do that, but they are disciplined by precedent and by the fact that their decisions can be reviewed by a court of appeals. There is a deep structure to American law, an implicit set of principles that determine the norms that will be applied to each case. The hard question is: How did they get there? I don't think that you need look any further for an answer to that question than the inside of your own head, for I will suggest that there is an implicit structure to the human mind that brings order to normative thinking.

In what follows I will attempt to point you to the inside of your own mind. If my thesis is correct—that the human mind itself is the source of the order in normative thinking—it follows that, since you are human, I should be able to point to it in your own thinking. This is likely to get a bit obscure, so bear with me.

The source of law

The question of where law comes from has bothered me for a long time. Why is it ever legitimate for one person to fine or incarcerate another? I was not satisfied with the answer that, "That is just the way it is." or, "Because we have always done it that way." or, "Because there is a social contract in which everyone has agreed to be disciplined by law." I never agreed to be disciplined by law. In fact, I don't recall anyone even asking me if I wanted to agree to it.

I made no headway on that question until an event that I will retell here involving my children. My older daughter was a great sleeper. Get her near her bed by 8:00 in the evening and she was asleep. My younger daughter was a terrible sleeper. She would go to bed at 8:00, but my wife and I would hear her playing in her room when we went to sleep after midnight. Parents don't trust nature in these matters, so my wife and I developed several strategies for getting her to shut out the light and go to sleep, the most successful of which was reading her a story.

Even the most well-written children's books, however, get tedious, so there came a night when I told her that if she would go to bed and turn off her light, I would be up in a moment to read her a story, fully intending to let her go to sleep without the story. When I checked her a half hour later, she was sound asleep and my wife and I congratulated ourselves on having turned a big corner in child-rearing.

It was a different story the next morning, however. My daughter was quite aware of what I had done: I had told her that I would read her a story, then intentionally failed to turn up in time to read her the story, or to wake her up to listen to it. So what was wrong with that? It simply was not "fay-oo". Where had this business of fairness come from? She was, of course, dead right. Telling a person that you will treat them one way, then treating them another, to their detriment and your benefit, is not "fair." That is a principle that is deeply embedded in American law, and she, at age 3, stated it almost word for word.

As if that were not enough, my older daughter, excited by this talk of fairness and dismayed to learn of all the book reading that had been going on while she was asleep, wanted to know why it was fair that we read stories to her sister but not to her. Well, I explained, we had to read stories to her sister to get her to go to sleep. That, she replied, would explain why we *wanted* to read stories to her sister, but it didn't explain why we didn't want to read stories to her. Since both of them equally enjoyed having stories read to them, it was illegitimate to read stories to one of them and not the other for purely selfish reasons. Yet another deep principle of American law.

There is a tendency when this kind of thing happens for a parent to think that his children are special, and I must confess that I thought that I had two future giants of legal thought on my hands. But I began to notice other children and it quickly became apparent that they were as adept at detecting injustice or unfairness as my own. All children, to be sure, are adept at pursuing their own self interest, at demanding what they want. But for children so easily to be able to articulate what they *deserve* and to back it up with reasoned argument struck me as amazing. These are children, mind you, whom it takes years to teach which eating implement to use to eat peas (i.e., not your fingers), yet they are capable of deep and subtle normative analysis while their skills with the language are still rudimentary and most concepts are yet to be developed.

The principle that my younger daughter articulated is, in law, called the principle of *due process:* Treat people the way that you tell them you will treat them. My older daughter's principle is *equal protection:* You may treat people differently only on the basis of actual differences between them that require the different treatment. It is probably a close question whether reading a book to one child and not the other because the one will not go to sleep without it is a sufficient difference between them to support the different treatment, but my older daughter got the argument right. When one has power over another, as a parent has over a child, these principles are, in fact, operative.

It is common in law to view principles like due process and equal protection as *constructs,* as propositions that have been invented to solve a particular problem (here, the problem is controlling people with power). I think that that is incorrect. I think that they are *emanations* from the human thought process itself, outcroppings, in other words, of mental processes that are innate. If that were not the case, it would be hard to justify the use of juries, for the jury is a group of rank amateurs in law who are trusted to render justice in each case. How is it that we can trust them to apply the rules of law to the facts of the case and render a just verdict?

There must be something in their makeup that enables them to do the very subtle thinking required of a normative decision, a deep and immediate understanding of the considerations that a normative question entails. Where does that capability come from?

Fairness

The word "fair" is anathema to most law professors, for it is used by law students to explain everything. What is wrong with the rule of contributory negligence? "It is just not fait "The trouble with that statement is not that it is wrong but that it is unilluminating. Many law professors simply ban the use of the word "fair" in their classes, yet it is a concept that is of central importance to understanding our own normative thought.

The word "fair" is the name for an emotion, like the words "happy" or "mad." When asked what is wrong with the rule of contributory negligence, the student should say, "It just does not *feel* fair." Unfairness is a feeling of, what, incompleteness? disorder? mistreatment?

To unearth the source of law in our own thinking we must identify the perceptual and cognitive conditions that trigger the emotion of unfairness. What conditions prevail that result in that feeling? To get a catalog of the conditions that people in the past have perceived to be unfair all we need do is go to a law library and read some cases. There are countless stories that will trigger that emotion. The house painter who painted the wrong house and wanted the owner of the wrong house to pay him for the paint job. Unfair! The uncle who told his nephew that, if the nephew would go to college, he would pay the tuition, but failed to pay the tuition, resulting in the college repossessing the nephew's car in payment for the tuition. Unfair! The elderly woman who was induced to pay $36,000 for ballroom dance lessons on the promise that it would make her youthful and glamorous. Unfair?

What is it about those situations that generates the feeling of unfairness? Boat designers use the word "fairness" in a way that might help us understand its cognitive meaning. A boat's hull is said to be "fair" if it curves in every direction in a regular manner. The test of the boat's fairness is to bend a wooden batten—a long, thin strip of straight-grained wood—along the curve of the hull and see if the hull touches the wooden batten at every point.

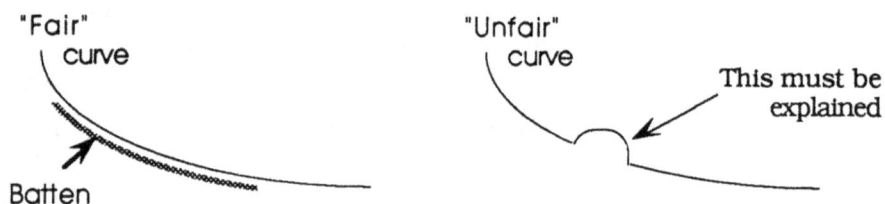

Figure 3.13   Testing a curve for fairness.

In Figure 3.13 the curve on the right is not fair. The curve does not conform to the curve of the wooden batten, which is the standard of fairness. The dent in the middle of the curve destroys it fairness. The boat builder who checks his hull for fairness and discovers this dent will experience a jarring emotion—the feeling that comes from the perception of unfairness.

Note that the perception of unfairness is identical in form to the binocular process of normative analysis that I described in Figure 3.1. The boat batten provides the *norm*. The fairness of its curve is the standard against which the hull is compared.

The feeling that comes from the perception of unfairness will generate tension in the mind of the boat builder, who will immediately seek to determine the cause of the unfairness. Did one of the workers go crazy with a disk sander and gouge it out? Does the unfairness reflect a deeper problem in the framing of the boat? Or is the unfairness part of the design of the boat?

I suggest that the feeling of unfairness is the same in law as it is in boat building. It stems from the perception that something is different from what was expected. It generates tension in the person that drives her to unearth the cause of the unfairness, *to justify* the unfairness.

Return to the boat builder for a moment. He looks at the dent and it looks intentional, not the result of a momentary lapse by a worker. He checks out the boat's framing. It looks fair (that is, it conforms to what he expected to see). Gathering the plans for the boat in hand, he compares that section of the boat with the plans and discovers that the boat designer intended the dent to exist as a housing for a through-hull fitting that would be installed later and would "fair out" the dent.

That discovery will *justify* the unfairness in the mind of the boat builder, eliminating his tension over what was unexpected. The local unfairness of the hull's curvature is justified by a deeper fairness between the shape of the hull and the intention of the designer.

That, I would suggest, is the role of the perception of unfairness: It directs our attention toward that which needs to be explained and generates the tension needed to do the work to justify it. The emotion of unfairness would appear, then, to be a necessary companion to the emotion of fear. The perception of fear generates a tension that drives us to resolve it by flight or fight or negotiation. But there are many more subtle threats to our well-being, like a boat hull that is not sound or a set of social relationships that is in danger of falling apart. For those we need a more subtle detector. That detector is the perception of unfairness and the emotional tension that it generates.

Consider the situation that prevails in most doctor's offices. The average salary of the doctors will be ten to twenty *times* has high as that of the average staff member. That is clearly a major difference between the people involved. But is it an *unfairness?* Is it a difference that is unexpected, that will jar you into seeking its justification? Well, is it? Is that difference just part of the normal "curvature" of income distributions that you expect to see? If it is, skip the next paragraph, for I mean to explore it a bit further, as it raises a question of fairness in my mind. Pursuing it should point out the similarity between the boat builder's and the lawyer's sense of fairness.

But, you might ask, who am I to question the fairness of this practice? After all, the staff members are free people and they go to work willingly each morning. That is. indeed, a justification. If a person willingly subjects himself to something, there is hardly any point in our asking if it is fair (why is that?). But that explanation does not fully remove my feeling of tension, for I wonder if the staff has *willingly* accepted the difference. Is it not possible, for example, that there is an imperfection in the market over which the staff has no control that accounts for the difference in pay? Is it not possible that the staff members are in a fully competitive segment of the market, where their competition with each other keeps their wages down, while the doctor segment of the market is somewhat monopolized, making their wages artificially high? If that is the case, the willingness of the staff workers does not justify the difference, for they are faced with a choice that has been manipulated by the doctors to their own advantage (a violation of the principle enunciated by my older daughter). Here would be an unfairness that was not justifiable on the basis of the willingness of the staff to work.

I am suggesting that law is, at its root, an institutional process for justifying unfairness and for rectifying unfairness that cannot be justified. Unfairness itself is a perceptual/cognitive/emotional process in each person that identifies those differences that need explanation and generates the motivation necessary to do it. I am also suggesting that the cognitive skills necessary to resolve the unfairness are present, at least in rudimentary form, in each person. My daughters' ability to generate deep principles of legal analysis without instruction was not singular.

As with any such process, it differs from person to person and is shaped by the social environment. Some people apparently lack the ability to see themselves as causes of unfairness: they are called "psychopaths" or "sociopaths." And some societies themselves exhibit sociopathic tendencies, discriminating between people on the basis of irrelevant differences between them, such as race. Most members of such a society seem to be able to adopt the social ethos, deforming their own sense of fairness according to the common bias. Yet even in the most unjust of regimes there are those whose sense is not fooled by the common wisdom.

If something like this process underlies law, that would explain how a system of law like ours could grow in a coherent way with neither direction from the top nor an explicit set of well defined guiding principles. It would also explain the perception that law evolves, that our understanding of law grows, little by little, with our experience. With time, our experience with justification grows and the bases upon which we justify social differences becomes more explicit. The principles have emerged from the stew of cases as if they had a life of their own.

Where does Jeffrey's case stand?

The legal thought process just described would suggest that we might not have as difficult a time getting a judge to overturn the rule of contributory negligence as we feared. We may be able to make the judge *feel* the unfairness of Jeffrey's case directly, without having to spell out the principles that were misapplied in creating the rule. We have, after all, a difference that cries out for a justification—the difference between Jeffrey and the twenty million or so other members of his generation who are still alive. And we have a cause that also cries out for justification—the driver of the car, who differs from the great majority of drivers, who have never run their cars into a seven-year-old.

The unfairness of this situation demands justification. For a court to refuse to consider Jeffrey's case by applying the rule of contributory negligence seems like a mechanical, institutional application of rule that is just not fair.

The great strength of a legal system that leaves the principles of law implicit, rather than setting them out beforehand, is that they emerge from experience and can change with experience. This is called the common law system. The judge and jury are directly confronted with the facts of each case. They sense the unfairness that the plaintiff demands justification for directly, through the story told by the plaintiffs witnesses.

The judge will, of course, refer to precedent, to similar cases that have been decided in the past. The judge may go further to explore the principles implicit in those decisions. But the judge's job is not simply a cognitive one—to do an artful job of applying prior principles to the existing case. The judge is not an *administrator* of law.

Figure 3.14   The source of common law.
Law books represent precedents, the witness represents facts, and the judge provides a judgement based on these.

The judge will see before her the effect of her ruling on actual people. If applying prior law would leave her in a state of tension, leaving her with a sense that unfairness has not been justified, she may fashion a rule that produces a more satisfying result. If we can tap the judge's sense of fairness, the rule of contributory negligence should not bar Jeffrey's case. Even if we can't do that, however, Montefiori's testimony should give a solid basis for claiming that Jeffrey, while headstrong, was not the cause of his own death.

All in all. Jeffrey's case looks lively, if not simple. There is surely a great deal of tension left in it, more than enough to cause us to look further into the case.

CHAPTER FOUR

Finding a defendant

Our feeling that there is life in Jeffrey's case puts us up against a fact that we have thus far ignored: The driver of the car hit and ran from the accident and has not been identified. Who will we bring Jeffrey's case against? We need to look further for the identity of the driver. Officer McGinty describes her search for the driver of the car:

John Newland, the owner of the car, reported the car stolen by a call to the station at 4:45 PM, about two hours after the accident. He reported that his son, Timothy, had driven the car from home on an errand, parking the car on the west side of State Street, about seven blocks north of its intersection with Purley. He then crossed State Street and went into a convenience store on the east side of the street.

He emerged from the store after five minutes or so and saw that the car was gone. There was no one in sight who might have seen the thief. He went to several stores on each side of State Street asking if anyone had noticed what happened to his car. Susan Pace, a travel agent in an office next to where the car was parked, had noticed a male teenager, dressed in a sweat shirt and jeans, get into the car and drive it off. Susan Pace confirmed her discussion with Timothy Newland, but was unable to further describe the teenager.

Three sets of fingerprints were taken from the car when it was recovered from the Brewster Police, but none of them matched any prints on record with the Lexington Police or National Criminal Information Center. The car was otherwise devoid of physical evidence that might establish the identity of the driver.

The investigation of the case is closed.

The investigation may be closed, but the tension of the case remains. What are we to do? One possibility is to conduct our own investigation. We learned earlier that Officer McGinty's techniques are less than perfect, for she missed Mr. Montefiori, who had witnessed the accident. Rereading the accident report, we note that Jeffrey lived in Ashville, a town eighty miles from Lexington. He had clearly not gotten to Lexington on his own (an inference). How did he get there?

A telephone call to Jeffrey's mother, Margaret Stapleton, provides the answer.

> Jeffrey and I were in Lexington that day to talk with Emily Paul. Emily lives in the house on the northwest corner of State and Purley. She is an artist's agent who has had great success representing piano players.

> Jeffrey's career had progressed to the point where I felt that his piano teacher, Ron Fritzer, though a fine teacher, was no longer an adequate agent. Ron had arranged Jeffrey's last tour, which included four concerts in the far East, but I didn't feel that they had given Jeffrey the kind of exposure that he deserved.

> We got to Emily's around eleven in the morning. She had him play a selection of pieces, noting that he did a particularly fine job with Chopin; then she made us lunch. After lunch Emily and I talked business and I guess Jeffrey went out into the yard to play.

> The next thing I knew, I heard screaming coming from the street. I looked out the window and saw Jeffrey lying in the street in a pool of blood. Two cars were stopped behind him and their drivers were calling for help. Emily called the emergency number while I ran to help Jeffrey. He seemed to be conscious when I got to him. He kept asking, "What happened? What happened?" You know the rest.

Where does that leave us? Has Margaret's story laid matters to rest, or opened new questions in your mind? We clearly have a special case in Jeffrey. Anyone who can manage Chopin at all is, in my book, special. A child of seven who does a "fine job" with Chopin is a person who happens only once or twice in a century. Jeffrey's death was more than a grave personal loss.

Margaret doesn't seem quite so appealing. It is perhaps understandable that she should get wrapped up in her discussion with Emily Paul, but is it understandable that she lost track of Jeffrey from the end of lunch until she heard the screaming in the street? She doesn't even mention hearing the car that hit Jeffrey skid, though we know from Montefiori that it did skid and from the accident report that the skid marks were 35 feet long. She must have been quite preoccupied with her discussion to have missed that sound (an inference).

Should we pursue this line of inquiry? Margaret is, in a sense, as much a victim of Jeffrey's death as he was. To subject her behavior to scrutiny seems like adding unfairness to tragedy. But if she was in some measure responsible for Jeffrey's death, is it not incumbent upon law to examine her behavior to determine if it was justified?

That may be, but how can it make any sense for us to pursue the case against her? She is the one who approached us about this case. Could we very well tell her that there was a little good news—Jeffrey has a good case—and a little bad news—the case is against her? Oddly, we could. The explanation lies in the fact that Margaret is covered by a million dollar liability insurance policy. If she is liable to Jeffrey's estate for his death, it will be her insurance company that will pay the judgment. Margaret may well be pleased at the prospect of being found liable for Jeffrey's death. We had better pursue that possibility.

Did Margaret "cause" Jeffrey's death?

In order for Margaret to be responsible in any sense for Jeffrey's death she must have *caused* it. It would be nonsensical to hold her responsible for his death if she didn't cause it, just as nonsensical as it would be to hold you responsible for it. That much is obvious. But why is it obvious? Why is it that the law holds people responsible only for what they cause? The answer to that question is not immediately apparent.

It is the fact that a human being can cause something to happen that makes that person a moral actor, an agent who is responsible for that which she causes. To say that a person "caused" an event to happen is to imply that the person could have chosen to do something else that would have caused the event not to happen. So, for example, we suspect that if the driver of the car had been paying attention to what was happening, he would have been able to avoid hitting Jeffrey. If the choice made by the person results in an event that causes harm to another, we conclude that the person "caused" the harm.

By placing such a reliance upon the choices that each person makes, the law takes a strong stand against the theory of physical determinism. Determinism holds that events are not caused but simply follow after one another according to the laws of physics. If anything can be said to be a "cause," under this view, it is the laws of physics themselves. Situations simply follow, one from another, under the control of physical laws. There is no room for the idea of moral responsibility under the doctrine of determinism. Choice, under that view, is simply an illusion.

However problematic to the physicist, choice is a subjective reality—we sense ourselves as choosing to drink a cup of coffee rather than a glass of wine. When we pause for a moment to consider that decision, it seems to us that either alternative is a relevant one, that we might choose coffee and we might choose wine. It is unthinkable that the choice that we finally make is simply the working out of physical laws. We sense ourselves as the *animating force* in what follows, as the reason why we later drink the cup of *coffee*.

It is this subjective sense of ourselves as an animating force, and the recognition of the same force in others, that is the ground upon which law is based. Human beings are, as *a matter of law*, capable of choosing to bring about one set of events rather than another. When they choose to do ill, or to do something that causes ill, they must answer in law for that choice.

Legal concepts are suffused with that sense of human causation. We say that the driver of the car *controls* the car, implying that the driver is the animating force behind the car, causing it to move and determining its speed and direction. We say that a person *intends* an act, implying that if he did not, the act would not have happened. We say that a person agreed to do something, implying that the person could have chosen not to do the thing.

Law would make no sense without the assumption that humans make choices, and those choices are effective in bringing about events. We don't hold guns or cars responsible for the ill that they cause. They simply obey physical laws. But we do more, following, to some extent, the dictates of our own desires. When ill follows from one of those desires, we are responsible for it.

That foundation for law is not all that secure. What is law to do, for example, if it can be shown that drug addicts all suffer from a deficiency in brain chemistry? Did the addict cause the addiction? did the addict in any meaningful sense *choose* the addiction? or was its real cause the laws of physics? Did the addict acting under the dictates of the addiction cause ill when he robbed a store and shot the owner, or was that the laws of physics at work again? As science explains human behavior ever more deeply in physical terms, the foundations of law are shaken, for it is a fundamental principle of law that no person should be held responsible for that which he could not control.

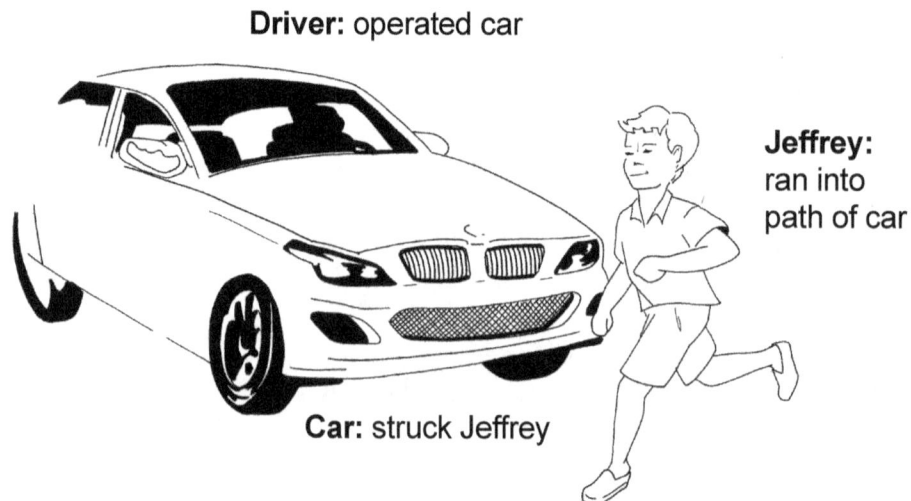

Figure 4.1   The chain of physical causation

That problem does not rear its head in our case, however. Margaret was operating under no physical disability as she chatted with Emily. She simply lost track of Jeffrey. Nothing forced her to do that, as far as we can tell. But did that *cause* Jeffrey's death in any meaningful sense?

Margaret is not present in the picture of the physical causation of the accident. Jeffrey is there, for if he had not run into the path of the car, it would not have struck him. The car is there. The driver is there, for even the physicist would say that the driver's hand on the steering wheel and feet on the accelerator and brakes were relevant antecedents to the path of the car. But note that the physicist would not say that the driver *controlled* the car. "Control" is a legal characterization of the relationship between car and driver.

We could say that Margaret had a hand in the physical chain of events leading up to the accident, for she physically transported Jeffrey to Emily's house. But where does that get us? We could also say that the gas station attendant had a hand in the physical chain of events when he filled Margaret's car with gasoline for the trip. So what?

We cannot solve legal problems with physics, for what we are after is the person or persons who were *responsible* for the event. Why wouldn't we think of blaming the gas station attendant? Because he had no choice about whether or not to give Margaret gasoline? Because when he gave her gasoline he had no idea of the bad end the trip would come to? Either of those reasons is sufficient to let the gas station attendant off the hook, but notice that both of them rely upon subjective concepts—he had no *choice;* he had no idea—that are invisible to the physicist.

The law uses what is called the "but for" test of causation: A person is a cause of an event if the event would not have happened, but for the actions of the person. Applying that test to Margaret: If Margaret had prevented Jeffrey from leaving Emily's house, would the accident have happened?

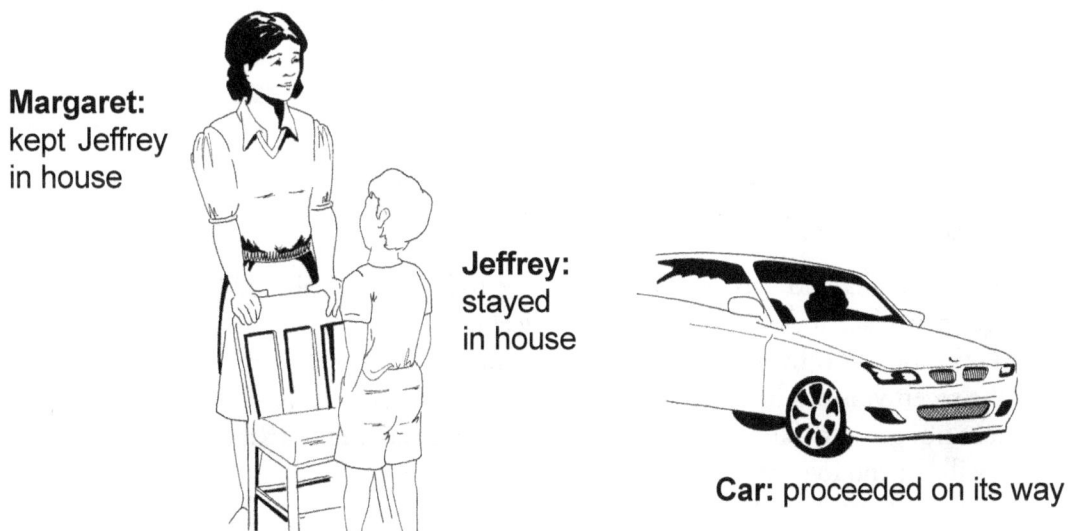

Margaret: kept Jeffrey in house

Jeffrey: stayed in house

Car: proceeded on its way

Figure 4.2   The chain of events, had Margaret looked after Jeffrey.

Clearly not, since there is no sign that the car would have struck the house. *But for* Margaret's failure to keep Jeffrey in the house, then, Jeffrey would not have been hurt.

Margaret is, in this odd sense, a cause of Jeffrey's death.

Under the same test, you and I are also causes of Jeffrey's death, for if either of us had kept Jeffrey in the house he would be alive today, as well. But that is ridiculous. Neither you nor I ever heard of Jeffrey. Oddly enough, it is not ridiculous. It may be pointless, but it is not ridiculous. The but for test of causation is a very easy one to pass.

To say that Margaret was a cause of Jeffrey's death is not to say that she is *responsible* for it. The question now is whether or not she had a *legal* duty to undertake the act, the failure of which was her contribution to Jeffrey's death. That is what gets you and me off the hook, for there is not even the faintest hint that either of us had a duty to protect Jeffrey. That is not the case with Margaret. Mothers do have a duty to protect their children.

A mother's duty to her child

To determine whether or not Margaret was responsible for Jeffrey's death, we must apply the same sort of binocular analysis that we used in the last chapter to examine Jeffrey's fault.

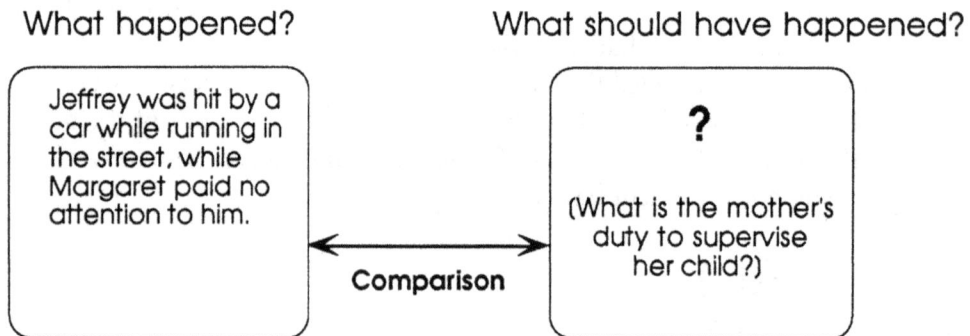

What happened?   **What should have happened?**

> Jeffrey was hit by a
> car while running in
> the street, while
> Margaret paid no
> attention to him.

> **?**
>
> (What is the mother's
> duty to supervise
> her child?)

← **Comparison** →

Figure 4.3   Determining Margaret's fault requires us to
                  determine the norm that she should be held to.

We know what did happen, but how are we to know what should have happened? The first place to look for a norm applicable to Margaret—the first place every lawyer looks—is into our your own sense of duty. Do *you* think that the mother of a seven-year-old has a duty to constantly keep an eye on the child to see that he does not get into danger? I have no idea what your answer to that question will be. It will depend to some extent on your own experience.

My own experience suggests to me that the mother of a seven-year-old has no such duty. My feeling is based on an experience that I had as an eight-year-old. Without asking anyone's permission, I rode my bicycle from my home in a Boston suburb through the streets of Boston to my father's place of business on Beacon Hill, a distance of perhaps twelve miles. My father was stunned to see me and told me to ride back home. When the matter of the trip came up at dinner, my mother was delighted with my adventure. Not even the fact that my five-year-old brother had ridden along with me on the back of my bike bothered her, though my father was not of the same opinion.

In my experience, then, Margaret's behavior raises no question. Her behavior was surely less egregious than my mother's, but I never had reason to question my mother's level of responsibility and don't to this day. Left to my own devices. then, I would find no disharmony between what happened to Jeffrey and Margaret's behavior. But if I am functioning as a lawyer in a case, is my own sense of proper behavior sufficient to send Jeffrey's case packing?

It may be. Lawyers are free to refuse to take on a client for any reason they choose. If I don't think that Jeffrey has a case against his mother, I can turn it down. But I may want to question my own sense of proper behavior and seek to confirm it. I might talk it over with other people to see if my sense of Margaret's duty is generally confirmed by the experience of others.

In the first analysis, then, each person is the source of the norms that are applied in law. It is our reflection upon our own sense of responsible behavior that enframes our initial assessment of a situation. That is, of course, the way all people do it, whether they are lawyers or not. But the lawyer has a slightly different responsibility than the non-lawyer, for consequences follow from the lawyer's assessment. If I apply my own norm of motherly responsibility to Jeffrey's case, it may die. If I was wrong about that norm, I will have caused an injustice. As a lawyer I have a responsibility to look for a more general source of norms. The obvious place to look is to the law itself. What do the cases say about the obligation of the mother to supervise her child?

The doctrine of intrafamily immunity

The cases don't say much, which is surprising, for parenting is an ancient activity and one would expect that it would have come under considerable legal scrutiny. The explanation for the paucity of cases is that until recently a child could not sue his parent for an injury caused by the parent. If the child attempted to bring suit, it was dismissed by the court, citing the doctrine of intrafamily immunity: each family member is immune from a suit alleging non-intentional injury to a family member.

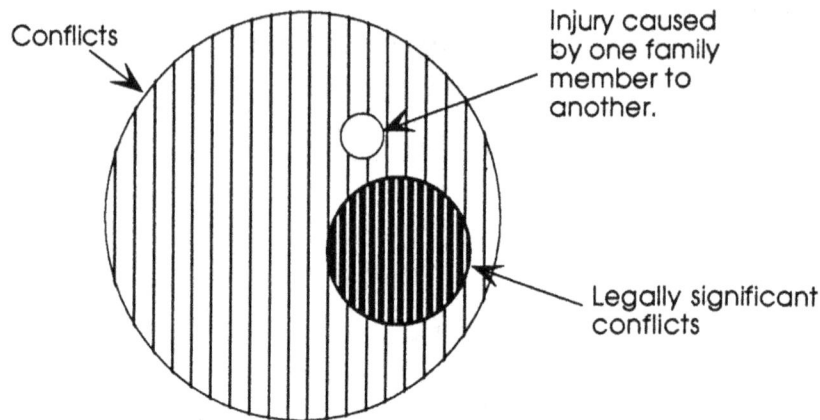

Figure 4.4   Under the doctrine of intrafamily immunity, courts would not consider injuries caused by family members.

That doctrine placed conflicts involving family members outside of the realm of conflicts that the court would entertain. If the behavior of one family member rose to the level of *criminal* behavior, as when a parent beat a child. the law might intervene by charging the parent with the violation of criminal law, though even that was rare. In no case, however, would the court entertain a suit for money damages by one family member against another.

The effect of that doctrine was to limit behavior within the family to the realm of *moral norms.* Each person had his own view of proper treatment of children by parents, of what treatment was "right" and what was 'wrong.' But none of those views had legal consequences, none became *legal norms.*

Over the past twenty years, however, courts have begun to entertain suits by a child against his parent. With little effort we will locate the case of <u>Holodook v. Spencer,</u> a 1974 case from New York, that is directly on point. That case was brought on behalf of a four-year-old against his parent for injuries that he sustained when he fell from a slide in a playground. The child's complaint alleged that his father had allowed him to "stray from his immediate control." The legal name for this theory is "negligent supervision." Putting that theory into the terms that we have been using:

Principle: Parents are responsible for the well-being of their children.

Norm: A parent may neither harm the child nor allow the child to come to harm.

Rule #1:

A child whose injury results from a harm done by the parent may recover damages from the parent for **battery**.

Rule #2:

A child whose injury is caused by the failure of the parent to keep him out of harm's way may recover damages from the parent for **negligent supervision**.

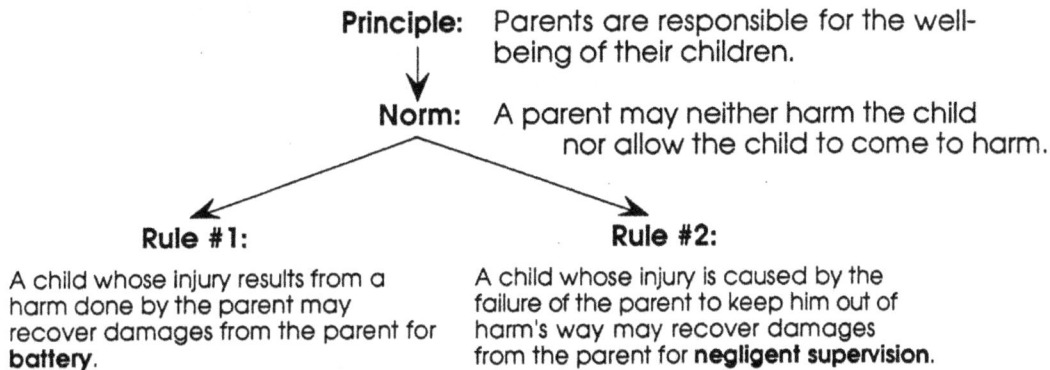

Figure 4.5   The principle underlying the child's
action for negligent supervision.

The lawyer who represented the four-year-old plaintiff in the <u>Holodook</u> case was up against the doctrine of intrafamily immunity, which barred the child's suit. To get the court to overturn that doctrine, the lawyer had to find a legal principle so deep and so strong that it would compel the judge to *overturn* the doctrine. As we saw in the last chapter, however, our courts are reluctant to voice such principles, partly out of the fear. perhaps, that the principles will be used as the lawyer in this case wants to use them, to overturn accepted doctrine.

Reasoning from precedent

The lawyer in the <u>Holodook</u> case was able to find such a principle: Parents are responsible for the well-being of their children. That principle was nowhere stated as such in New York law, but it was clear from countless cases that it must be implicit in New York law. A long line of New York cases, for example, required parents to provide their children with the necessities of life, including education. The New York cases did not support the principle that the parent must *maximize* the prospects of the child. But they did support the principle that the parent must provide, at least minimally, for the well-being of the child.

The lawyer then argued that the principle required this norm: A parent may neither harm the child nor allow the child to come to harm. That norm must follow from the principle that the parent is responsible for the well-being of the child, since the child's well-being is diminished by injury, whether at the hands of the parent or of another whom the parent has failed to protect the child from.

From that norm follows two rules. The first rule gives the child a cause of action in "battery" against the parent who harms him physically. The second gives the child a cause of action in "negligent supervision" for allowing him to come to harm. The lawyer argued that Rule #2 should allow his plaintiff to prevail against the father who let his child fall from the slide.

The court in the <u>Holodook</u> case rejected that argument and dismissed the case. Interestingly, it accepted Rule #1, allowing a child an action in battery for harm caused by the parent. But it rejected Rule #2, holding that a child has no cause of action against a parent for negligent supervision. In essence, the court edited the lawyer's theory of the proper norm in this way:

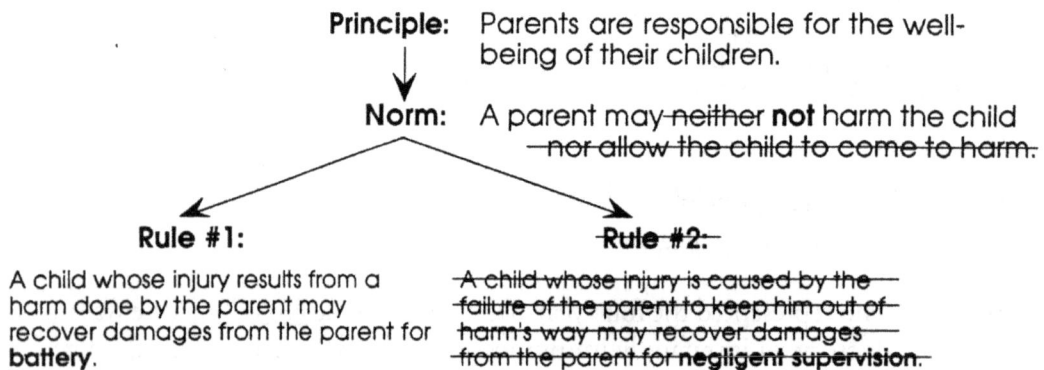

Principle: Parents are responsible for the well-being of their children.

Norm: A parent may ~~neither~~ **not** harm the child ~~nor allow the child to come to harm.~~

Rule #1:
A child whose injury results from a harm done by the parent may recover damages from the parent for **battery**.

~~**Rule #2:**~~
~~A child whose injury is caused by the failure of the parent to keep him out of harm's way may recover damages from the parent for **negligent supervision**.~~

Figure 4.6   The court's rewrite of the norm and rule in the <u>Holodook</u> case.

The court rejected the contention that each parent must keep the child from coming to harm, which caused Rule #2 to fail for lack of deep support. On what basis did it do that? The court clearly felt that injuries to children are inconsistent with the child's well-being, for the court did accept Rule #1. What, then, is the difference between harming the child, which the court found contrary to the principle, and allowing the child to come to harm, which the court did not find contrary to the principle?

The court gave several reasons, one of which would, I think, have earned my mother's avid support. Growing up, said the court, means that the child must develop a sense of responsibility for himself. He must learn about risk, how to identify it, how to avoid it. To do that the child must experience risk. Each parent must, therefore, be free to expose the child to risk, else the child will fail to develop the self-confidence and self-protective capabilities necessary for adult life. To subject the parent to a review of her decision in those cases where the child failed to avoid the risk and was hurt would burden the parent's decision with judicial second-guessing. The parent must be free to exercise her own judgment as to the capabilities of the child.

The court's argument is, in fact, supported by this statement by Margaret Stapleton in our case:

I never gave a second thought to looking after Jeffrey that afternoon. Jeffrey was an extremely clever child with a strong independent streak. Even as a three-year-old, if he got the feeling that I was spying on him or supervising what he did, he would get himself into real trouble just to show me. If I left him alone, he was always careful and quite clever in his own self-preservation.

If I had tried to keep a close eye on him that afternoon at Emily's, there is no telling where he would have run off to. I found that he was always safe on his own when we visited foreign countries, so long as we had a talk beforehand about what was safe and what wasn't.

But what if Margaret was wrong? There is, after all, a strong tendency for a parent to invent justifications after the fact if something goes wrong. The New York court's ruling in Holodook means that the parent's justification will never be examined by a court.

California courts take a different view. They adopt, in essence, both of the proposed rules set out in Figure 4.5, allowing the child a cause of action for negligent supervision. But what norm, what standard of behavior, does the court hold the parent to? According to the California Supreme Court in Gibson v. Gibson, "We think the proper test of a parent's conduct is this: what would an ordinarily reasonable and prudent *parent* have done in similar circumstances?"

What kind of a norm is that? It is not a norm at all. It is simply a *procedure* for the jury to follow after the fact to fashion its own norm.

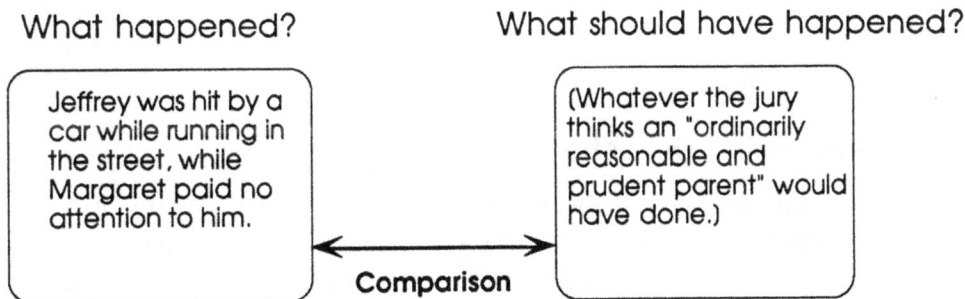

What happened?   What should have happened?

```
 ┌──────────────────────┐               ┌──────────────────────┐
 │ Jeffrey was hit by a │               │ (Whatever the jury   │
 │ car while running in │               │ thinks an "ordinarily│
 │ the street, while    │◄────────────► │ reasonable and       │
 │ Margaret paid no     │               │ prudent parent" would│
 │ attention to him.    │               │ have done.)          │
 └──────────────────────┘  Comparison   └──────────────────────┘
```

Figure 4.7   The California view does not set out a norm for evaluating the parent's conduct, but leaves it until after the fact.

During the trial the jury will look at the facts of the situation and reach its own decision as to what an "ordinarily reasonable and prudent parent" would have done under the circumstances. How is it to know what such a parent would have done? It decides that itself: What, dear jury, would we have done if we were Margaret Stapleton on August 8, 1990? If the parent's behavior did not measure up to what the jury thinks that it, as the ordinarily reasonable and prudent parent, would have done in retrospect, it will find that the parent violated her duty.

The California approach gives us some sense of what was worrying the New York court in the <u>Holodook</u> case, for it allows the child to bring virtually any case to the jury. Once in the hands of the jury, there is no way to tell what it is that they will find reasonable and prudent. If they come from a different social class than the parent, or are as a group more cautious, or fail to understand the family's ethnic or socioeconomic context, or are simply inflamed by the prospect of an injury to the child after the fact, the parent will lose. Worse, since the jury cannot know the child, its standard will be fashioned in the abstract, not derived from the nature of the child himself.

The California rule gives the parent no guidance before the fact. It does not set out a norm to guide the parent's care for the child. How is the California rule consistent with the principle that the parent is responsible for the well-being of the child? It does not ask if the parent was acting responsibly. It asks if the parent was conforming to standards of child-rearing that were ordinarily reasonable and prudent. That is a very different thing, for it means that a parent is responsible not for the well-being of the child but rather for raising the child in conformity with whatever the ordinarily prudent parent in the community does.

Could such an approach not demoralize parents and result in less well-being for their children? Could not concern for future liability cause them to be overly cautious, over-protective in raising their children? And what of parents of children like Jeffrey, who take very poorly to direct supervision? Does the California rule not put those parents at war with their children, putting them under lock and key to avoid the chance that the kids will hurt themselves?

The response of law to change

Pause for a moment to consider where we are. We started with a pretty simple question: What norm of behavior should Margaret's behavior that afternoon be held up against to determine if she was at fault in her care for Jeffrey? We began by reflecting upon our own experience, asking what *we* thought she should have done. That led me to think that her behavior was reasonable, based upon my mother's treatment of me as a child. But then I wondered whether my own sense of what is proper behavior for a mother was a proper standard.

We then took a look at the law and ended up worse off than we started. We wound up comparing two answers to the question, New York's limited parental immunity rule and California's rule of no parental immunity. Neither view, as it turned out, gave us a norm to apply to Margaret. The New York view would shield Margaret from any law suit. The California view leaves it to the jury after the fact to come up with whatever norm it wants to apply. What a waste of time!

Isn't law supposed to be the source of LAWS? Of clear, authoritative norms of conduct against which we can measure individual conduct? What are we to make of the goulash that we dove into when we innocently went looking for a norm to apply to Margaret?

The law used to have a very simple rule to give us: Parents are immune from suit by their children. Period. But, as clear and simple as that was, the wheels fell off of it. Courts began chipping away at it, first letting the child whose parents had stolen property from him sue to get it back, then letting the child who was beaten sue for redress, then, at least in California. letting the child who had come to harm while under his parent's control, sue the parent for that harm. The simple rule of intrafamily immunity was replaced by a mess of conflicting rules as courts entertained cases by family members. Don't judges have any sense?

There are clearly stronger values at work in law than simplicity and consistency, else courts would never have stepped off the dock of intrafamily immunity into the storm-tossed sea of rules that today they paddle around in. Those values clearly have something to do with "fairness," for it does not feel fair to bar a child who has been injured by a parent's neglect from holding that parent responsible in law. But they have surely made our job as lawyers (and, perhaps, as parents) more difficult.

This situation is universal in law. An existing standard begins to deteriorate under the force of social change or new moral sensibilities or new understandings of reality. But new rules do not emerge fully formed to replace old ones. There emerges a crop of alternatives, which compete with each other. Will the New York view prevail, or will states begin to move to the California view? Or will a third view emerge and prevail?

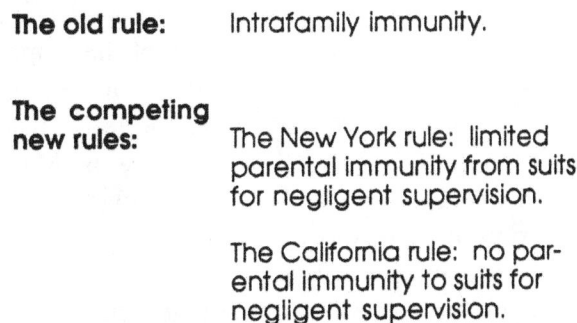

The old rule: Intrafamily immunity.

The competing new rules: The New York rule: limited parental immunity from suits for negligent supervision.

The California rule: no parental immunity to suits for negligent supervision.

Figure 4.8   Competition among new rules to replace the old.

This process of legal change has been likened to *evolution.* The demise of an existing rule opens up a new ecological niche, as it were. It creates a space that must be filled by a new member of the species. Many new candidates for that spot are generated. In physical evolution the new candidates are generated by the processes of mutation and selective reproduction. In law, the new candidates are the rules that are generated by competing legal systems. As in physical evolution, the new candidates compete with each other until one prevails.

To work, an evolutionary process must be *polycentric*—it must have many sources of new candidates to fill the niche. In physical evolution that requirement is provided by the fact that any set of parents can produce offspring with new characteristics. In law, that requirement is filled by the vast profusion of *law-giving agencies.* We have seen, for example, that New York and California have each generated a new rule of parental responsibility. There is nothing to keep the courts of each of the fifty states from coming up with its own rule. The legislatures of each of the fifty states could get into the act as well, passing statutes that enacted a new standard.

The courts and legislatures of each state are legitimate law-giving agencies. That amounts to one hundred possible sources of new candidates, which is polycentric. In truth, law is far more polycentric than that, for, within each state there are multiple courts, any one of which can generate a proposed new rule. Add to those the state and federal administrative agencies that generate law, plus the local courts and city councils, and we see that the legal system has a rich inventory of agencies that can generate new rules.

To work, an evolutionary process must also have a way of sorting through the new candidates, throwing out those that are not fit. In nature, that is done through direct competition between members of different species for material survival. The population of the species that can best exploit its niche will rise, eat up all the available food, and starve the competition into extinction.

How is that process of consolidation accomplished in law? Each state has the power to choose its own laws. How is it that the laws of different states don't radically diverge over time? What accounts for the fact that, over time, the number of different laws that address a problem (e.g., what should be the child's right to bring action against his parents?) falls, as one after another of the proposed rules fails?

There are a number of different forces at work in this process, but we can feel one of the most important in our own minds: Do you feel that the New York rule or the California rule should apply to Jeffrey's case against Margaret? Or do you think that neither of them makes sense and so would provide one of your own? Your answers to those questions are part of the evolutionary process in law. If you pick the California rule, you will bring suit against Margaret, urging the court to adopt the California rule. If you are successful in that argument, you will have been the agency by which the California rule is propagated further into the niche created by the demise of the rule of intrafamily immunity. You will have been a force for the consolidation of the California rule of law.

If you don't like either of the rules, you may come up with your own proposed rule and urge a court, or the state legislature, to adopt it. In that case you will be functioning as a source of new candidates, rather than as a force for consolidation. In either case, you, as the lawyer, are the element that carries the evolutionary force in law, just as the chromosome is the element that carries the evolutionary force in nature. Unlike the chromosome, you choose which candidate you will back. You *decide* what force to exert upon the system.

Lawyers, like chromosomes, have a hard time seeing themselves as a formative force in an evolutionary process. To the lawyer, it usually feels that she is simply making a decision about whether or not to represent a client or what theory to pursue in a case. But those decisions will play against the decisions made by countless others in a competition for the generation and selection of legal norms.

Should Jeffrey sue Margaret?

Our role as forces in the evolution of law may or may not bring comfort to us as we try to decide whether or not to pursue Jeffrey's case against his mother. None of the cases that we have found has given us any guidance as to the legitimacy of Margaret's behavior on the day of the accident. Was it right or wrong?

If you have been taking Jeffrey's case seriously, you should be in a state of considerable tension at this point. We are running out of potential defendants. The driver of the car cannot be identified. There doesn't appear to be anyone else who we can plausibly say caused Jeffrey's death. But the case against Margaret is in limbo. To have a case, we need a norm, something that will allow us to evaluate her behavior. The law provides no norm. What are we to do?

The only thing we can do is fall back upon ourselves. Do you think that what Margaret did was a breach of a duty that she owed Jeffrey? If you do, and if you can enunciate reasons why you feel that way, you may be able to convince a jury that she breached that duty to Jeffrey. If you can get a court to adopt the California rule, which leaves it to the jury to decide the proper norm to apply to Margaret, you might be able to prevail in a suit by Jeffrey against Margaret.

As for me, I will not take Jeffrey's case against Margaret. I don't see any unfairness in her behavior; it conforms, in other words, to what I expect as reasonable behavior from mothers. You might *imagine* from my story of my mother's response to my trip to Boston that I think that parents must have considerable freedom in deciding the level of supervision to subject their children to. Children will be injured; no doubt. Irresponsible parents will abandon their children; no doubt. I do not think that juries acting after the fact can meaningfully put themselves in the place of the parent. I do not think that any parent should have to raise a child under the threat of meaningless scrutiny. I do not think that that rule is consistent with the principle underlying the parent's obligation to her child.

Who am I to make such a decision? Don't I have an obligation as a lawyer to pursue every possible avenue of redress for my client? Perhaps, but Jeffrey is not yet my client. What I am saying is that, if all Jeffrey has is an action against his mother, he is not ever going to be my client. Another lawyer, more enamored than I with the California rule, may take on his case. You may take his case. But I will not. My reading of the existing law does not lead me to question my own sense of unfairness in this case. As between Jeffrey and Margaret, my mind is in a state of zero tension.

That is not to say, however, that I have resolved all of my tension about Jeffrey's case. There are still loose ends that whisper that my thinking on this case should not yet end.

CHAPTER FIVE

Pursuing a defendant

It is time to consider the possibility of a case against the owner of the car, John Newland. According to Officer McGinty, John asked his son, Timothy, to go to the store on an errand on the afternoon of August 8. The car was stolen from its parking place on State Street while Timothy was in the store.

On its face, this is not a promising situation. Is there any sense in which the owner of a car *causes* the harm that follows when it is stolen? There were presumably many cars parked on State Street that day. The thief chose Newland's car from among them. How are John or Timothy Newland in any sense the cause of the injury to Jeffrey? Had John's car not been parked where it was, would the thief not simply have stolen another car?

Jeffrey's case is hanging from a reed so slim that a practicing lawyer might well pursue this case no further. But we are by nature resolutely thorough. The tension in Jeffrey's case is not completely resolved. We will pursue his case until it is. We need more information. The easiest place to start is with another call to Officer McGinty, who by now is getting a bit testy with our repeated inquiries.

> Both John Newland and Timothy have clean driving records. John has had bad luck with car thieves, however. This was the third time he had reported his car stolen within a two month period.
>
> When we picked up the car from the Brewster police, the keys were in the car.
>
> Lexington has experienced a wave of car thefts over the past nine months. We generally average about two car thefts per month per thousand registered cars. But this year we have had over ten per month. We have no idea what is causing that jump, and nothing we do seems to make a difference in it.

The keys were in the car when it was recovered? By inference that would mean that Timothy left the keys in the car when he went into the store. That could explain why the thief stole John Newland's car and not one of the others parked on the street. That justifies a trip to the Newlands' home, a small farm on the outskirts of Lexington. Pulling into the driveway, we spot the car that hit Jeffrey. It is only four years old, but it is in bad shape. Both rear fenders are badly banged up and the rear bumper is partially torn off on the left side. Without being obvious about it, we can't see the spot behind the right front wheel where the car hit Jeffrey. John is pleased to talk with us and invites us into the parlor of the old farm house.

> Timothy is nineteen years old. He has worked full time with me on the farm since he quit high school. He is a good driver, but he is somewhat absent-minded.
>
> On the farm it is natural to leave keys in the ignition of the farm equipment. Timothy seems to have developed a habit of doing that with cars. The car was stolen twice in June. He left the keys in the car both times. The second time it was stolen it was involved in a minor accident. The police recovered the car from a ditch where the thief left it.
>
> After the second theft, I prohibited Timothy from driving the car for three months. On the day of Jeffrey's accident, however, I was unable to go to the store and I asked Timothy to go there for me.

John's statement contains some interesting propositions—propositions, that is, that generate tension. Tim was in the habit of leaving keys in the car. That habit had, on two prior occasions, resulted in the theft of the car. One of those thefts had resulted in an accident. We begin to suspect that this was not the normal situation of a person who, through inadvertence, leaves his keys in a car.

Using law as a guide

One of the things that stunned me as a young lawyer was that the lawyers who I got to know knew hardly any *laws*. When I asked them about that, they cheerfully, even proudly, confessed that I, who had just taken the bar exam, knew far more laws than they did, but before long I would forget most of them. When they needed to know authoritatively what the law actually held on a point, they said, they would look it up. During the years that I worked with them, I hardly ever saw them look up any laws. On the occasions when that had to be done, they usually gave the job to me.

The practice of law is clearly not a *knowledge-based* activity, at least not in a simpleminded sense of getting law from over here and applying it to facts from over there. If it isn't knowledge-based, what is it? I pursued that question with them and other lawyers from time to time, but never got much of an answer. The best I could get from them was that law is an activity of the mind that is based upon a set of general frameworks, understandings of an area of law that each lawyer builds for himself. A lawyer who has a reasonably developed framework should be able to *make up* the rule of law on any given point. The only reason to see what the law actually said was to confirm that the law that one had made up was, in fact, the law that was recognized, or to discover what the law said on a point that was so close that either of two mutually exclusive rules was plausible.

To this point in Jeffrey's case I have relied upon the normative framework that is implicit in your mind, your own sense of rightness and wrongness, as a guide to his case. You may have found some of my explanations of his case obscure, but I will wager that you have had no difficulty resolving the specific points of his case—was he injured? should his claim be barred because he ran into the street? did Margaret do anything wrong?—in your own mind.

At this point I want to make the law more explicit, both because the case against the Newlands raises more subtle questions than the ones that we have thus far considered and because I want to give you a framework for analyzing the case that is as close as I can make it to one that a lawyer actually uses. I must caution you that the framework of law that follows is, as nearly as I can put it into words, my own. I have made it up, just as every lawyer who practices in the area of law involved in Jeffrey's case has made up his or her own framework, different from mine.

The mental framework that guides my thinking is, in fact, visual. As I have tried to draw it, however, I have generated diagrams that don't make sense to anyone else (mental visualizations seem to be intensely personal), so I will set it out as nearly as possible in words:

> A person who creates a risk of injury to another is liable in damages if that risk results in injury, so long as the person knew or should have known of the risk created, unless it would be unreasonable for the person to avoid the risk.

Figure 5.1   My general principle of liability for injury.

Notice that it is a principle of *law,* for it sets out the consequences that follow from the satisfaction of each one of its elements: "... is liable in damages ...." That clause sets out the teeth of law, the consequence that will be foist by law upon the unfortunate person who satisfies all of the elements of the framework. This is no idle principle of manners: "It would be really nice if...

For the Newlands, those consequences would be extremely unfortunate. The only source of wealth that they have from which they could pay damages to Jeffrey is their farm. It has a present market value of over $600,000, for it lies in the path of prime residential development as the town of Lexington expands. John Newland has steadfastly refused to sell the farm, for it has been in his family for six generations and farming is all that he knows how to do. If his behavior satisfies the principle set out above, or whatever version of that principle is applied by a court of law, he will lose that farm.

As we think through the case against the Newlands, then, we will be sobered by the realization that for them this is no laughing matter.

Spotting the issue

Let us apply the general principle, element by element, to the Newlands.

◆ "A person ..." John and Timothy are clearly persons. There is no room for tension on that element.

◆ "... who creates a risk of injury to another ..." John, who knew that Timothy had a way of leaving his keys in the car, nonetheless loaned it to him to drive on an errand for John. Timothy apparently left the keys in the car. Does any of that constitute "creating a risk of injury? We might be comfortable with the idea that the thief created such a risk, if we infer from what we know that he was nervous about driving the stolen car, probably speeding, and perhaps so distracted that he didn't see the risk to Jeffrey as soon as he should have.

We might see Jeffrey as creating the risk by chasing the paper around in the street, though that may be a bit strong, given the nature of seven-year-olds. We might even see Mr. Montefiori as creating the risk by letting the paper blow out of his hands. But did John or Timothy *create* the risk?

The most that we can say is that they may have created a situation that *increased* the risk of injury, if we imagine that something that they did *induced* the thief to steal the car. Could this have been a situation in which an irresponsible kid, walking along the street casually glancing into the parked cars, spotted the keys in the ignition to the Newland car and was thus *inspired* to steal it?

To me, that is the heart of the possible case against the Newlands. Notice that it all hinges upon an inference about the thief's mental state: Did something that the Newlands did create a *state of mind* in the thief that led to the disaster? Inferences of this sort are irretrievably problematic, for they are incapable of objective verification.

That inference will be derived from the other inferences that we glean from the facts, and there is one lurking here that troubles me: Why did the thief steal the Newlands' car? It is, as has been described, a bit of a junker, surely not a car that would appeal to either a professional car thief or a joyrider. There were other cars parked on State Street that afternoon, many, if not most of them, more appealing to a thief than the Newlands'. Could it be that the thing that singled out their car was the presence of keys in the ignition? Could it be that the thief was not at all in mind of stealing a car that afternoon, but was inspired to do it by the presence of the keys in the ignition? If so, there is some reason to charge the Newlands' with *creating* a risk.

◆ "... if that risk results in injury ..." There is no question that Jeffrey suffered an "injury." But did it result from the risk that was created by the Newlands (assuming, under the last point, that they created a risk)? Leaving keys in a car increases the risk that it will be stolen, but does it increase the risk that the stolen car will cause injury to another?

We could approach that question *empirically:* Is there statistical evidence that stolen cars are more frequently involved in accidents than cars that have not been stolen? The answer is emphatically *yes." Stolen cars are four times more likely to be involved in accidents before they are recovered than if they had been driven the same number of miles by their owners.

This link between the risk and the injury is *statistical.* No statistic can show what happened in this case. From the facts that we know, in fact, it may be that the driver of the car was doing an exemplary job of driving the car, but Jeffrey created an impossible situation. What weight can we give to that statistic?

◆ "... so long as the person knew or should have known of the risk created ..." When John Newland's car was recovered from the Brewster police, Officer McGinty called to tell him that it had been the cause of Jeffrey's death. He was dumbfounded. Neither had the faintest idea that leaving the keys in the car would result in anyone's death.

It appears, then, that it is not true that they "knew" of the risk created. Since we cannot get inside their heads, we will have to take their word for that. They will pass the descriptive prong of the test: They didn't know of the risk. But what of the normative prong: *Should* they have known of the risk?

The normative prong calls for a normative comparison:

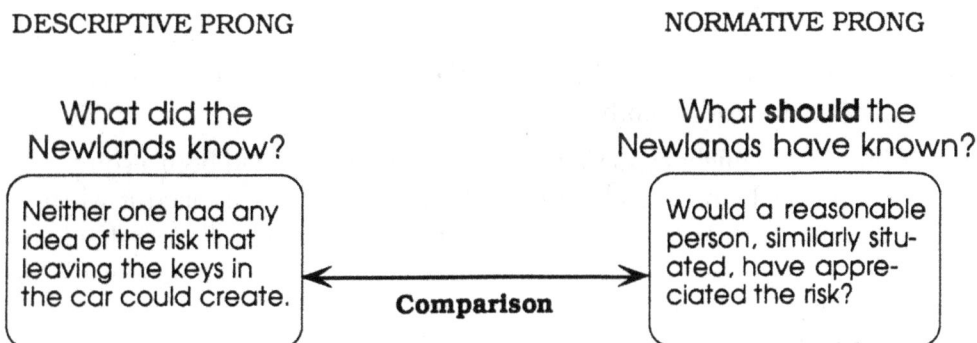

DESCRIPTIVE PRONG   NORMATIVE PRONG

What did the   What **should** the
Newlands know?   Newlands have known?

| Neither one had any idea of the risk that leaving the keys in the car could create. | ◄——— **Comparison** ———► | Would a reasonable person, similarly situated, have appreciated the risk? |

Figure 5.2   The descriptive and normative prongs of the knowledge test.

Who is the "reasonable person" who is the test for what the Newlands should have known? If the case goes to trial, it will eventually be the jury that decides, as the reasonable person, what they should have known.

For now, we must consult the only reasonable person who is ready to hand, namely ourselves. Putting ourselves in the position of the Newlands, is the risk from the stolen car something that would have been apparent? We might well differ on this (as might the members of the jury). Leaving keys in the car is something that just about everyone has done inadvertently, never thinking about the consequences beyond the risk of theft.

But the Newlands were different. Their car was stolen twice in the month of June and involved in an accident one of those times. Would not the reasonable person to whom that had happened have been aware not simply of the risk of theft, but also of the danger of an accident following a theft?

I am not absolutely sure about what I would have done under those circumstances, but I think that it would have crossed my mind that it was very lucky that no one had been hurt when the car was driven into the ditch. I think, in other words, that a jury might well conclude that the Newlands should have known of the risks of injury created by a stolen car.

◆ "... unless it would be unreasonable for the person to avoid the risk." John Newland knew how to avoid the risk: Don't let Timothy drive the car. He relaxed that prohibition on August 8, sending Timothy to the store on an errand because he was "unable" to do the errand himself.

How do we decide whether or not that was unreasonable? We ask what consequences would have followed if the errand had not been done. If, for example, John was suffering from a serious heart ailment and needed medicine immediately but was unable to go to the store himself, we would all agree that it would be reasonable to send Timothy to pick it up, even at the risk of another theft. If, on the other hand. Jeffrey was simply doing a normal errand that could wait, we might conclude that it was unreasonable for John to send Timothy.

Further, we might expect (an inference) that if there had been a compelling reason for John to send Timothy, he would have mentioned it when we talked to him, since that would put him in a better light. But we should not put too much weight on that inference. We better make a note to ask him why he sent Timothy to the store.

Where does the case against the Newlands stand? The general principle gave us a framework against which we could assess the case. Now let's tote it up.

Element:	**Tension level:**
(1) A person ...	0
(2) ... who creates a risk of injury to another ...	100%
(3) ... if that risk results in injury ...	30%
(4) ... so long as the person knew or should have known of the risk created ...	51%
(5) ... unless it would be unreasonable for the person to avoid the risk.	40%

Figure 5.3   My tension level on each element of the case.

Of the five elements of the case we have eliminated all tension as to one of them—the Newlands are each "a person." There is, however, considerable tension as to the other four, at least as I assess this case. The most problematic element to me is the conclusion that the Newlands "created" the risk of injury. It is possible, as we have seen, that something that they did *inspired* the theft of the car. If that were not possible, the tension on this element would, in my mind, fall to zero. That would kill the case against the Newlands, for it would eliminate one of the five elements of the case and all five are required to constitute a case against them.

Figure 5.3 is my representation of a mental process that is central to the process of legal thought: spotting the issue in a case. Each element of the principle constitutes a potential issue; each element must be proved by the plaintiff. If the defendant is able to destroy any one of those elements, the plaintiffs case will fail. The elements of the case are the battleground upon which it will be fought.

When the facts of the case, and the inferences that follow from them, are organized according to the elements, the elements that are *at issue* in the case are identified. In this case, four of the five elements are at issue. That is not a pleasant situation for the lawyer who is looking at the case from Jeffrey's standpoint, for it means that she will have to fight the case on four fronts at once. From the amount of tension in each of the four elements, it looks to me like it will be a very tough fight.

You might very well, and very reasonably, disagree with me about that.

Figure 5.4   Differences between lawyers in their assessment of cases arise from differences in their concepts of the law and in the way that they process information, as well as from differences in their reading of the facts.

Lawyers often disagree about what the issues are in a case. For one thing, they may be working from different legal frameworks—they may have a different principle, with different elements, in mind, as do the two lawyers in Figure 5.4. For another, they may differ in the tension that they associate with each element. If, for example, you think that it is clear that someone who leaves his keys in his car is creating a risk (thereby putting the tension associated with that element at 10% or less), you and I will have a very different view of this case.

   Identifying the issues in a case gives you a sense of what to pursue next, of the most productive path of further inquiry. At this point in Jeffrey's case we have a tiny grasp on the great sea of facts in which it is awash. We don't know the color of Jeffrey's eyes or his height. We don't know what was in the trunk of the Newlands' car at the time the accident happened. We don't know what the weather was like, how fast the car was going when it hit Jeffrey, what it was that Timothy was going to buy at the store, or the condition of the car tires.

It would be enormously time-consuming to draw a complete picture of the events surrounding Jeffrey's death. We cannot spend the time to do that. We must decide what it is that we want to know. How do we do that?

Do we want to know Jeffrey's eye color? Why not? Because it is *irrelevant*. What does that mean? It means that as far as we can tell from our present understanding of the case, his eyes could be any color, including bright yellow, and it would have no effect upon any of the *issues* that are in a state of tension in our minds. Assessing the facts as we know them against the framework of law that is applicable to the case points our efforts toward gathering information that is most relevant to the case.

Pursuing the issues

Given the assessment of the case in Figure 5.3, what information should we pursue next? Lawyers differ in the strategies that they use to develop cases. My own tendency is to look at the most burning issue—the one with the greatest tension—first. That must be tempered, however, with a consideration of how much additional information will be needed to resolve the issue and how difficult it will be to get that additional information.

Element 5, while not in great tension, may be resolved very easily, so that might be a good place to start. You will recall that Element 5 provides that a person is not responsible for a risk that he creates if it would be unreasonable for the person to take action to prevent the risk. The risk that we are concerned about here is the risk that the car would be stolen because the keys were left in it. John could have avoided that risk by refusing to let Timothy drive the car. If there was a compelling reason why John let Timothy drive the car on the afternoon of August 8. it might have been unreasonable for him to keep Timothy at home. We should be able to unearth that reason with a quick telephone call to John.

> I sent Timothy to the store to get the newspaper. The paper boy had failed to deliver the paper that morning.
>
> There was no particular reason why I wanted to read that day's paper. I enjoy reading the paper at lunch and I missed it that day.
>
> I was all tied up repairing the tractor and I was worried that by the time I could get to the store all of the news-papers would be sold.

Hmm. I don't know about you, but I don't think that that is a very compelling reason for John to have sent Timothy to the store. John was quite aware of the chance that

Timothy would leave the keys in the car again. Would it have been unreasonable for him to have waited until he was through with the tractor to get the newspaper himself, or to miss it for the day?

John's statement has reduced the tension in my mind that arises from that element.

Element:	Tension level:
(1) A person ...	0
(2) ... who creates a risk of injury to another ...	100%
(3) ... if that risk results in injury ...	30%
(4) ... so long as the person knew or should have known of the risk created ...	51%
(5) ... unless it would be unreasonable for the person to avoid the risk.	**5%**

Figure 5.5   The effect of new information on the assessment of the case: The tension on element 5 drops to 5%.

The tension on that element is not completely resolved in my mind, for I can imagine that a member of a jury might think that John had a compelling enough reason to send Timothy to the store for the paper. At 5% the tension is high enough to remind me that the matter is not completely closed, but low enough that I can put it to rest for now and get on with the issue that really bothers me: Did John or Timothy *create* the risk that resulted in Jeffrey's death? To resolve that I will have to talk with Timothy.

> I swear that I didn't leave the key in the car that day. Before I left home dad gave me a little lecture about the key. When he handed it to me he tied a string to it to remind me to take it out of the ignition.

> I don't know how the thief got the key. All I know is that when I bought the paper at the store I put the change in my pocket and the change fell out on the floor. I guess that pocket had a hole in it. Then I realized that the key was missing. I guess it fell out of that pocket.

If we believe what Timothy says, and he is easy to believe for he strikes us as utterly guileless, he didn't leave the key in the car. He tried to act responsibly, but was inept. Does his attempt to do the right thing cleanse him of fault? Or does the fact that he didn't check his pocket put him back into the soup?

Timothy's story generates a mental picture (a string of inferences) of what might have happened that afternoon. As Jeffrey pulled up to the curb, the man who would steal the car was standing on the sidewalk, perhaps idly lingering, perhaps coolly watching for a car to take on a joyride (the inference that he was a professional car thief is eliminated, for me, by the poor state of the car itself and its low value). Timothy carefully took the key out of the lock and put it into his pocket as he got out of the car. Somewhere between the car and the door of the store across the street the key fell out of his pocket. Seeing that, the thief retrieved the key from the street and took the car.

If that picture of the event is valid—and there is no way that we will ever know whether or not it is—Timothy's situation under the general principle above is not good. That principle assigns liability to one who *creates* a risk. According to the picture that I have just drawn, Timothy could be said to have created a risk, for we could *characterize* the dropping key as an inspiration to the thief to steal the car, as behavior that <u>caused</u> the car to be stolen when, without it, the car would not have been stolen.

Notice that this characterization requires us to infer something that can never be proven—the mental state of the thief. It may have been that the thief was a person who had personal animosity for Timothy, who vowed that the next time he saw Timothy's car he would steal it no matter what. Or the thief could have had a weird aesthetic attraction to beaten up Fords that made the Newland car irresistible. If the thief had either of those mental states, Timothy's behavior was irrelevant; dropping the key on the street would not have inspired the theft of the car.

The trouble with that is that both of those inferences badly strain the facts as we know them. Timothy just doesn't seem like the kind of kid who would have sworn enemies, dedicated to doing him ill, though we might want to check that with him. And an aesthetic love of beaten up Fords is probably so rare that the chance that the thief was possessed of it is so unlikely as to be worth ignoring.

Of the possibly infinite number of inferences that we could draw from the facts as we know them, the inference that Timothy's dropping the key in the street inspired the on-looking thief to take the car is a lively one. By "lively" I mean that I can well imagine myself convincing a jury that that is the best way for it to visualize what happened on that day. You can test that yourself. Have I convinced you that it is the strongest inference? You are a potential member of the jury that I will have to argue this case to. Can you think up a string of inferences that is more compelling than mine?

The contingencies in legal reasoning

Pause for a moment to consider how enormously contingent legal reasoning is. My reasoning in this case is, first, based upon a general principle of law that I made up. I don't know that I will be able to convince a court to accept it. for I know for sure that each judge and lawyer has his or her own version of that principle and it may conflict with my own.

Based upon that made up principle I have assessed the case, making layers of inferences from the facts that I know. Some of those inferences are empirically verifiable, like the inference that a professional car thief would not steal the Newlands' car. But the most crucial inferences are not empirically verifiable, like the mental state of the thief. No one will ever know what it was, but determining what it was is crucial to the case.

To test the inferences that I have made I must hold them up against yet another huge contingency—the jury that I imagine presenting Jeffrey's case to. I have no idea who that jury will be. Even if I did, I could not get inside their heads to see if they were following my reasoning on the case.

To top it all off, I have only my own mental tensions to guide me. If there is something faulty in that dynamic, my treatment of the case will be way off. If, for example, there is something in my private life that is causing me great tension, that tension might overwhelm the delicate tensions that have been generated by my thinking about the case (clients are rightfully ill at ease if their lawyer is going through a divorce or an illness). Or there could be tensions from my job that interfere. The law firm for which I work could, for example, be so desperate for new business that I am under great tension to bring in any case, however remote. That force could easily distort my reading of Jeffrey's case.

We can check our interpretation of the event with Susan Pace, the travel agent who saw the thief take the car, to see if she can shed any light on the scenario that we have built.

> As I told the police officer, I got a good look at the kid who stole the car because he was hanging around in front of the travel agency for quite a while before he took the car. I just can't remember what he looked like.
>
> I did see him get into the car. Now that you mention it, I do think that he picked up something from the middle of the street before he got into the car.

That tends to confirm our reconstruction of the scenario, but what exactly does her statement mean? She did not offer the information that the thief had picked something up in the street. We had to ask her about it explicitly. Did that jog her memory, or did it plant the idea in her mind? Does it reflect what happened or what we want to have happened? We will probably never know, but we will now know that if we need her to testify on this point at trial the idea is firmly planted in her mind.

Doesn't the thief's wrong erase Timothy's wrong?

We have worked awfully hard to find fault on Timothy Newland's part, when all along the thief was guilty of a far graver wrong. Doesn't his wrong relieve Timothy of responsibility for his fault, assuming that he was at fault?

Consider this. I own a small store. One afternoon I clean the pistol that I keep behind the counter, reload it, and carelessly leave it on the counter. A thief, intending to rob me, grabs the pistol and accidentally shoots himself with it. Will I be liable to him for damages for his injury? Did I *create* the risk that the robber suffered from? I don't think so.

But what if the robber accidentally shot a customer? The fault still seems to lie solely with the robber unless it was true that it was the sight of the gun on the counter that induced the robber to use a gun in the robbery. If the robber was planning to use a knife, but grabbed the gun when he saw it, the increased risk to bystanders associated with the gun is partially caused by my carelessness. However bad the robber, his evil does not eliminate the fact that my carelessness worsened the prospects of the people who were in my store.

That conclusion can be justified if we look at the relationship between the shop owner and the thief in this way:

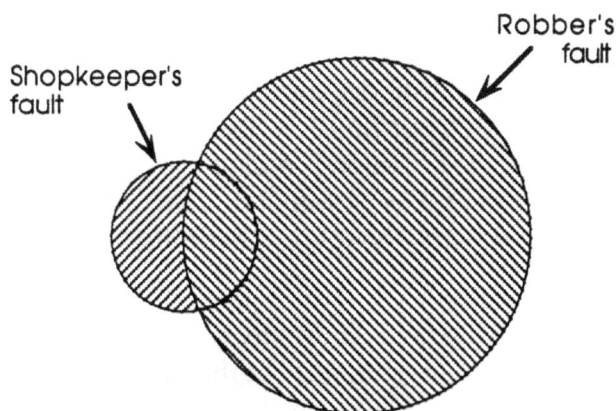

Figure 5.6   The shopkeeper's fault is not entirely
              superseded by the robber's fault.

The shopkeeper's carelessness, while less egregious than the robber's fault, is not entirely obscured by the robber's fault. A part of it—the part played by the motivating force exerted by the sight of the gun—lies outside of the fault attributable to the robber. The actions of the robber do not absolve the shopkeeper of responsibility for that action.

Timothy's situation is slightly different. Where a gun is solely an instrument of harm, the car, while potentially dangerous, is largely beneficial. It would be expected that the owner of a car, unlike a gun, would leave it in public. Leaving the keys to the car in public, however, invites abuse. If it did that in our case, it is arguably like the gun in the above example. And if it stimulated the thief, Timothy played an active role in Jeffrey's death that is separate from that played by the thief.

This does not eliminate our concern about the causal nature of Timothy's actions, however. We have treated the thief as a wrongdoer, which is surely correct when it comes to the theft of the car. But it does not automatically follow from that that the thief was at fault when the car struck Jeffrey. It is entirely possible that the thief was without fault in that accident. Jeffrey's death could be wholly attributable to his action in darting after the newspaper in the street.

If the thief was driving as a reasonably prudent person would under the same circumstances and made every effort to avoid Jeffrey (that is, if he passed muster under the general principle in Figure 5.1), he is not at fault in the death of Jeffrey. How are we to tell? It is time to talk with Officer McGinty again.

The speed limit on Purley Street is 35 mph. The skid marks on the pavement did come from the tires of the Newland car, according to the state police forensics laboratory.

That means that the driver of the car did attempt an emergency stop at that point, presumably to avoid hitting Jeffrey. A skid of that distance would slow that Ford by about 25 miles per hour. So the driver could have been driving at the speed limit, maintaining a good lookout, have hit the brakes at the first warning, and still have hit Jeffrey hard enough to cause the injury that was observed.

It is entirely possible (by which I mean, "A jury could conclude ...") that the driver of the car was not at fault in Jeffrey's death. The thief is surely at fault for the theft of the car, but it does not automatically follow that he was at fault in the impact upon Jeffrey. Nor does the fact that he left the scene of the accident prove that he was at fault. The facts do not exist that would definitively establish the thief's fault. The jury will have to reach a decision on this crucial issue on the basis of far too little evidence.

Does the possible innocence of the thief absolve Timothy of fault? If the thief was driving responsibly, the most that we can say of Timothy is that he set in motion a set of events that led to very good driving and a death that resulted from the fault of the victim himself.

The thief's innocence would absolve Timothy of responsibility for Jeffrey's death, for then all Timothy could be charged with is inducing the thief to take a joyride. If the joyride was a responsible one, not exposing others to risk greater than the irreducible risk posed by any moving vehicle, Jeffrey's death would have been caused by a risk that only he could have reduced.

This means that if Jeffrey is to recover damages from Timothy he must show not only that Timothy's actions caused the car to be stolen but also that the driver's actions (or inactions) caused him to die.

All of these considerations were necessitated by our uncertainty over the element that Timothy "... created the risk that resulted in injury ...." Those considerations have not, however, eliminated that uncertainty. We have generated a plausible argument for the proposition that Timothy's actions inspired the theft of the car and for the proposition that the thief was driving irresponsibly, though that argument is weaker. To win, the jury will have to buy <u>both</u> of those arguments. That is possible, but not very likely. I would say that my tension on this element of Jeffrey's case against the Newlands has fallen to 75%. Nor does there seem to be any way to reduce it further, for we have explored every source of information that is relevant to it.

The effect of an ordinance

To this point our analysis of the case against the Newlands has been guided by the general principle in Figure 5.1, which is my framework for analyzing injury cases like this one. As it happens, there is something more concrete for us to go on in this case—a local ordinance, adopted by the Town Council of Lexington three months prior to this accident, that provides as follows:

> It shall be a misdemeanor, punishable by a fine
> not to exceed $100, for any person who parks
> an automobile within the limits of the Town of
> Lexington to leave his or her keys in the ignition.

Figure 5.7   Section 13-3.2n of the Lexington town ordinances.

Finally, a <u>real</u> law. This ordinance was passed by the Town Council in response to the rash of automobile thefts that have occurred. How does it affect our thinking on Jeffrey's case? Does it make Timothy's behavior on that day criminal?

It is not clear that the ordinance applies to Timothy. According to him, he removed the keys from the ignition. We may, however, suspect the truth of that statement, since he had gotten into trouble from leaving keys in the car on two previous occasions. A jury might conclude that he had left the keys in the car. But even if he removed the keys from the car, didn't he violate the *spirit* of the ordinance? One way or another he allowed the keys to the car to come into the hands of the thief. That is clearly what the ordinance aims to prevent (inference).

Timothy's violation of this ordinance could have quite an impact on the jury's thinking. At the least it would convey to them the seriousness of Timothy's actions. It might even convince them that Timothy was guilty of criminal behavior. Could we get the judge to allow us to bring the ordinance into the case?

In a trial the judge decides what law and facts may be presented to the jury and what may not. He will refuse to let the jury see things that are misleading, inflammatory, or irrelevant to the case. Is there anything misleading, inflammatory, or irrelevant about the ordinance?

The ordinance sets out a standard of behavior—removal of keys from the ignition. That norm was arguably violated in this case. Yet we would not be charging Timothy with a violation of the ordinance. Only the town can do that. We would be attempting to borrow the standard of behavior from the ordinance and apply it to our case. Is it legitimate to take a standard of behavior from one context (i.e., a criminal law) and apply it in another context (i.e., a civil action by Jeffrey against Timothy for damages)? Putting that question in its legal format: Is the ordinance relevant to Jeffrey's case?

This question is far more difficult than you might think. There is no general answer to it. The judge in each case must decide the relevance of a law from one legal domain when a lawyer attempts to introduce it into another legal domain. To see why that is the case, look again at the principle set out in Figure 5.1. That principle, while admittedly my own version of the one that would guide the court, is sufficient law to cover Jeffrey's case. There are no holes in it; we do not need to search around for other laws to fill a hole. We were not at a loss when we analyzed Jeffrey's case against the Newlands. Timothy knew that leaving his keys in the car was a bad idea. We don't need the ordinance to show that he should not have done it.

Yet it does set out a very specific standard of behavior: Leaving keys in the ignition is illegal. But does the violation of that standard make it wrong? Perhaps we need to understand the ordinance itself a bit better. Another call to Officer McGinty should tell us what we need to know.

> That ordinance is a joke ... maybe I should call it a "consciousness-raiser." The Town Council was bothered about the rash of auto thefts and wanted to do something. They passed the thing and the first day it was in force we ticketed the Fire Chief for leaving his keys in the car so it would be picked up in the newspapers. We haven't given a ticket for it since, and we are not planning to.

The purpose of the ordinance appears to be to put a dent in the auto theft rate by getting the people of the town to make life a little more difficult for car thieves. Leaving keys in a car would not appear to be *wrong* in a normative sense, just *expensive* in an economic sense. It would, therefore, be incorrect, even inflammatory, to use the ordinance to establish a normative standard of behavior for Timothy. I would guess that the judge at trial would declare the ordinance irrelevant to Jeffrey's case and prevent it from being introduced into evidence.

Positive law and organic law

The Lexington ordinance is law of a very different type than the law that has guided our thinking about Jeffrey's case. It is *positive* law, law that is promulgated to achieve specific objectives. It is "positive" in the sense that the objective that it seeks to achieve is defined and the law is crafted to achieve that objective, *positively.* The objective of the Lexington ordinance was apparently to teach people to take their keys out of the ignition. That objective did not justify the actual enforcement of the law. The Town Council used it as a device to raise public consciousness about the problem, never intending that it be enforced.

The law that we have applied to Jeffrey's case is of a very different sort. It arose, as we have seen, from our perception of the facts surrounding Jeffrey's death. Those facts raised questions in our mind, driven by our sense that there was something that needed to be explained. Our understanding of the case *was guided* by law, not by laws but by a legal framework built out of the experience of courts in similar cases.

This type of law is "organic" in the sense that it arises out of the experiences of life, of interaction within the social "organism." The experiences of life are the source of the norms that determine whether or not a given behavior is "right" (i.e., conforms to the norm) or "wrong" (i.e., violates the norm). We trust juries to decide cases, even though they are amateurs in law, because they are experts in life, experts at the norms that underlie rightful behavior.

The distinction between positive and organic law helps to explain our difficulty deciding whether or not the Lexington ordinance should be applied to Timothy's behavior. It was a standard of behavior derived from one type of law which we tried to apply in the other. As a positive law it was intended to reduce car theft by increasing the cost of stealing cars. We wanted to use it in to establish a standard of Timothy's *wrongful* behavior. It simply did not apply.

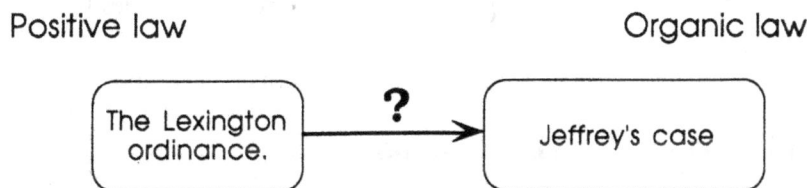

Figure 5.8   The problem of applying a standard
                from one realm of law to another realm.

The distinction between positive and organic law also helps to explain why the members of the law firm that I worked for spent so little time in the law library looking up the law. Our firm practiced organic law. That is, it dealt with problems like personal injuries, breaches of contract, and divorce that arise out of daily life. Once the lawyers in the firm had built a mental framework covering a sector of problems, like the one in Figure 5.1, they were able to analyze the factual situations that came before them without reference to specific laws. The only time they did any legal research was to see whether there were any provisions from the positive law—like the Lexington ordinance in our case—that had a bearing on their cases.

Practicing positive law is very different. The ultimate positive law area is tax law, so I will use it as an example. The aim of tax law is not to sort out conflicts between people, as is the aim of organic law, but to raise revenue to finance government. Tax law is a fund-raising instrument of the state. There is nothing organic about it: tax law is whatever the legislature says it is. In one state, for example, the legislature defines the sale of a car as a taxable transaction, in another state it is not a taxable transaction. There is nothing organic about car sales that makes them innately taxable or non-taxable, as there is about reckless driving that makes it "wrong." Car sales are taxable if the legislature says they are.

Practicing in a positive law area is very knowledge intensive, for here it matters what the *laws* say, and it is not possible to develop an intuitive sense (i.e., a "framework") of what they will say. The tax lawyers whom I know *live* with their copies of the Internal Revenue Code and its regulations. They constantly refer to it as they deal with tax problems. They will occasionally give an off-the-cuff, intuitive answer to a question, but in my experience they are quite often wrong when they do so.

Positive law is based upon *policy decisions,* upon the ends that the legislature wants to pursue. If it wants to promote industrial innovation, for example, it will tweak many provisions of the tax code to cut the costs of firms that pay for research and development. When the political agenda shifts to cutting personal taxes, it will untweak the provisions that promoted innovation and go to work on the personal deductions and the tax rate. The tax lawyer must constantly refer to the rules of law to see what it provides this year.

Organic law is far more durable. The social and personal realities from which it is derived do change over time, but at a far slower pace than the desires that underlie policy decisions.

Striking another person in anger was wrong in Biblical times and it is wrong today.

The antinomy between law and justice

The different flavors of positive and organic law reflect competing concepts of law so ancient that I suspect that they are rooted in the human thought process itself. By the time that words were first written down in any language, different words were used for each concept. The word "law" comes from the Indo-European (the root language of Greek and Latin, as well as everything from Hindi to Gaelic, including English) root "leg-" and means "to collect" or "a collection." "Justice" comes from the root "yewo-" and means "to swear" or "to accord that which is properly due."

A sense of the difference between these concepts can be gleaned from a comparison of words that share the same root.

leg-	yewo-
law	justice
legal	just
illegal	unjust
legislature	jury
legislator	judge
lecturer	jurist
negligence	injury
intelligent	juridical
syllogism	jurisprudence
legitimate	perjure

Figure 5.9   The difference between "law" and "justice" evinced by differences in the words that stem from the same root.

"Law" connotes authority—a *legislature* that lays down *laws* that are *legitimate* and distinguish that which is *legal* from that which is *illegal*. *"Law"* connotes "positive law," as I used it above. One expects law to be *intelligent*, perhaps even set out as *syllogisms*, but certainly as clear as a lecturer (*originally* meaning *lawgiver*, which may explain why people don't like to be lectured to) could make it.

"Justice," by contrast, connotes morality, right and wrong—a *judge* and jury listen to a witness, who hopefully does not *perjure* herself, give sworn testimony, and apply principles of *jurisprudence* to render a *just* result, one that accords both parties that which is properly due them. "Justice" connotes the "organic law" that I referred to above, the law that arises out of fair-minded *jurists* who listen to the facts of a dispute.

There is no necessary correspondence between law and justice; it is altogether possible for a law to be unjust (as with say, the laws that enforced slavery) or to be entirely neutral (as with, say, the law that declares the corn muffin to be the state muffin of Massachusetts).

Does it count against a law that it is unjust? If justice were seen to be the *sole* purpose of law, a law that was unjust would be illegitimate and a society would presumably provide institutional mechanisms for revoking such a law. But justice cannot be the sole purpose of law for two independently sufficient reasons. First, since it is grounded on our moral sense, it is never wholly clear what justice entails. Is it what most of the people think it should be? Or what judges think it should be? Or scholars? We may *test* laws against our concepts of justice, but we cannot *determine* them with it.

The second reason is that law is an important vehicle for producing social order, for producing desired patterns of behavior. The Lexington Town Council, for example, used its lawgiving power to declare leaving keys in a car a crime in an attempt to reduce auto theft. From its viewpoint, auto theft was "disorder," which it would use law to rectify. The unavoidable purpose of law is to produce order. That purpose may be in harmony with justice, but it also may not, as countless despotic regimes have amply illustrated.

The eternal contest between justice and order is, I suspect, a reflection of a profound ambiguity in our own thought processes. We value both, yet they inevitably conflict. Someone said that what each of us wants is justice for ourselves and order for everyone else. We want, in other words, that which is *due us,* so long as everyone else behaves the way that we want them to behave. Periods of great disorder are often periods of great injustice as well, as law is used as a force to restore order at the expense of individual rights. People seem to accept injustice as the price of order, suggesting that of the two values, order is the more basic.

Individuals appear to differ in the balance that they personally desire between these values. Some are confused by even minor disorder, while others, perhaps more self-confident, are comfortable even amid chaos. It is likely that you and I differ to some extent. One way to tell if that is true is to ask yourself if you agree with my assessment of the relevance of the Lexington ordinance. I found it irrelevant, a cheap attempt by the Town Council at reducing disorder that shed no light on whether Timothy's behavior was wrong. You may well disagree. You may even find my characterization of it ("cheap attempt") a little offensive. The Town Council is, after all, a duly constituted lawgiving agency. It has the authority to make law, and the law that it makes should be followed. Timothy failed to follow it (at least in its spirit). That is wrong.

You might ask how it is that I could seriously ask a court to apply the ordinance against Timothy if I brought the case on Jeffrey's behalf, given that I do not think that it should be relevant. The standard answer to that question is that if I took Jeffrey's case I would be under a duty to prosecute his case vigorously, presenting any argument that had a reasonable hope of success, whether I personally thought the argument was valid or not. That answer is professionally faultless, but I must confess that it is not, to me, emotionally satisfying. As I consider whether or not to take Jeffrey's case, then, I will take into account the fact that, if I take it. I will be required to argue that the court should take the ordinance seriously. That argument would exact some psychic discomfort. The anticipation of that discomfort creates a tension that weighs in my decision.

If you feel differently about order and justice, this may cause you no pain whatsoever. In fact, you may be excited by the discovery of the ordinance, fully able to make a heartfelt argument to the court for its adoption.

CHAPTER SIX

Deciding whether to take the case

The time has now come for us to decide whether or not to take Jeffrey's case. We have no obligation to take the case. Every lawyer is free to decide who she will represent. Should we represent' Jeffrey? How would we represent Jeffrey? He is dead, after all.

Who would our client be?

When Jeffrey died, his property went to his "estate." An estate is a fictional entity that the law invents to answer what would otherwise be a difficult existential question: Who owns the property of someone who has died? The estate holds the property until a court can determine who its rightful owners are.

Jeffrey had earned a considerable amount of money from his piano concerts. That money became the property of his estate when he died. The estate also "owns" the right to bring a cause of action for redress of the wrongs associated with his death. That cause of action did not die when he died. It may be asserted by his estate.

But who, in particular, can bring suit? The law designates the person who can act on behalf of an estate. The court appointed Jeffrey's parents, Margaret and Tom, to act as co-administrators of his estate. They will be our clients if we take the case, acting on behalf of the Estate of Jeffrey Stapleton. Margaret and Tom are also Jeffrey's only "heirs." They will inherit any property that he owned. That means that if Jeffrey's case against the Newlands results in a recovery of money damages to his estate, that money will eventually go to Margaret and Tom. Which presents a bit of a problem.

You will recall from Chapter 4 that we were at some pains to determine whether or not Jeffrey could sue Margaret for damages for negligent supervision. There are states that would entertain such a suit, though it was my judgment that allowing such a suit was ill-conceived (a judgment that you might well have disagreed with). There is a serious question in this case, however, about the legitimacy of Margaret's behavior. We do have her statement that Jeffrey was a very independent child who had always looked out for himself, so she felt free to ignore him that afternoon. But a jury might well conclude that that was a self-serving statement, generated more to deflect a feeling of guilt than an accurate account of Jeffrey's mental state. A jury could determine that Margaret's behavior strayed too far from the norm of proper motherly oversight.

I don't think that we have any business raising that question in a suit by Jeffrey against Margaret. But if Margaret and Tom stand to personally benefit from a law suit against the Newlands, that question once again rears its head. Would it be legitimate to force the Newlands to pay money to a woman who was herself partially to blame for her son's death?

That possibility jangles my sense of fairness. I can't quite put that feeling into words, but it has something to do with the principle that a person should not benefit from his own wrongdoing. The law, after all, does not let a murderer collect on an insurance policy covering the life of his victim, even if he was the named beneficiary. Margaret is hardly a murderer, but it is troublesome to think that she might recover money from the Newlands, whose fault, as we have seen, hangs by a very subtle string of legal analysis.

The principle that guides my analysis of these cases (Figure 5.1) does not give me a basis for resolving this tension. It does not deal with relationships between parties who are themselves at fault. This is a situation in which I feel a need to expand my framework by consulting the law.

A bit of legal research reveals a 1978 New York case that dealt with almost exactly the same situation as the one that we face here: <u>Nolechek v. Gesuale.</u> In that case the father of a sixteen-year-old child who had been killed when he drove his motorcycle into a steel cable that the defendant construction company had strung across the road as a barrier, sued the construction company as administrator of the estate of the child. The construction company felt that the father was at fault for providing the child, who was not a licensed driver, with the motorcycle and allowing him to drive on public roads.

To assert their theory of the father's fault, the construction company filed a *counterclaim* against the father, essentially requesting the court to deduct from any money that it might have to pay the estate any amounts attributable to the father's fault. The father requested the court to dismiss the counterclaim. The trial court did dismiss it, but the Court of Appeal of New York reinstated it, saying that it would ...

> ... be repulsive to permit the parent to recover from a third party guilty of "concurrent" negligence for the death of his child while preventing the third parties from counterclaiming for contribution against the parent.

I don't know exactly what to make of the statement that it would be "repulsive" to let the father recover, but it sounds to me as though that judge's sense of fairness was jangled the same way that mine was in this case. Organic law cases are heavily colored by, even driven by, emotion. It is very hard for humans to give words to their emotions or to construct a logical structure upon which they are based, for they are based upon feelings, not logic. Judicial opinions in these areas are rife with terms like "repulsive" that refer directly to emotions, which is as it should be. While it is not very illuminating for the judge to report on his emotions, it is honest.

Burying emotion in empty rationalizations hides what's going on.

If we file suit on behalf of Jeffrey's estate against the Newlands, then, we can expect that the Newlands will make some sort of claim against Margaret for a contribution to the amount that they must pay. That may reduce the amount that the Newlands will have to pay, but it will probably not eliminate it, for the Newlands' fault operated prior to, and independent of, Margaret's. There is still some life in Jeffrey's case.

Putting a dollar value on Jeffrey's life

The possibility of collecting damages is the engine that drives the pursuit of cases like Jeffrey's. There are other engines that could drive it as well. One is our own mental tension in the ease. We may become so curious about the case that we are willing to volunteer our time as lawyers to get some resolution to the problematic elements of the case. Lawyers have pursued cases out of sheer interest, but that would be a slim reed indeed upon which to base a legal system. Such a force might drive academics to a life of selfless devotion to ideas, but few legal cases raise questions as interesting as those that drive academics.

Another possible engine is the desire of people for public vindication. Margaret Stapleton may be so struck by the unfairness of Jeffrey's death, or so desirous of exonerating herself from any responsibility for it, that she will front the costs of bringing the Newlands to rights. But she may instead want to put the whole thing behind her or lack the resources that it would take to bring action.

The possibility of collecting damages is an engine that operates without the vagaries of relying upon plaintiffs who want vindication or lawyers who are driven to resolve the tensions of the case in their own minds. Dollars are an almost universal motivator. Why should a society be so concerned about generating litigation that it provides such a powerful motivator? I will leave that question to your own tender considerations.

There is a curiously psychedelic quality to the task of putting a dollar value upon a person's life. How much was Jeffrey worth? It is not clear, to be honest, that that question has any meaning. One thing that we have learned from economics is that the idea of "worth" has no meaning in money terms beyond what people are willing to give up in order to get it. If, for example, you are willing to forego two trips to New York in order to have one trip to Vancouver, we are on fairly safe ground saying that the trip to Vancouver is worth twice as much as the trip to New York. If the trip to New York would cost $1000, we could conclude that you should be willing to pay up to $2000 for the trip to Vancouver.

There is, however, no market in human beings. We cannot ask how much someone would be willing to give up in order to get Jeffrey, how much he would bring on the auction block. The mere idea is repugnant. Are not human beings of such inestimable value that we cannot put a value on them? Clearly, but if we are to bring suit on behalf of Jeffrey's estate we must do just that. And we must do it without any guidance from market prices.

It would be expected that any activity so inherently devoid of meaning would be governed by rules that don't make a great deal of sense. Here, the law will not disappoint you. In calculating the value of Jeffrey's loss the law allows us to take three things into account. First, the past and future costs of caring for him. Those costs in this case are minimal: $800 for emergency medical services and $3400 for his funeral.

The second component of his loss is the value of his pain and suffering. We know from Margaret's statements that Jeffrey was conscious after the accident ("He seemed to be conscious when I got to him. He kept asking, 'What happened? What happened?'"). We can imagine the horrifying mental state that Jeffrey was in. We could find out from the medical personnel how long Jeffrey was conscious. What would we do with that? How do we put a dollar value on his mental state? Let's leave that to the jury and pencil it in at, what? $1,000 $10,000? $100,000? $1,000,000? Here, mental tension serves as no guide to me, for each of those numbers leaves me with the same amount of unrequited tension.

The third component of damages, Jeffrey's loss of future earnings, is something that we can get a firmer grasp upon. We can conceptualize the task in this way:

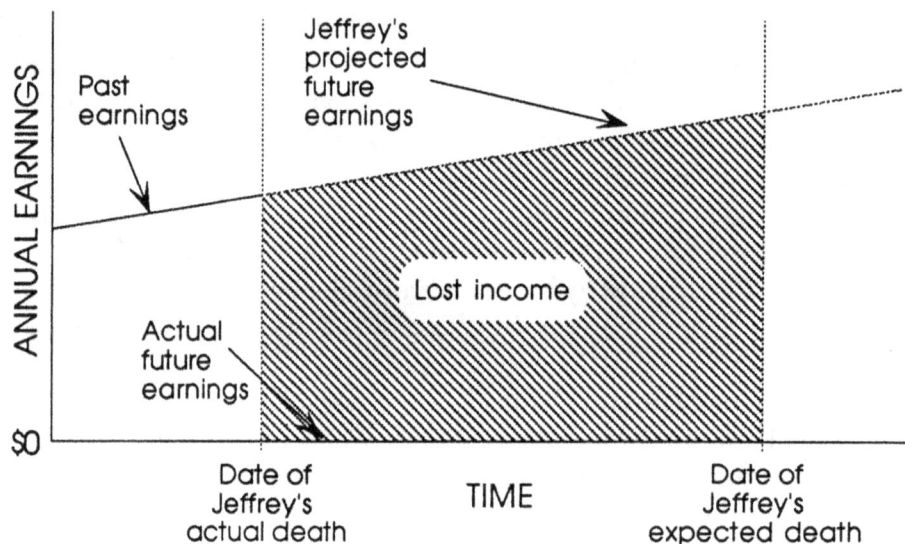

Figure 6.1   A framework for conceptualizing Jeffrey's lost future earnings.

An injury that causes a person to miss time from work results in a "hole" in their future earnings, represented by the shaded area in Figure 6.1. The size of the hole will depend upon how much time it takes the person to return to her normal pattern of earnings. If the injury was so severe that the person will never return to her full earning potential, the lost earnings must be projected over her entire expected working life.

In Jeffrey's case, of course, the hole in his expected earnings is total. To put a dollar value on it we will need to know what his career expectancy as a concert pianist would most likely be and what the most likely income stream from that career would be. Projecting a person's income is, at best, a chancy business. There are so many contingencies in a person's life that it is simply impossible to forecast the future with any certainty. Yet that uncertainty is not Jeffrey's fault; he did not commit suicide. The uncertainty is the fault of those who caused his death. They should not be able hide behind it in order to shield themselves from responsibility (that is a normative statement; upon what principle, stated earlier in this chapter, is it based?).

To put a dollar value on Jeffrey's future career we will need some expert help. The obvious place to start is with Ron Fritzer, Jeffrey's piano teacher and business manager.

> In the course of my career as a piano teacher I have had 12 students who made their living as concert pianists. Several of them began their concert careers as children, but none were as young as Jeffrey or received such critical acclaim. His concert tour of the far East was a critical sensation.
>
> The closest parallel to Jeffrey that I can draw is to a woman whose career I have managed since childhood. She is now 36 years old. Her income this year was $65,000 from her regular appearances with the BSO, $135,000 for two concert tours, and about $35,000 from her recordings. After deducting $60,000 for expenses, she made about $175,000 for the year.
>
> She is very good, but not in the league with Jeffrey. I would expect him to make at least as much as she does by the time that he is twelve years old. After all, he made more than $70,000 on his first tour.
>
> The career of a concert pianist of the first rank is a long one. I would expect that Jeffrey would have been an active player at least until he was 60, and that his income from recordings would have continued long after that.

If we were going to trial we would need more specific information than that, but it is enough to give us an idea about whether or not this case is worth taking. If we take Fritzer at his word, Jeffrey could expect to make $175,000 per year from age 10 to age 60, possibly beyond. That is $8,750,000. We would expect the defendant to argue almightily over that sum, but we can take it as a rough estimate of his lost income for our purposes. Adding it to the out-of-pocket costs and Jeffrey's pain and suffering, we can think of Jeffrey's loss as being on the order of $10,000,000.

Notice one troublesome implication of allowing a person to recover for lost future income. People differ enormously in their incomes. Little Tony, Jeffrey's favorite playmate at school, is a marginal student, devoid of talents and possessed of a serious problem with his attention span. Tony is a great kid, but if we were projecting his expected future income we would be hard pressed to come up with a number even one tenth as large as Jeffrey's.

Does that raise a normative question in your mind? Is there not a sentiment alive in this society that all people are equally valuable? If we base a damage award on a person's expected future income, which is some measure of their value to the other members of society, are we not making an objective dollar estimate of the value of each person? Perhaps the sentiment of equal human value is wrong. Perhaps what we sense is that humans are equally worthy of respect, but they are very different in economic value.

This, I should mention, is not a question that courts spend much time worrying about. The court is fully capable of enunciating one set of values in one case and employing a conflicting set of values in another. The problem of comparing human value is, however, one that is popping up ever more frequently in law, particularly in the field of medical treatment, where the need to ration medical treatment is forcing us to make troublesome comparisons between the worth of different individuals.

Discounting for the probability of failure

Putting the number $10,000,000 on Jeffrey's loss gives us a place to begin with our assessment of the value of the case. We must now discount it by a number of factors, prime among them the risk that a suit by Jeffrey's estate against the Newlands will simply fail. How do we assess that probability?

The place to begin is with our own mental tensions about the case. In order to win, we would have to prove every one of the elements set out in Figure 5.3. We will have to show that the Newlands created the risk to Jeffrey, that the risk that they created killed him, that they should have known of the risk, and that they could reasonably have avoided the risk. Each one of those elements is still in a state of tension in our own minds.

Worse, our exploration of the case thus far makes it unlikely that we will find facts that conclusively prove any one of them. They will all be "at issue" in the trial, which means that the Newlands' lawyer can be expected to mount a serious attack on each one of them. If any one of them fails, Jeffrey's case is lost. How do we convert our own uncertainty about each one of them into an estimate of the jury's likelihood of finding in favor of Jeffrey?

Lawyers are, in fact, quite unable to explain how it is that they do this, but I think that something like converting tension values into probabilities is what is going on in their minds. To see how that might work, we will list the tension values set by our analysis of the case in the last chapter:

Element:	Tension level:
(1) A person ...	0
(2) ... who creates a risk of injury to another ...	75%
(3) ... if that risk results in injury ...	30%
(4) ... so long as the person knew or should have known of the risk created ...	51%
(5) ... unless it would be unreasonable for the person to avoid the risk.	5%
(6) *The driver of the car was at fault when he hit Jeffrey.*	50%

Figure 6.2   Our most recent tension settings on the elements of Jeffrey's case.

Recall that our analysis of the case against the Newlands added a sixth element to the case: the need to prove that the driver of the car was at fault. The mere fact that he was a car thief does not prove that the driver was at fault in the collision with Jeffrey. If no reasonable driver could have avoided Jeffrey, the thief was not at fault. If the thief was not at fault, all that the Newlands can be charged with is inducing the thief to take a joyride in their car.

   If the tension that we feel about each element of the case is an accurate reflection of our uncertainty about whether or not that element is present in the case, we can convert the tensions to probabilities:

Element:	Tension level:	Probability of success:
(1)	0	Certain
(2)	75%	1 of 4
(3)	30%	2 of 3
(4)	51%	1 of 2
(5)	5%	19 of 20
(6)	50%	1 of 2

Figure 6.3   Associating probabilities with mental tension levels.

The probabilities reflect the likelihood that a jury that sees this case as we do will reach a judgment on each one in our favor. This immediately raises a question about how likely a jury is to see the case the same way that we do. The jury will be in a very different situation than the one that we have been in as we have analyzed the case.

It will see only the *evidence* that the judge allows into the case. Have we based our assessment of the case on anything that the judge will not let us present to the jury?

I don't think that we have. I think that every "fact" that we have relied upon thus far can be presented into evidence, pretty much as we have seen it. But there is another question: Will the jury see those facts the same way that we do? There is a chance that our thinking has not been fair-minded, that we have allowed our desire to find a case for Jeffrey to systematically bias our evaluation of the case (that is, to artificially reduce the tensions associated with each element). If that is so, a reasonable jury, taking seriously its duty to do justice to both parties, will evaluate the evidence very differently than we have done.

Once again, I think that our analysis of Jeffrey's case has been resolutely fair-minded. But how can I tell? If I have looked at Jeffrey's case through rose-colored glasses, the tensions that I gave to each element in Figure 6.3 will be too low. On the face of it, however, that is hard to believe, for some of those probabilities are very low. The probability that I assign to the second element is, for example, only one chance of success in four. That is, I think that if I put Jeffrey's case before four different juries only one of them would find that the Newlands had *created* the risk.

Does that mean that there is only one chance in four that we will prevail? Our chances are nowhere near that good. If the jury goes against us on any one of the six elements, we will lose. To figure our probability of victory on the case as a whole we must multiply together the probability of victory on each element.

Element: (1)   (2)   (3)   (4)   (5)   (6)

Probability of success: 1.0 X .25 X .66 X .5 X .95 X .5 = **.04**

Figure 6.4   Calculating the probability of success in the case.

That would indicate that we have a 4% chance of prevailing in Jeffrey's case! One chance in 25. Bring this case to trial 25 times and expect one jury to rule in Jeffrey's favor. What a crapshoot!

But wait a minute. Justice is not supposed to be a crapshoot, is it? If the Newlands' fault caused Jeffrey's death, they should pay. If not, they shouldn't pay. If law were that simple, it wouldn't take people to do it. Fault and causation are human judgments, each of which is composed of countless sub-judgments like those that have gone into our thinking on each of the elements of the case. People's judgments differ. From those differences comes the probability that the case will produce the series of judgments that produce the desired result.

In cases where there is a great deal at stake, there is a growing practice in law to conduct a mock trial of a case to a paid panel of jurors before it goes to court to get a reading on the case. Short of that, the lawyer's assessment of the case is hers alone.

Testing this assessment against experience

As it happens, we are in a position to evaluate our assessment of Jeffrey's case in a way that lawyers never are. The case of <u>Stapleton v. Newland</u> has been presented to entering law students at the school at which I teach for eight[1] years, with facts that are pretty much as I have set them out here. The class is broken into twelve-member jury panels, who watch the trial and render their verdict at the end, just as a normal jury would.

We haven't kept precise records of the results of those jury verdicts, but my sense is that about 60% of the juries have returned with defense verdicts (no liability on either defendant), 40% with verdicts for the plaintiff against one or both defendants. Those proportions have differed from year to year, depending partly upon differences in the lawyers trying the cases and the students who play the role of witnesses.

How can we square my estimate of a 4% chance of victory in this case with the fact that 40% of the law student panels (that is about 40 panels over the past eight years), came in with verdicts for the plaintiff? My estimate of the strength of the plaintiff's case is apparently off by a factor of ten!

One obvious answer is that law students favor the position of plaintiffs more than they should if they applied the law fair-mindedly (as I, of course, have done). There is some reason to suspect that that factor is, in fact, at work. As the general tenor of the times swung conservative during the 1980's there was a notable shift toward verdicts for the defendant. Political attitudes definitely affect legal judgment. If normal juries are, however, as plaintiff-oriented as law students, I should have taken the bias in favor of plaintiffs into account in my calculations.

There are a number of specific factors at work in <u>Stapleton v. Newland</u> that could account for the difference between my assessed likelihood of success and the law student results.

◆ *The sympathy effect.* Nowhere in my analysis of the case have I consciously taken into account the affective differences between the plaintiff and the defendants. To an extent that continues to amaze me, many law students developed a real attachment to Jeffrey, expressing apparently genuine regret for his demise, despite the fact that the trial was a mock exercise. The Newlands generated some sympathy as well.

The strongest emotional effect, however, was universal disgust with the driver of the car. The effect of that was to erase the point that I have made that the Newlands' liability hinging upon the finding that the thief was at fault when he hit Jeffrey. The law student panels very generally felt that, since he was a thief, *ipso facto* everything he did with the car was a wrong.

---

1   That's eight years as of 1990. Gibbons kept on teaching until 2005.

Element: (1)   (2)   (3)   (4)   (5)   ⊠

Probability of success: 1.0 X .25 X .66 X .5 X .95 X ⊠ = **.08**

Figure 6.5   Removing element 6 from the plaintiffs case doubles
the plaintiffs overall probability of success.

That feeling removes element 6 from the plaintiffs case. The jury just did not want to hear that the thief should be held to the same standard as any other driver. Removing element 6 from the equation doubles the probability of the plaintiffs success to 8%—one chance of success in 12. It does not, however, get us to 40%, so there must more factors at work.

◆ *The subtlety effect.* Learning of a case through a trial is a very different thing from learning about it in a book. A trial consists of the facts and whatever inferences the lawyers can sneak past the judge in the testimony of the witnesses ("Judge, I object; that question calls upon the witness for a conclusion." "Overruled."). In a book we pause to discuss the legal implications of the facts as they arise. The trial proceeds at a pace set by the court. A book proceeds at a pace mutually established by author and reader. The reader is free to pause for reflection, to review the material, to make notes.

The effect of this, confirmed by my interviews with the jurors in our mock trials, was that there were copious facts which had simply passed them by and other key facts that they failed completely to see the significance of.

If the plaintiffs case and the defendants' case were equally subtle, this effect would favor neither party—the jury would be equally ignorant as to both. That is not, however, the case. The keys to the defense of this case lie in elements 2 and 6, both of which call for the kind of resolutely sophisticated thought that even the most well-intentioned jury cannot muster within the limits placed upon them as jurors.

Log another one for the plaintiff.

◆ *The bandwagon effect.* As we have analyzed this case I have been careful to keep each one of the six elements of the plaintiffs case logically distinct. It was the distinctness of each one of the elements that allowed me to multiply their probabilities to arrive at the overall likelihood of the plaintiffs success.

The jury does not keep these elements distinct. They emphasize one factor, or perhaps two, to the virtual exclusion of the others. In my experience, juries that found for the plaintiffs overwhelmingly cited the fact that Timothy Newland had a bad habit of leaving his keys in the car, while those that favored the defendant felt that anyone can leave his keys in the car and it would be ridiculous to hold him responsible for all the ills that could follow. Not a single jury panel that I am aware of focused on the question of whether or not Timothy's behavior *induced* the thief to take the car, which is the point that I consider the lynchpin of the plaintiffs case.

It is the judge's job to prevent the bandwagon effect, to prevent the jury from jumping onto one point and letting it override the others. The judge's instructions to the jury carefully lay out each element of the case and tell the jury what its effect on the case will be. In addition, the jury may be provided with questions that force it to make specific findings on each element.

Our experience indicates that these efforts to control the bandwagon effect are irredeemably feeble.

◆ *The money adjustment.* I have said that if the plaintiff fails to prove each one of the six elements of the case, the plaintiff recovers nothing. If the defendant didn't wrongfully cause the injury, the defendant is not liable. But what if the defendant didn't do anything wrong, but he did cause the injury? Or what if he didn't really cause the injury, but he did do something wrong? Or what if the injury was really bad?

There is a tendency for a jury to deal with holes in the plaintiffs case not by terminating the case, but by reducing the amount of money that it gives in damages. That is clearly what was going on in the law student jury panels. About half of the panels that found for the plaintiff gave him only the amount of the actual out-of-pocket costs associated with Jeffrey's death. Upon interview, they said that they didn't think that the Newlands had done anything wrong, but it would be intolerably sad to send the Stapletons home with nothing.

Of the other twenty panels, only a few came in with damages over $100,000. Most panels steeply discounted the plaintiff's recovery by the weakness of his case.

The practicing lawyer is keenly aware of these effects and will take them into account in assessing the case. In fact, the last effect—the money adjustment—is an essential part of the lawyer's analysis. To assess the monetary value of the case, the lawyer will multiply her assessment of the probability of success by the amount of the loss experienced by the plaintiff.

Probability of success	X	Amount of loss	=	Expected recovery
.08	X	$10,000,000	=	$800,000

Figure 6.6   Calculating the expected recovery in Stapleton v. Newland.

Notice that I doubled the probability of success from 4% to 8% to indicate my judgment that element 6 of the case is going to be next to impossible to convey to the jury. It is (fortunately for Jeffrey) the defendant's job to convey it to the jury, so dropping it out of the case helps the plaintiff.

We have not completed our evaluation of the case, however, for while it appears that the case is worth $800,000 in the abstract, that money must be paid by someone concrete, and it is not clear that there is anyone around with that kind of money.

Finding the deep pocket

If the possibility of recovering damages is the engine that drives cases, the presence of a defendant with money is the fuel for that engine. The fuel in the case is the Newlands' farm, for that is their only asset. They are not covered by insurance against a risk like the one that happened in this case. We have seen that the farm's estimated market value is $600,000, which immediately reduces the valuation that we put on this case. If the jury awarded Jeffrey more than $600,000, it would be impossible to collect the excess from the Newlands.

Identifying the farm as the only source of money further complicates matters. The farm is owned by John Newland individually. Timothy has no assets whatsoever beyond a few tattered shirts.

To this point we have treated the case against the Newlands as a lump. Now we must look at Jeffrey's case against each of the Newlands independently, for it is possible that the jury could come in with an award against Timothy, but not against John. If they did that, could we recover the damage award against Timothy by levying against John's assets? Must a parent pay for injuries done by his child?

The short answer to that is "no," unless the parent can be charged with negligent supervision of the child. That is the doctrine that we ran into in Chapter 3. There, however, we were wondering whether Jeffrey could sue his mother for negligent supervision. We found that California will allow the child to sue his parents for injuries that he would not have received if they had kept an adequate eye on him, but New York wouldn't. I decided to drop any thoughts of a suit by Jeffrey's estate against Margaret.

Here, the doctrine of negligent supervision applies in a different way. It provides that if the child injures someone else (not himself), that person can recover against the parent if she can show that the injury would not have occurred if the parent had exercised proper supervision.

Was it negligent for John Newland to send Timothy on an errand with the car? This question is, in essence, a seventh element in Jeffrey's case. In financial terms it is the crucial issue, for a judgment against Timothy alone is worthless. The jury will have to rule specifically against John if Jeffrey is to have any chance of collecting damages.

The law provides no norm against which to measure John's behavior. There are cases that are close—a parent, for example, who was held liable for giving the keys to a car to a child who was drunk. But there are no cases in which a parent who loaned his car to a sober child with a clean driving record was held liable for negligent supervision. Where is the norm by which John's behavior is to be measured to come from?

This will be a question for the jury. The jury will provide the norm after the fact by deciding whether a "reasonable" parent would have acted the way John did in this case. There are some facts in the case that will help John out, that will tend to convince the jury, that is, that he acted reasonably. According to Timothy, John gave him a stern lecture before he drove off and tied a string to the key to remind him. And according to Timothy, he did not leave the key in the car.

It is highly possible (what does "highly possible" mean in probability terms, 1 chance in 4?) that a jury could find that Timothy was at fault in this matter, but not John. If that happened, the value of the case would be zero, for Timothy has no assets against which to collect a judgment. To account for that possibility we must reduce our expected recovery by one quarter. That reduces it from $800,000 to $600,000, which, as we learned earlier, is the market value of the Newland farm. Hmm.

Should we take the case?

By our most sophisticated analysis, Jeffrey's case has an expected return of $600,000. Our standard fee in cases of this type is a contingent fee of one third, so we would expect the case to result in a fee of $200,000. That fee is by no means certain, however. In fact, there is a far better than even chance that we will receive nothing. There is no chance that we will receive more than that, for even if the jury comes in with a bigger award there are no assets out of which it could be paid. Is the chance of getting $200,000 worth the effort that it will take us to get it?

That question calls for a standard economic analysis. Lawyers are generally not gifted at economic analysis, but when it comes to calculations of this sort no one does it better. We will need an estimate of the cost of the suit in terms of the time that we will have to devote to it. The case looks as though it will be a fairly easy case to prove. There are not many witnesses. We have talked with most of them and they seem believable. We will spend, let's guess, two hundred hours on the case.

Next we need to take into account the delay before we would receive the fee. Personal injury cases take about three years to come to trial after the complaint is filed, so we must discount the expected value of our fee by the fact that we will not likely see it for a few years. There is little chance that we will be able to settle this case, for any interesting settlement would require John Newland to sell his farm. He is likely to hold out as long as he can before parting with it.

The third factor that we need to account for is our willingness to accept risk. There is a strong chance that we will receive nothing for our efforts in this case. On the other hand, there is a chance that we will receive $200,000 for two hundred hours of work, a non-laughable rate of $1000 per hour. People differ greatly in their willingness to take such a gamble. It is likely, in fact that you and I will differ on it.

You may be risk averse, needing to see a steady flow of income in the future. I on the other hand, may prefer risk, being excited by the possibility of earning $1,000 per hour. If our practice is otherwise generating a reasonable flow of income, I will prevail strongly upon you to agree with me to take Jeffrey's case.

Is that all there is to it? All of our thinking on Jeffrey's case comes down to a financial decision as to whether or not we should take the case? Is there no thought about whether or not it would be right to take the case? Doesn't our own normative sense, our sense of right and wrong, have some place in the decision about taking the case?

Those questions raise personal questions about the lawyer's role in the legal process. There is a very respectable body of opinion that argues that the lawyer's own normative sense should play no role in the decision about whether or not to take cases. Under this view the lawyer is simply an instrument that is at the disposal of the members of society as they resolve legal conflicts. The lawyer is free to base the decision upon her own financial objectives, for the lawyer is not a slave who the members of society can call upon to do their bidding. But a lawyer's sense of the merits of the case should play no role in the decision, beyond serving as the basis for an evaluation of its likely outcome.

The other view argues that the lawyer has a responsibility to society that goes beyond a simple responsibility to the client. The lawyer should not allow himself or herself to be used as the instrument of injustice. Legal actions apply force to people: they disrupt lives and cause fear, as Jeffrey's case surely would in the life of John and Timothy Newland. If the legal action is not legitimate, if it is not based upon the resolution of a legitimate injustice, the threat that it brings to the life of another is itself an injustice.

In truth, I don't think that either of these views is very influential, for I think that lawyers resolve this question for themselves on an emotional level that is beyond such philosophizing. Some are pleased to see themselves as hired guns. They enjoy cases that are likely losers, for it is the odd chance of winning that gives them the excitement they need to pay attention to what they are doing. Others have a hard time divorcing themselves from the case. Their role has forced them to think fairly about the case and once they have done that they cannot separate themselves from the evaluation of its legitimacy. To them, the case is a loser for very good reasons. It would not be legitimate to ignore those reasons or to allow oneself to be the vehicle for ill.

At the end of all of these considerations you and I discuss the case over a sherry at Pomeroy's Wine Bar. You want to know how I actually feel about the case. Would I take it? Even in such relaxed surroundings, talking with a fellow lawyer, I will be evasive. I will couch my answer in the trappings of professional responsibility.

I don't think that we should take the case. There is too much about it that troubles me. To me, the tensions raised by the case are a very personal matter, not simply something that should be converted into probabilities to determine the expected value of the case, as in Figure 6.3. Those tensions are my emotions, my feelings about the merits of the case, and I neither can nor will let them go away in deciding whether or not I should use my own time and talent on the case.

I am bothered by the effect that filing suit in this case would likely have on the Newlands. Filing suit is incredibly easy. I have a bank of standard complaint forms in my computer. I could produce a complaint against the Newlands in this case in less than fifteen minutes and have it on file in the court by 9:30 tomorrow morning. It could be served on the Newlands within the week. I feel a sense of personal responsibility for that process. Perhaps you are right, perhaps that is letting my own feelings interfere with Jeffrey's rights. Perhaps you should take the case.

I am bothered by a lot of other things about the case. The Newlands have some very strong defenses, but they are subtle. I am worried that a jury may not understand them, or allow its passion to overwhelm it. I am worried that the lawyer the Newlands hire will not understand their case or will do a poor job with it.

"It sounds to me," you might say, "that you think that the Newlands *should* win." I do think that they have the stronger case, but I think that Jeffrey's case is legitimately arguable. I could live with a jury verdict for either the defendant or the plaintiff in this case. I would bow to the wisdom of those twelve people. I would, that is, if I had a little greater faith in the system, a greater faith that the advocates for plaintiff and defendant both understood the case, took their job seriously, and were of equal persuasive power, a greater faith that the judge would shape the issues for the jury to resolve in a way that the jury could comprehend, a greater faith in the jury's fair-mindedness, to listen to all the evidence, to connect the case with their own sense of fairness.

I guess I think that Jeffrey's case is too difficult a case for the legal system to do justice to. I will leave this case for another lawyer to pursue.

PART II

EXPLAINING OUR ANALYSIS

CHAPTER SEVEN

The control system model

We have resolved Jeffrey's case. The question now is, How did we do it? What was going on in our minds as we evaluated the facts of the case, made inferences about what had happened, and applied law to the case as we came to understand it?

Why do we need to understand how we did it? Is it not enough to realize that we did do it? Legal thinking is just something that we humans are good at. Why not leave it at that? There are many good reasons to understand the way we think, but I will mention only one: As you thought through the case you made a number of mistakes. You ignored facts that later proved to be crucial; you misunderstood some of the norms that applied to the case; you got confused on some points, many of which are may still be a bit of a muddle in your mind.

Legal thinking is something that we are good at doing badly. Legal thinking comes naturally, all right, but it is not something that we naturally do well. Biases distort what we see; emotions intrude upon the way we feel about the parties to the case; short term memory fails us as we lose track of loose ends; laziness prevents us from looking deeply enough into the law. If we understand what "bias" and "laziness" are, if we understand the way that emotions affect our thinking, perhaps we will be aware of them, more able to spot their effects and avoid them.

Whatever our minds were doing as we thought through Jeffrey's case, it is clear that that thinking took place in our brains. To fully understand our thinking we would have to describe what is going on in our brains. What is an *inference* in terms of brain activity? When we say that we "inferred" that Timothy dropped his keys in the street, what neuronal activity was entailed in that thought?

It is not possible to explain thinking in terms of brain activity. During each minute that we thought about the case many, many billions of neurons fired off in our brain. Most of them had nothing to do with thinking about the case. Some controlled our heart beat, others our body temperature and breathing. We are many decades, perhaps centuries, away from understanding what all that brain activity does, let alone how something as simple as an inference is actually done in biological terms.

To explain thinking we must simplify the problem by modeling thinking with abstractions. A model railroad, for example, is very different from a real railroad. Missing are the dirt that coats everything in a real railroad, the sheer size and weight of the cars and engines, the thrill of traveling over the countryside. What is left in the model is the part that the one who builds the model finds *interesting*—the tracks and switches and cars running through a make-believe countryside.

The aspect of legal thinking that I think is interesting is the *organization* of legal thinking. I cannot account for the *content* of legal thinking, for the feelings that you have for the parties or for the decisions that you made. It seems to me that we all differ in those feelings and values, and differ in a way that I cannot account for. But we are similar in the way our thinking is organized. We organize data about a case into things that we call "facts." We draw "inferences" from the facts. We base our decisions on those inferences and adduce "reasons" to support our conclusions.

Legal thinking is systematic. That is to say that, whatever the flow of thoughts actually going through the lawyer's head, those ideas fall into regular patterns. It is that fact that allowed you to understand what I was talking about as we went through Jeffrey's case. My thinking, however different from yours, fell into patterns that you could "understand." It is those patterns that this model of legal thinking will account for.

To say that legal thinking is systematic implies that it evinces the properties of a "system." A system is a set of things that are *causally related*. Your hand is a system that translates physical tension on the tendons that connect it to the muscles in your arm into the movements of gripping, holding, and letting go. Your hand moves systematically, which is to say that tension on a tendon produces coordinated movement in a bone and in the skin that is connect to it. Were the first joint on your index finger to move in a different direction from the second joint, you would be rightfully distressed, for that is not a permitted movement of the hand system.

Your thinking is similarly systematic, though like your hand it can break down. If you feel, for example, that Timothy did nothing to cause Jeffrey's death, it would be a violation of your mental system if you concluded that he should nonetheless be made to pay for it. Ideas, in this case the idea that a person is only responsible for that which he causes, exert a pull on your thinking just as the muscles in your forearm exert a tension upon the bones of your hand. Those ideas *cause your* behavior. In this case, presumably, that behavior would be a verbal statement to the effect that, "I don't think that Timothy should have to pay damages to Jeffrey's estate."

Modeling thought, however, will require a more complex system model than the one that would model your hand. Your hand is a mechanical device. It could be modeled with a physical model that showed how physical tensions on tendons caused changes in the position of the bones. Where your hand *accepts* control from the rest of your body, your mind *exerts* control on the rest of your body. To account for that we will have to model your mind as a *control system,* a system that exerts control over things like hands. The control system model that I will use is the work of William Powers. See Recommended Readings: Powers (1973). For tutorials and models you can run on your Windows computer, see Powers (2008).

To get a sense of how Powers' control system model works, try a little experiment. Put your right hand palm down on a flat surface with your fingers close together. Now move your index finger to the left until the tip of the finger is an inch away from your middle finger. Try it.

What is going on in that experiment? The movement of your hand and finger were controlled by the muscles in your forearm. Those muscles, in turn, were controlled by signals from your brain. You were not conscious of those signals, which is very fortunate, for it took many thousands of nerve signals to move your hand and finger. If you were aware of them, your mind would have been so flooded with information that you would have lost track of my instructions. What you were conscious of was my instructions, which established a *desire* in your mind to move your index finger until it was an inch away from your middle finger. My instructions created a desire in your mind, which generated without conscious effort the signals necessary to carry out that desire.

Powers' model explains thought and behavior as a system that translates desires into actions which yield the desired outcome; that is what is meant by "control." Your mind controlled the behavior of your hand to bring it into alignment with the standard that I established, namely, that the tip of your index finger be an inch from your middle finger. That standard exerted what I called in Part I a "tension" on your mind, a sense that there was something that needed to be done. Your behavior eliminated that tension. Or did it? How close did you come to the standard? You might want to do the experiment again, this time with a ruler in your left hand so that you can check to see how close you actually come to a one inch separation.

Legal thought and behavior are a good deal more complicated than that involved in the hand movement experiment. In Part II I intend to explain what was going through our minds as we thought through Jeffrey's case in Part I. Our thinking in that case will serve as the experience that I will attempt to explain. First, however, we must place legal thinking within the context of thinking in general. Legal thinking, as you have seen is pretty much like any other kind of thinking. To see how it differs, we must first gain a sense of what it differs from. That is the text of the next three chapters. In Chapter 10 we will apply Powers' model of thinking to our own experience of Jeffrey's case.

Understanding thermostats

To get a grip on the control system model we will begin by considering a control system—the home thermostat—that is a good deal simpler than our minds. Understanding how it works will give us a sufficient understanding of control system theory to get on with the job of understanding legal thought.

If you were to pop the cover off of the thermostat in your home you might see something that looks like this:

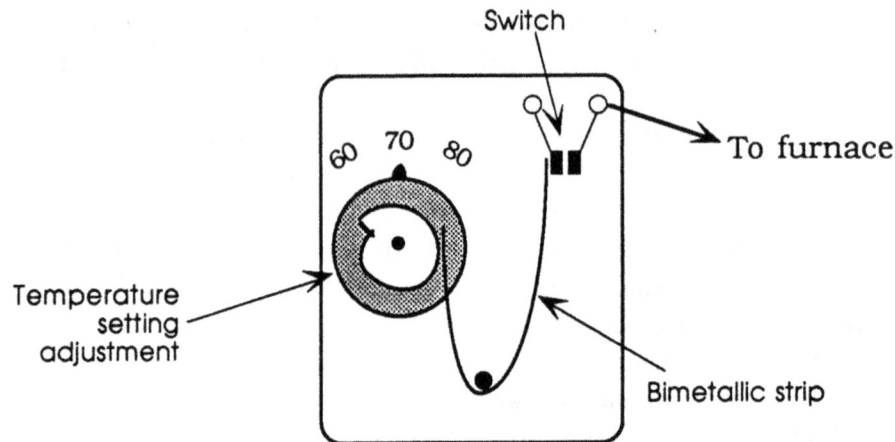

Figure 7.1   The innards of a home thermostat.

There are several types of thermostats, but the type shown here is quite common. You set the temperature by rotating the knob on the left to the temperature that you desire. That applies a pressure to the left end of the bimetallic strip that is proportional to the temperature that you have set (the higher the temperature, the greater the pressure on the strip).

The other end of the bimetallic strip pushes against a spring-loaded switch. When it pushes against the switch with enough force to overcome the spring, the contacts on the switch close, sending a signal to the furnace which tells the furnace to deliver heat.

The bimetallic strip is the active component of the thermostat. It is made up of two strips of metal that are bonded together (hence, "bimetallic"). Each of the strips expands at a different rate when it is heated, which means that as the strip changes temperature it bends. In Figure 7.1, the right end of the strip bends to the right as it cools, exerting greater pressure on the switch, until the pressure is great enough to close the switch. As the temperature of the room rises, the bimetallic strip warms up and the right end of the strip bends to the left, relaxing the pressure on the switch and allowing it to open when the temperature of the room reaches the level set on the adjustment wheel, thereby shutting off the furnace.

As simple as it is, the thermostat illustrates all of the functions of a control system. Those functions can be diagrammed in this way:

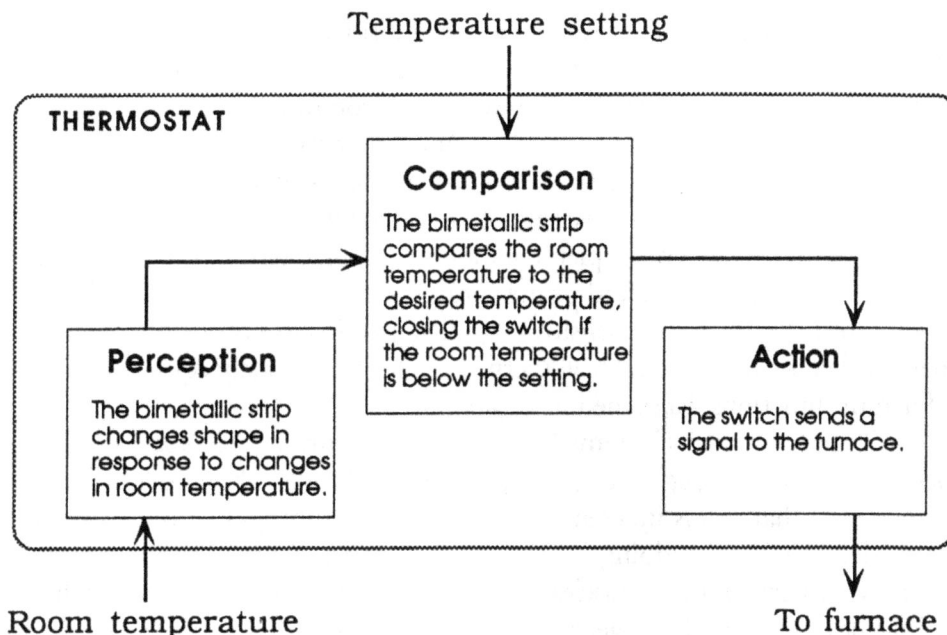

Figure 7.2   A functional diagram of the working of the thermostat.

The thermostat deals with two items of information: the temperature of the room, which it senses through the bimetallic strip, and the desired temperature setting, which is set on the adjustment wheel. It compares those two values, and if the room temperature is below the level set on the adjustment wheel it closes the switch, sending current to the furnace. The switch stays dosed until the room temperature rises enough to bend the bimetallic strip to the left, relaxing the pressure on the switch and letting the contacts on the switch open.

Notice that the thing that animates the thermostat is its detection of a difference between the temperature setting and the room temperature. In control system theory that difference is called an "error." The control system acts to reduce or eliminate that error by telling the furnace to generate more heat.

Notice also that the action of the control system is quite dumb—all it does is tell the furnace to turn on or to turn off. It does not tell the furnace how long to burn or how much heat to deliver. It just tells the furnace to turn on, and, when the room temperature has reached the desired temperature, to turn off. It is quite a simple mechanism, but in that simplicity resides its power.

A control system is a "negative" feedback system because of the way it is put together. Its action, turning on the furnace, generates a response—a rise in room temperature—which it in turn perceives. The perception of its own actions is called "feedback." By engineering convention temperature setting (TS) is positive, the perception signal (PS) negative. Comparison: + TS – PS = Error. The error drives the action, which serves to reduce or eliminate the error.

Positive feedback can be created but creates a runaway condition, as when you hold a microphone in front of the loudspeaker it drives. Negative and positive feedback have nothing to do with blame or praise, common lay usages of the terms.

Figure 7.2 is a functional diagram of a control system. A functional diagram describes the functions of the system—the way that it acts—in the abstract. The actual system can be *implemented* in a variety of ways. The thermostat pictured in Figure 7.1, for instance, is just one implementation of a thermostat. In other thermostats a mercury switch is used instead of the spring-loaded mechanical switch in Figure 7.1, or a tube of temperature-sensitive liquid is used instead of the bimetallic strip. However they are implemented, all thermostats are functionally equivalent; they all perform the functions diagrammed in Figure 7.2.

I will use functional diagrams like the one in Figure 7.2 to describe the inner working of human thought. I am suggesting that human thought is a lot like a thermostat. If that seems inherently unlikely, even insulting, pause for a moment to consider what you are doing at this instant. You are reading this line of text. To do that, your neck and eye muscles must move, pointing your eyes ever rightward on this line of text, until you get to the end of the line and must return to the left. How do you make them do that?

You don't actually *make* them do that in any conscious sense, do you? (There *are* people who must consciously make themselves do it and use their finger as a guide to their eyes.) All you know is that you have a desire to read the text—you *want* to read it. Everything else follows unconsciously from that. I am suggesting that your desire to read this text is, in a sense, like the temperature setting on the thermostat. Once you have set that desire (that is, once you have decided to read this line, rather than closing the book and getting on with something else), a process very much like the thermostat takes over and issues commands to your neck and eye muscles (as well as to your eyes and to your hands, if you are holding the book) to carry out your desire.

Occasionally your neck and eye muscles make a mistake. They may make your eye skip some words, or skip a line of text. That may generate an error signal—at that point you become aware that your eye controllers have made a mistake and act at a higher, conscious level to rectify it. Your perception that you have skipped a line generates an error signal ("Woops, where am I?"), which you rectify by finding the correct line of text. I can let you feel what that where am I?"), which you rectify by finding the correct line of text. I can let you feel what that is like by duplicating the line of text above. That messes up your eye control system, creating an error and forcing you to take conscious control to get back on track.

Tricks like the one I just played on you are irritating. Your first perception was probably that the printer had made a mistake. Then you realized that I had repeated the line on purpose to demonstrate what an error signal feels like.

You are now operating under the control of the purpose of reading this book. You can change that purpose, for example, by deciding to "skim" the book, rather than reading it thoroughly. Do that right now. Tell your eyes to skim the balance of this paragraph. (Then reread it to see what you missed.) Changing your desire from a desire to read the text to a desire to skim the text is like a change in the setting on the thermostat. It changes the commands that your brain sends to your neck and eye muscles, causing them to jump greater distances between the chunks of text that your eye focuses upon.

There are several important differences between a human and a thermostat which require us to further develop the general control system model described in Figure 7.2. The first difference lies in the fact that a thermostat cannot generate its own desires, while a human can. Notice that in Figure 7.2 the *value* of the temperature setting comes from outside the thermostat, from the setting put on it by a person. Humans have their own values, their own purposes, desires, norms, standards, aspirations. They are self-animated in a way that a thermostat cannot be. That requires an addition to the control system model.

Making lemonade

In his seminal work on control system theory William Powers used an illustration which in its sheer simplicity and homeliness conveys the main idea of the theory clearly. He explored the process of making a glass of lemonade. If you have never made lemonade, think of it in terms of mixing any beverage for which you have a refined sense of the way it should taste.

Making lemonade from scratch involves mixing water, sugar, and lemon juice into a satisfying drink. Most commercial lemonade is, to my taste, not satisfying—it is usually too sweet. As a result, I only drink lemonade that I have mixed myself. Here is my approach. Since lemons come in lumps, one lemon at a time, while sugar and water can be added little by little, I begin by squeezing a whole lemon. Then I add some water and sugar, and taste the mixture. I expect that the first taste will be too strong (not enough water) and too sour (not enough sugar) because I cannot take out water or sugar if I have added too much. Occasionally I get it right the first time, but usually I have to add more water and sugar. Eventually, the taste of the lemonade conforms to the taste that I am after and the task is complete.

As you can tell from that tale, I don't make lemonade often—perhaps once every two or three years. If I did it more often I would probably have a recipe in mind that would set out the proportions and speed up the task. The interesting thing, however, is that, as rarely as I do it, I *never make a mistake* (well, hardly ever; occasionally I add a bit too much water and have to cut another lemon). The lemonade always turns out right. Since I can test it continually, I can always produce a glass of lemonade that is exactly "right."

The process of making lemonade can be diagrammed as a control system:

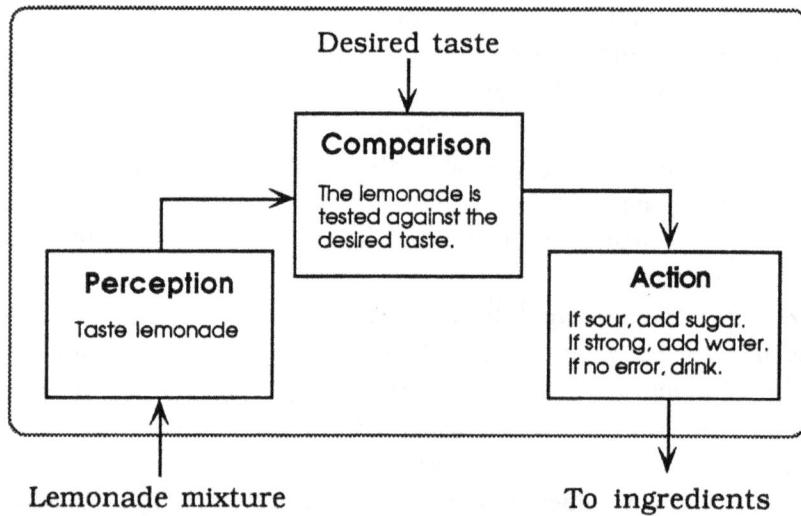

Figure 7.3   A functional diagram of making lemonade.

As with the thermostat, there are two inputs into the lemonade making system: the perceived taste of the lemonade and the desired taste of the lemonade. As with the thermostat, those two inputs are compared. If the taste departs from the desired taste, an error signal is generated that directs my action to eliminate it by adding water or sugar. If the actual taste conforms to my desired taste, the procedure is at an end and I am ready to get on to the drinking stage.

Unlike the thermostat, the value that drives this system—the desired taste of the lemonade—is contained within the larger system, the person, himself.

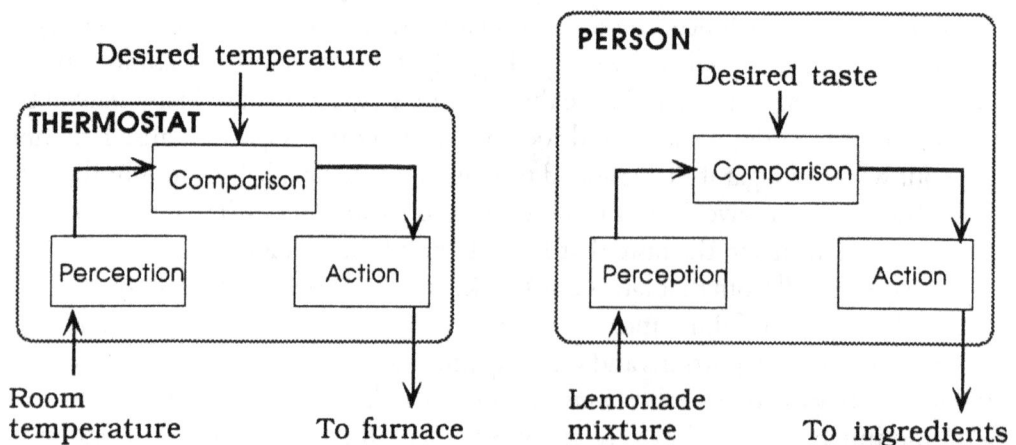

Figure 7.4   A functional comparison between a thermostat and
a person, showing the difference between them in
the source of the desires that animate them.

The desired room temperature set on the thermostat comes from outside the thermostat, from the same place the desired taste of the lemonade comes from—namely, from me. Unlike thermostats, human beings are *self-animated* control systems.

As humans pursue their desires, they have at their disposal dumb control systems, like thermostats. Consider your situation as you read this. You are presently pursuing a desire to read this book. That desire is generating a great deal of behavior—page turning, eye and neck movement—that is presumably allowing you to satisfy the desire; you are perceiving the book, line by line.

At the same time, however, other perceptions are pouring into your mind that have nothing to do with the book. The chair that you are sitting on is pushing up against your body, generating a constant flow of signals that you are largely unaware of (until I mention it), which your mind uses to interpret that all is well as far as body position is concerned. The temperature receptors in your skin are also sending a stream of messages to your brain that let it make constant minor adjustments to your body temperature without any thought on your part.

If those adjustments get out of hand—let's say that, in order to keep you warm enough, your brain is sending strong messages to your muscles to contract, which you feel as shivering—you may become consciously aware that all is not well on the body temperature front: "Hmm. I am freezing." That is an "error signal," a notice that there is a difference between the temperature that you would like to be and the temperature that you are. That error signal generates the feeling that I referred to in Part I as *tension,* a feeling that something more must happen. That tension drives you to action.

You have at least two possible strategies for eliminating the error, and its attendant tension: (1) put on more clothing, or (2) raise the temperature of the room by setting the thermostat to a higher level. You have, in other words, a *repertoire* of alternative actions, both of which will bring about the desired result.

How do choose from your repertoire? Control system theory does not, at the moment, have a very good answer to that question. Economists think that economics has as good answer, so let's ask for a moment how an economist might explain your choice between putting on more clothes and turning up the thermostat.

To the economist, every choice produces *costs.* If you decide to turn up the temperature of the room, you will burn more fuel. In fact, since the thermostat will raise the temperature of the entire house (unless you have multiple heating zones), it will burn a lot more fuel than what you need to stay warm while you read. That is a big waste, unless there are other people in the house who are also cold or unless you anticipate that you will soon be moving to other parts of the house.

On the other side of the ledger (to use a metaphor that economists resonate with), the decision to put on more clothing is not costless either. You will have to stop reading the book and move to get a sweater (which you would presumably rather not do), but you will have to do that with the thermostat as well. The extra clothing might be somewhat uncomfortable to wear. Worse, the extra clothing will not be as effective at producing exactly the right body temperature as setting the thermostat. Putting on a sweater will raise the temperature of your torso, but perhaps leave your legs too cold. If the sweater is a little too heavy, you may find that you have to take it off in a few minutes. To make the decision an economist would compare the costs of the alternatives:

LEDGER

COST OF RAISING THERMOSTAT	COST OF PUTTING ON MORE CLOTHES
Time and effort needed to make the adjustment 10	Time and effort needed to don more clothing 25
Cost of excess fuel 65	Discomfort of added clothing 5
	Cost of expected further fooling around with clothing to produce the desired temperature 55
TOTAL COST 75	85

Figure 7.5   Cost analysis of decision about warming up.

To decide between the alternatives, you compare the costs of each and choose the action that will impose the least costs. If your cost analysis was like the one in Figure 7.5, you would choose to raise the thermostat rather than put on more clothes, though the costs of the two alternatives are so close that you might do the worst of all possible things (in economic terms), namely, sit for minutes in a dither as you tried to make the decision.

To the economist, people are *rational maximizers* (if they are sane), which means that they always try to get the most of that which they value for the smallest sacrifice in other things that they value. The "costs" of an action are the perceptions that must be sacrificed in order to pursue a given perception. If you are cold, pursuing a better perception (i.e., the perception of getting warmer), means that you will have to give up other things that you could do with that time and effort. That is a cost. You will try to minimize that cost.

To make this explanation work, economists posit some kind of internal accounting system. In Figure 7.5, the costs of each alternative are represented in numbers. But what do those numbers mean? They are a measure of the sacrifice that a given behavior will entail. From introspection it surely does not feel as though we do this calculation between alternatives numerically, though it is a convenient way of quantifying the decision-making process. Perhaps control system theory will one day explain how it is that we actually make decisions without the need to posit numbers.

As we apply the control system model to legal thinking in later chapters we will find that decision-making in law is a subtle process, far more subtle than the decision between raising the thermostat or putting on more clothes. At this point, however, we will assume that you have decided to bring your body temperature into alignment with your desired body temperature by raising the setting on your thermostat. Doing that creates a relationship between two control systems—you and the thermostat—in which you generate the desire that the other control system will pursue. That relationship can be pictured this way:

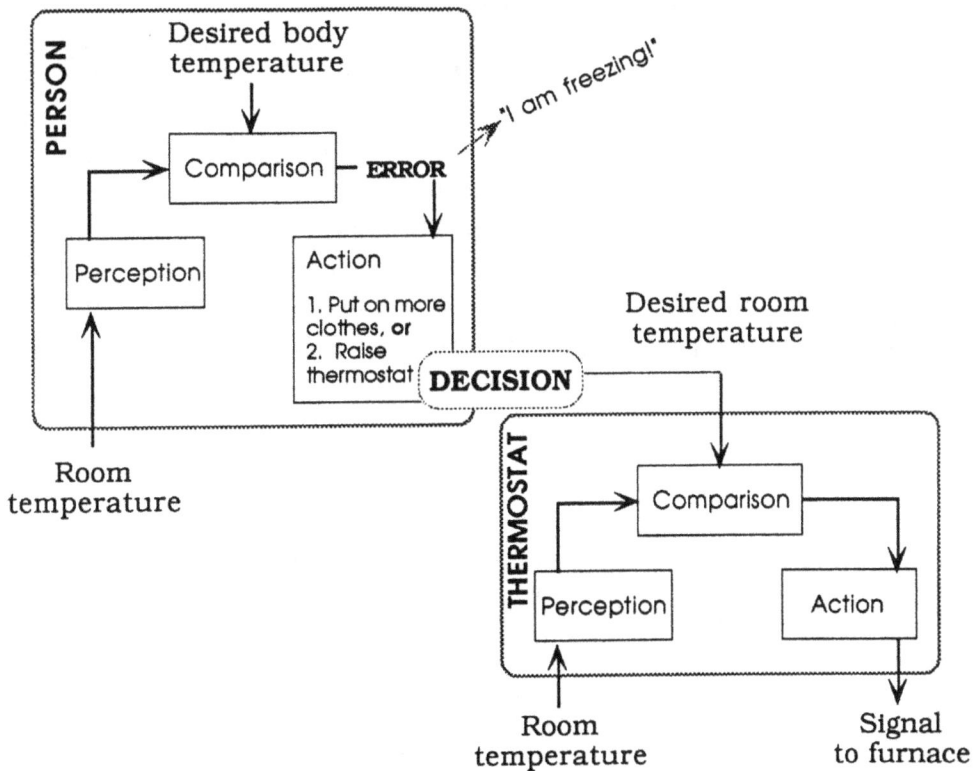

Figure 7.6   The relationship between a human
                 and a mechanical control system.

Notice that both control systems will sense the same feedback—the temperature of the room. But each will compare that temperature against a different standard. The thermostat will compare it against the value that you have set, keeping the furnace going until the desired room temperature is reached. Your body will use the room temperature to change its internal response to temperature change, none of which you will be aware of. You will be aware of the general level of your body temperature, of the measures that your body is taking to warm or cool itself. If the thermostat and furnace are working well, the temperature of your body will recede from consciousness and you will turn all of your attention to the purpose of reading this book. If you were not artful, if, for example, you turned the temperature up too high in an effort to get a quicker fix, you will get too hot and have to go through the procedure again.

Getting along with others

The thermostat is your slave. Were the only control systems that you had to deal with in your life dumb ones like the thermostat, there would be no need for law. Lacking their own sense of purpose, dumb systems wait obediently until a control system that has its own purposes, like you, comes around to animate them with new settings. It has been suggested that a large part of the success of personal computers is that they are so rewarding to control. They are themselves control systems, controlling such things as printers, modems, and disk drives. But they lack a purpose. They sit around until they are animated by a person. They reward the person with an uncritical willingness to do whatever is desired. Because they are so willing, however, when they fail to deliver because of a software or hardware failure, they can produce outrage.

Living with other human beings is altogether different. Each human being is a self-animated control system; each person is up to something. The actions of a person pursuing a purpose can enhance or diminish the ability of another person to pursue her own purpose. The ability of our actions to enhance the desires of others is the foundation for social interaction; their ability to diminish the desires of others is the foundation for law.

There is no need to spell this out at any length; we all have vast experience with social life. But I will point out the way that control system theory applies in the social context (that is, in control system theory's terminology, in the context comprised of multiple, interactive, purposive control systems). Return to the example of setting room temperature, but now put another person in the room with you.

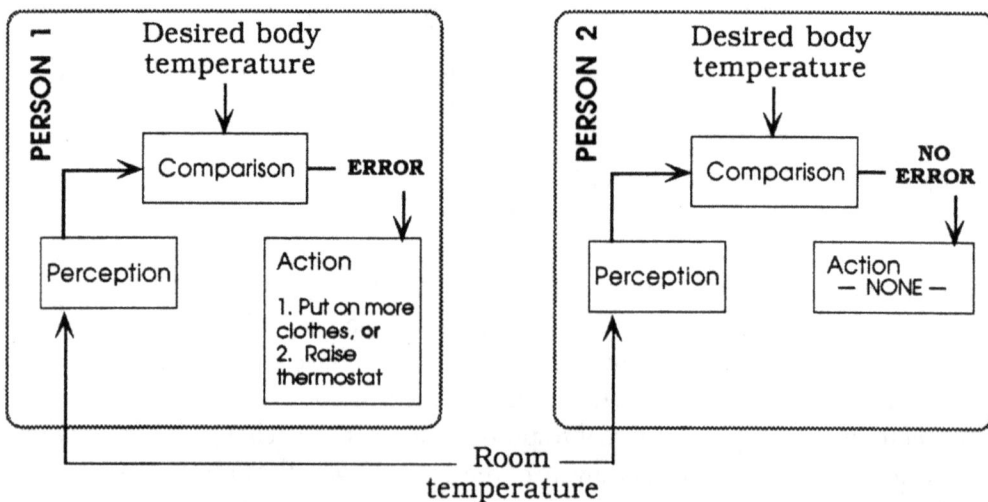

Figure 7.7   The relationship between two humans who are in the same room, one of whom feels comfortable while the other is too cold.

Each of you is experiencing the same room temperature, but you ("Person 1") are cold, while the other person ("Person 2") is comfortable. You are in a state of tension derived from the error signal from body temperature, while the other person is not. What to do? You could proceed as before, ignoring the other person. Doing that, however, will raise the room temperature, which is likely to create an error signal in the other person ("Isn't it getting awfully hot in here?"). Ignoring other people's error signals is, in fact, typical of young children, as they struggle with each other over their individual pursuits. But you are no child, so you will take the effect of your action upon the other person into account.

Why would you do that? Here are three possible reasons, each with a profoundly different implication for the legal system.

FEAR　　　　If I raise the temperature of the room, that will create an error signal in the other person ("It is getting to hot in here!"), who is likely to remonstrate with me about it ("**Turn down the heat!**"), creating an error signal in me and forcing me to act.

LOVE　　　　If I raise the temperature of the room, that will create an error signal in the other person ("It is getting hot in here!"), the mere contemplation of which creates an error signal in me ("Oh oh, I **have made someone unhappy!**"), causing me to eliminate it from my action repertoire. I'll put on a sweater.

RESPONSIBILITY　　If I raise the temperature of the room, that may create an error signal in the other person, so I'd better ask whether or not it is OK.

> NOTE: In Part II I will use statements like the ones in parentheses above to illustrate what the particular error signals I am referring to feel like.

Figure 7.8　　　Three different reasons to take another
into account in one's decisions.

You might not raise the thermostat because you fear the consequences. Doing it would have two effects: raising the room temperature and possibly provoking discomfort in the other. The first would remove the error signal stemming from your desire for a comfortable body temperature, but the second would create an error signal, even if all it did was interfere with the peace and quiet that you need to have to continue reading this book.

Conversely, you might not turn up the temperature because the mere thought of causing discomfort to the other person itself creates an error signal in you. I have termed this "love," for love appears to enable one person to appreciate another person's mental state as if it were her own. One person empathizes so strongly with another that his discomfort is her discomfort, her joy is his joy. In such a system, purposes and perceptions are shared in a way that each person's error signals incorporate the other's perceptions, and action is taken only if it will reduce the error of both people.

If Person 1 "loves" Person 2, Person 1 will put on a sweater without making a fuss (unless Person 1 also needs appreciation from Person 2 for the "selfless" act).

Fear and love are powerful motivators, but neither offers a perfect solution to the problem of integrating the behavior of independent actors. Love seems to have its own agenda independent of social control, which even the repetition of the duty to love one's neighbor seems impossible to affect. By contrast, fear is subject to social manipulation. Law can provide and enforce penalties for improper behavior. But enforcement is costly, both to those who must do it and to those whom it is directed at. And fear is not reliable: some people seem to act to spite the promised penalty, while others take consequences into account only if penalties are uniform and reliable. To them, the chance of getting caught every tenth time they do something wrong produces little fear.

Fortunately, there is a form of control that avoids the weaknesses of both love and fear. As you sit shivering with this book, considering whether or not you should put on more clothing or raise the thermostat, you will be aware that raising the thermostat will affect the other person. That is, you will recognize your *responsibility* for the discomfort that the other might feel if you raised the temperature setting. You will see yourself as the *cause* of that person's error signals. That recognition will induce you either to avoid that behavior or to ask the other person for his acquiescence to your desire to raise the room temperature.

Notice that responsibility operates in a self-contained way. It doesn't matter whether or not you know the other person, love him or hate him. The golden rule of responsibility extends to all persons. In the lilting terminology of control system theory, the idea of responsibility could be put this way. "Never take an action that will induce an error signal in another without gaining the other's acquiescence."

I would suggest that that principle was, though you were probably unaware of it, the basis for your evaluation of Jeffrey's case. It is what enabled you to identify the injury to Jeffrey (who suffered a terrible set of error signals until his very existence as a control system terminated), the potential problem of Margaret's behavior (the failure to protect her son from error signals), and the difficulty with the case against the Newlands (did their actions *produce* an error signal in Jeffrey?).

We talk about injuries, risks, and responsibilities in everyday terms without making explicit their underlying dynamics. In this book, however, we are seeking to understand how it is that we think about law. Seeing human beings as control systems gives us the opportunity to model both our own thought and our concept of ourselves and others as moral beings who are entitled to respect. Control system theory enables us to use a single model to describe both the way we are and the way we think we are.

In this chapter I have described how it is that a fundamental moral principle (i.e., Never take an action that will induce an error signal in another without gaining the other's acquiescence.) derives from the very process by which we *think about law*. I have yet to show, however, that control system theory offers a framework for understanding normative thought. In the next chapter I will describe a simple way in which our values and desires generate thought.

CHAPTER EIGHT

The pursuit of the good

A control system, be it a person or an animal, operates upon its environment to produce what it wants. We understand the behavior of a thirsty dog who is in search of water because it is easy for us to imagine that the dog "wants" water and is acting in a way that will satisfy that want. The desire for water animates a dog as it would a person.

A dog who is very thirsty will attack a dog who is blocking his path to water. That is also easy to understand, though here we perceive a difference between dogs and people. It is easy to imagine that a thirsty person would, like the dog, attack a person who was in his path to water, but that would raise questions—normative questions—that the attack by the dog would not raise. We would want to know, for instance, whether or not the thirsty person had first tried to deal reasonably with the person he attacked. We would want to know how thirsty he was and why the other person blocked his path.

There are two types of thought at work here. The first is the type of thought of the thirsty person (and presumably the dog, as well) as he attempts to satisfy his thirst. That type of thought is fairly straightforward and can be modeled quite easily in control system terms. That is the purpose of this chapter—to develop a model of thinking that underlies a person's pursuit of what he wants, of what he considers "good."

The second type of thought is our thought as we evaluate his attack upon the person who blocked his path. That is the type of thought that we are trying to run to ground. It is the type of thought that we employed in Part I as we evaluated Jeffrey's case. It is less obvious, more difficult to model, than thought that is in pursuit of a particular good. We will take the simpler case first.

The role of personal values

Why are you reading this book? To do it, you have set aside other things that you could be doing with this time. Or did you? If you are reading this book because you are sitting in a doctor's waiting room with nothing better to do and it is the only reading matter available, you did not have to sacrifice much in the way of other values to read it.

That is unlikely. You have likely put other values on hold to pursue whatever value it is that reading this book might satisfy. What value could that be? Not knowing you, I have no way to tell, but there are a limited number of possibilities. One is that you simply *enjoy* reading books of this sort for the pleasure of the mental activity that it brings. That would look like this in control system terms:

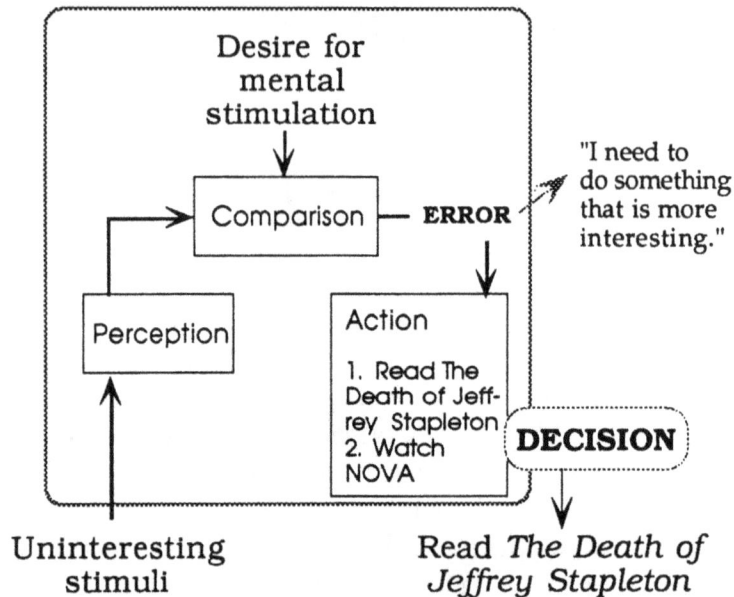

Figure 8.1   The process underlying your decision to read this book.

Your desire for mental stimulation was not satisfied; you were bored, or you were anticipating being bored, which created an error signal, inducing you to look around for something to do (we could call this "search behavior"). A NOVA program on the courtship behavior of puffins looked mildly interesting, but failed in the last analysis in its competition with reading this book. Your decision between the two was presumably based upon your anticipation of the pleasurable mental activity that each would generate. If, when you go to work tomorrow, your fellow workers are abubble over the excellence of the puffin show, you may regret the decision that you have made.

If that is why you are reading this book, we could regard your behavior as producing a "final good." That is, reading it is an action which you do directly for pleasure, not to serve any other end. Reading this book delivers some personal value; it *feels good*. Why would that be? Why would it feel good to you to read this book rather than the novel that you could be reading instead? Why are there people for whom reading never feels good?

There is no accounting, as they say, for personal tastes and values. No accounting, that is, for what makes a given person feel good. Interestingly, there is an accounting for what makes people feel bad. There is probably no one to whom a blow in the face feels good, or rejection by a loved one, or notice of a terminal illness. But there is no accounting for what people find good.

Some people like complex puzzles, others are simply confused by them. Some like a pat on the back, while others find it patronizing. Some like physical stress, while others avoid it.

Thinking and feeling

Control system theory offers no explanation of personal values, but it does explain how they relate to behavior. To see how it does that we will have to tweak our perception of the control system model. I have implicitly treated it as if it were a *cognitive* model, a model of the rational dimension of thought. In Figure 8.1, for example, I used words to describe the three system functions—"perception," "comparison," and "action." Those words are cognitive phenomena; they are the vehicles by which I convey knowledge. Using a cognitive vehicle to describe subjective phenomena, however, implicitly suggests that those subjective phenomena are themselves cognitive.

In part, they are. Reading this book conveys information to you, which you can store, manipulate, and retrieve as you can any other knowledge that you possess. But reading this book also generates *feelings*, perceptions that cannot be put into words. You may, for example, feel good about acquiring the knowledge in this book. That is a very different thing than simply acquiring the knowledge.

Consider the feelings associated with your perception of how much more of this book you have left to read. Cognitively, you can determine how much more there is to read either by squeezing the remaining pages between your thumb and forefinger ("Hmm. Still a lot left."), or by turning to the last page and noting its number. That information is not by itself important. The importance of it lies in the *meaning* of the number of pages left, in the *feeling* that that produces. If you are enjoying the book, the fact that there are only 80 pages left may make you feel regret that it will not go longer. If reading it feels tedious, 80 pages may feel like an intolerable burden. In either case the information is the same, but the feeling that it produces is not.

| Cognitive level: | 80 pages left |
| Affective level: | I don't think I can stand it. |

Figure 8.2   The relationship between the knowledge of the number of pages remaining in this book and the emotion that that thought produces.

Cognition is significant primarily because of the feelings that it produces. Cognition that produces no feeling is *meaningless*. Have you read the telephone book cover to cover? Why not? It is chock full of symbols; your perception of those symbols will generate knowledge. But it will be naked knowledge, knowledge devoid of significance. It will produce no feeling, at least no feeling that is worth having. It won't connect ideas together that have been floating around in your mind; it won't add to your repertoire of skills; it won't titillate or amuse or lead you somewhere in life.

We should understand the control system model, then, to describe not simply a relationship between cognitive phenomena (purposes, actions, and perceptions) but most importantly between the feelings that those cognitive phenomena generate.

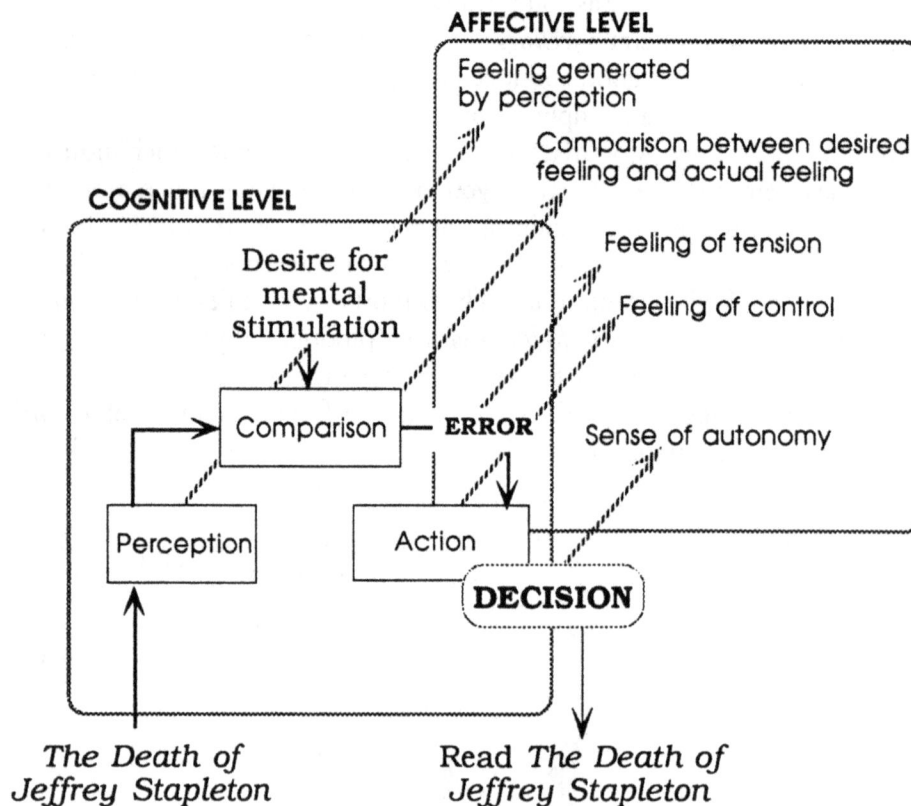

Figure 8.3   The affective level underlying the process of control.

In humans, each part of the control system has associated feelings. The error signal produces the feeling of tension. Actions produce the feeling of control, of acting to bring about the perceptions that we desire, of simple joy in the sheer fact of using our capabilities. Making decisions reaffirms our sense of ourselves as actors, as the causal force in our lives. Perceptions generate feelings directly, and it is those feelings that we compare against our desired feelings to determine whether or not our desires have been satisfied. Our desires are themselves wholly affective—they are states of *feeling* that we intend to produce.

All of this would be entirely obvious were it not for a fixation with intellectual processes that has afflicted those who have tried to understand thought since the time of the Greek immortals. The impulse to sever thought from feeling has generated an attempt to create a thinking computer. Computers have no affective processes; they don't feel anything. Under the argument that I set out above, that means that they cannot *understand* anything; nothing has any meaning to the computer. They are able to process symbols. They can attain "knowledge," if all we mean by knowledge is the acquisition and manipulation of symbols. A computer could, for example, "read" this book. It could record each of the symbols in the book and retrieve any one of them in an instant. Such a capability is a necessary, but by no means sufficient, part of thought. To constitute thought those symbols must mean something, they must produce a feeling. That part is wholly absent in the computer.

No lawyer who has ever represented a client would spend more than a moment with the notion that thinking is a solely cognitive process. In fact, a lawyer would be likely to wonder why I had made such a point of the emotional foundation of thought. Legal problems do not exist in an emotional vacuum. The solution to them affects the lives of real people and that awareness produces feelings in the lawyer at every step. It is that emotion, which is felt as tension, that animates and directs the lawyer's thought.

In the balance of this book I will use the cognitive version of the control system model, like the one set out in Figure 8.1, to describe legal thought. You should be aware at every point, however, that I intend it to represent the affective states associated with the cognitive processes set out in the model.

The hierarchy of purposes

It is not likely that you are reading this book because it makes you feel good in any immediate sense. I say that because I do not read books like this because they make me feel good, and I find it difficult to imagine that anyone does. Reading them is a means toward some larger end. What could that larger end be? There are any number of possibilities, but let us pick a straightforward one: You are reading this book because you have been assigned to write a report on it for a course that you are taking. Your purpose in reading the book is, then, derived from your larger purpose in taking the course, like this:

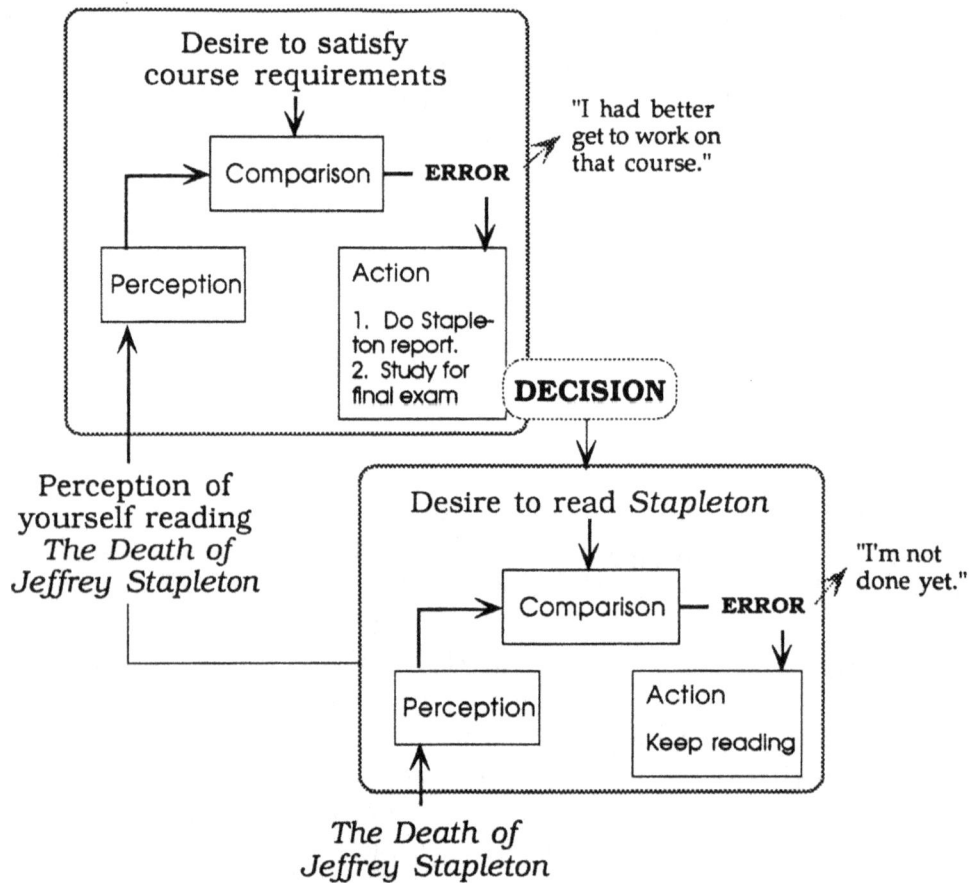

Figure 8.4   The hierarchy of purposes underlying behavior.

At this moment there are presumably several things that you could do to pursue your desire to satisfy the course requirements. You could, for example, spend this time studying for the final exam. Instead, you decided to work on the report. To do that you first had to read this book, or enough of it to form the basis for a convincing report. Your decision to work on the report created an error signal, which seems like an odd thing to call it. The "error" lies in the fact that you have a desire—to read the book—which is not yet backed by perception—you have not yet perceived all that is in this book. When you have, your perceptions will match your desires and the error signal will disappear; you will be done with it and you can move on to other desires free from the tension that remains while the book is unread.

This account is not yet complete, however, for we have not explained where your desire to complete the course requirements comes from. It may be that it is itself a final good. You may be a "professional student" who takes direct pleasure in completing courses. It is more likely that the course is itself an instrument in the service of a larger desire, such as achieving a college degree, which itself may be part of a larger aim to qualify for a particular career, and so on. Most of the purposes that animate our behavior are *instrumental.* They are purposes that serve larger purposes.

Lead an enjoyable life.
  ⮡ Pursue a rewarding career.
      ⮡ Qualify for the career.
          ⮡ Get a degree.
              ⮡ Satisfy course requirements.
                  ⮡ Read *The Death of Jeffrey Stapleton*.
                      ⮡ Move eyes across text.

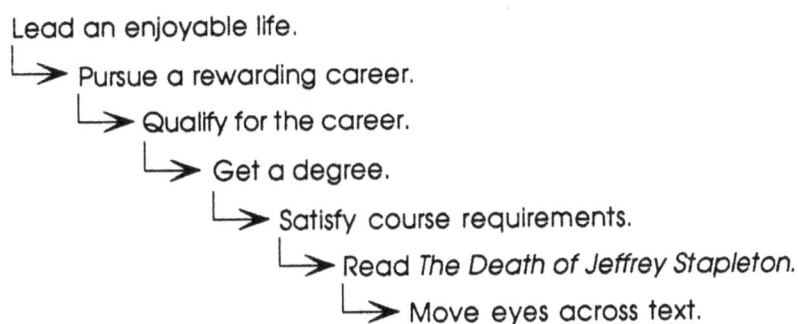

Figure 8.5   The complete hierarchy of purposes underlying reading this book.

Each purpose derives from the purpose above it. The lowest level purpose controls your eye movement across this line of text. It is in the service of the higher level purpose of reading this book. If you should eliminate the purpose of reading this book, the purpose that controls your eye movement would evaporate. Lower level purposes depend upon higher level purposes.

The hierarchy of purposes explains two phenomena that are otherwise obscure. First, why is it that we do things that do not feel good at the instant that we do them? While I surely hope that it is not the case, it is possible that reading this book is producing unpleasant feelings in you—you just don't like it. But you keep reading. Why? If you were reading solely for pleasure, you would have stopped by now. But if reading the book is a purpose that is in the service of a larger purpose, you will continue reading it as long as the good feelings that you anticipate from the higher purpose outweigh the bad feelings that you presently experience. They may induce you to try to wriggle out of the assignment that you have been given, but if that doesn't work you will continue to read.

How do you choose which desire to pursue next? One factor is clearly the strength of the given desire, the intensity of the tension that it produces. But if that were all there was to it, you would simply execute the action that figured to resolve the greatest tension.

It is not as simple as that. What is going on in your mind when you have the sense that you are doing something because "duty calls" to you to do it? You often forego doing something that would be highly rewarding in favor of doing something that is less rewarding because the latter satisfies a higher purpose. You may not get as much satisfaction, for example, from reading this book as from doing a lot of other things, but if reading this book serves the higher purpose of preparing you for a career that you desire, you will do it before you do things that are more pleasant.

It is almost never the case that you are fully in control of any perception. As you read this book, for example, you are only loosely in control of what you are perceiving. You may decide to skip lines or paragraphs, or to quit reading altogether. But, as you read, your perceptions are largely under my control. I cannot be sure that these words convey to you the sense that I intend, so my control over your perceptions is not anywhere near complete either. In fact, much of what you perceive from these pages will not result from control exerted by either one of us. It will be sheer serendipity. You will misunderstand part of what I am saying and make up your own meaning.

The less your desired perception relies upon a response from your environment, particularly from other human beings, the greater will be your control over it. If all you desire, for example, is to perceive your own inner states, as is the case when you do physical exercise or mental reflection, you should be largely in control of your perceptions. If you desire, however, to perceive yourself President of the United States, you will be able to exert little control toward that end. Running for President is so heavily dependent upon the decisions of countless other control systems over such a long period of time, that it will take a total effort (that is, the exclusion of most other purposes) for you to make even a plausible go at it.

Your ability to deliver desired perceptions is also dependent upon the repertoire of actions in your tool bag and upon the level of your skill at executing each one of them. The greater the number of different actions that you have at your disposal, the more likely it is that you will have one tailored to deliver the perception that you desire. The greater your skill in exercising an action, the more likely it is to be effective.

This account of human thought and behavior enables us to paint a picture of the mental state of the thirsty man whose story began this chapter. Like all of us, the thirsty man presumably had a number of perceptions that he desired to pursue. As time passed since his last drink, however, the tension generated by his body's demand for water increased to the point where it became conscious. Under normal circumstances, he could have eliminated that error signal in any number of ways, the most obvious of which would be drawing a glass of water from the tap. It should not have been necessary for him to beat another person to get a drink.

His was not a normal circumstance. Perhaps he found himself in the desert, perhaps he was being held prisoner without water by another person. As time continued to pass, the tension got stronger; he felt thirstier. Under normal conditions thirst is simply one of many tensions that needs to be addressed, as it increases in strength thirst threatens the integrity of the person as a whole. With his survival at stake, we would expect a person to exert whatever force he could muster in order to deliver the desired perception. We would not be surprised if the person attacked another who was barring his path to the water.

There is a great deal more to be said about a person's pursuit of what she desires, but this is not the place to do it for we are still a fair distance from our goal of explaining normative thought. Understanding the way we act to bring about the perceptions that we desire does not explain how it is that we evaluate behavior according to norms. What is going on in our minds when we ask whether the attack by the thirsty man was *justified?* To understand that we must develop the control system model further.

Positive law: the pursuit of the collective good

There is an area of law that can be adequately explained with the control system model as it presently stands—the positive law. You will recall from Chapter 5 that we considered the effect of the Lexington town ordinance making it a crime to leave keys in an automobile on Jeffrey's case. You might recall that I was against applying that law as a norm to determine the legitimacy of Timothy Newland's behavior, even though the law seemed directly on point.

That ordinance is positive law, law that attempts to produce a set of conditions that those who promulgate it think is *good*. In that case, the Town Council was alarmed by a jump in the rate of auto theft and reacted by passing the ordinance. When it is used in that way to produce the good, law is being used just as an individual would use any action to produce the good. The desired perception is different, for it comes not from a single person (unless the political system is a dictatorship) but from some collective body that has a recognized right to promulgate law.

We have seen that control systems can be implemented in mechanical systems (the thermostat) and in biological systems (humans and dogs). They can also be implemented in social systems.

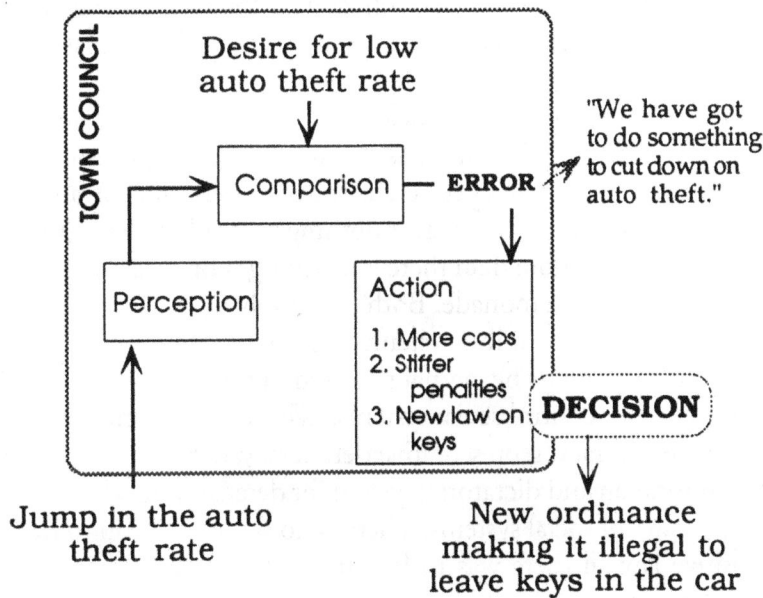

Figure 8.6   The Lexington Town Council as a control system

Perceiving the jump in the auto theft rate, the Town Council became alarmed, just as you would become alarmed if you perceived a discomforting jump in the temperature of the room that you are sitting in. That created a error signal, a difference between what the Council wanted to see and what it was actually seeing. As with individuals, an error signal produces *tension* in social systems. The auto theft rate became a big issue in the Council. The Council called on the Police Department for up-to-the-minute statistics and ordered the Chief to come to every meeting of the Council to keep it posted.

As with individuals, the Council had a repertoire of actions at its disposal to use to reduce the theft rate and thereby eliminate the error signal. To choose among them it had to look more closely at the phenomenon to see what was causing it. It appeared to the Chief that it was due to an increase in joy riding by teenagers rather than to professional auto thieves. For that reason the Council concluded that if drivers made it more difficult for the kids to steal cars by removing their keys from their cars the rate of theft for joyriding would fall. Its action was, then, to pass the ordinance.

The ordinance, unfortunately, was essentially unenforceable. The Chief estimated that he would have to double the size of his force to provide enough officers to check even a substantial portion of the parked cars for keys in the ignition. That cost could not be justified by the Council. As with individual decisions, the Council compared that cost against other desires that would have had to be foregone (Where was the money to come from? From the library budget? From the fund being raised for the new sports complex'?") and decided to pass the law but provide no means for its enforcement. Perhaps the law would be effective if they got the message across to the citizenry, so they staged a media event in which the Fire Chief was ticketed for leaving the keys in his car.

In a nation of laws, law is the vehicle by which the society pursues collective values. Positive law is a set of instructions to various parts of government (e.g., the police force) and to citizens that aims to change their behavior toward the achievement of a preferred state of affairs. There is nothing particularly normative, or moral, about this use of law, any more than there is anything morally significant about our decision to make a glass of lemonade. Both are simply a pursuit of the good.

Social systems, like mechanical systems, are not self-animating. Both must be animated by human desires. The eternal problem of social systems is deciding how individual desires are to control social systems. We have experimented with hereditary monarchy, meritocracy, representative democracy, direct democracy, and every manner of authoritarian and dictatorial system for determining whose desires count as the guiding desires of social systems. There is no stable solution to that problem.

Were positive law all there was to law, it would be quite easy to understand our thinking about it, for it would be very much like our thinking about our own desires. We would simply ask what the law stated and then ask whether the actions of individuals conformed to that law. If they did not, we would mete out whatever penalty was required to induce individual compliance in the future.

Much of law is that way. I return to the example of income taxes. Income taxes are an action of government to raise the resources to support its pursuit of the collective good.

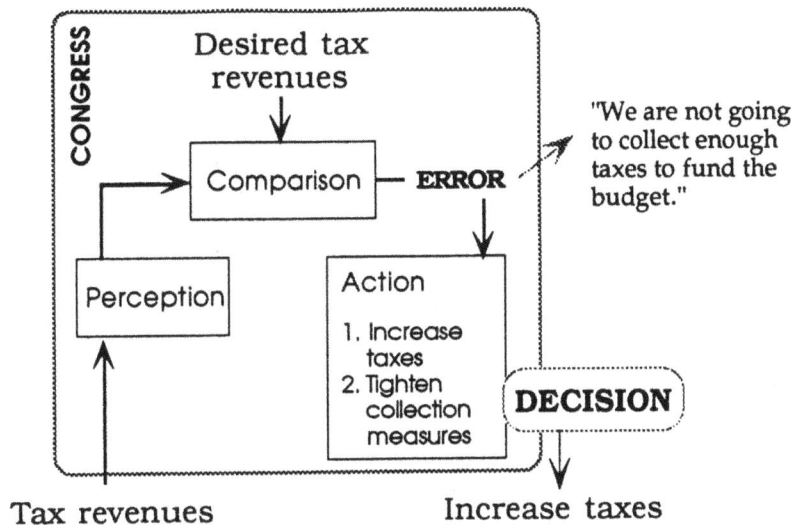

Figure 8.7   Taxation as a control system.

Desired tax revenues are established (loosely) by the governmental budget, by planned expenditures. If planned expenditures exceed projected tax revenues an error signal—an expected deficit—is created. The action to be taken is, then, whatever mix of tax laws and collection measures are needed to generate the desired revenues.

Government is no more free to pursue its vision of the collective good than you are free to pursue your vision of your individual good. As with you, government is limited by its environment. Neither you nor government may spend resources that you do not control. There is a limit to government's ability to control resources.

There is another kind of limit on both you and government as both pursue the good—a *normative* limit. Can the government summarily execute citizens who do not pay their taxes? Why not? The threat of summary execution would most certainly have a salutary effect upon its collection process. We could well imagine that, if execution were allowed, citizens would hand deliver their tax payments to the tax office weeks in advance of the due date to avoid the chance that the return would be lost in the mail or in the bureaucratic process. But summary execution is not a permitted collection measure.

There are constraints upon the positive law, upon the ability of the collective to pursue that which it desires. That constraint is LAW, the sense of law that we employed when we evaluated Jeffrey's case. Positive law defines that which is good. LAW defines that which is right or legitimate. The summary execution of tax evaders, however effective it might be at producing tax revenues, is not right. We must now ask where this sense of what is right and what is wrong comes from and how it acts in our thought.

CHAPTER NINE

Constraints upon action

Pursuing a desire is a great deal different from satisfying that desire. To satisfy it, you must act in a way that brings about the perceptions that you are after. Pause for a few moments to consider the desires that you have never pursued. Are there not things that you would like to do, but will never seriously attempt, things that you would like to have that are beyond the realm of the possible? You are a rare person indeed if every desire that you have ever had has either been satisfied or is still under realistic pursuit.

Some of your desires were sacrificed because of your decision to pursue other desires. Some of them were simply unattainable. I can recall, as a child, being captivated by the story of Icarus, who attempted to escape from the island of Crete on wings made by his father, Daedalus, but flew too near the sun, which melted the wax holding his wings together and dropped him into the sea. I spent a fair amount of time imagining what it would feel like to fly under my own power and how I would find a glue that would not melt in the sun. That imagined feeling has led me to experiment with hang gliding, but somehow the reality of dragging around a contraption composed of aluminum tubing and nylon never delivered actual perceptions that were close to the perceptions that I had imagined. Those imagined perceptions are, for me, unattainable.

Our actions are constrained by the laws of physics and, to a lesser extent, by the laws of economics. Like a rolling boulder, we are constrained forever to roll down hill. Unlike the boulder, we can decide to go up hill, to thwart the law of gravity, but that decision confronts us with the laws of economics. It requires us to spend time and energy, to give up other things that we could do with those resources. Going up hill is attainable, but only at the sacrifice of other perceptions.

The laws of physics determine what is possible. The laws of economics determine what is feasible. But there is another set of laws that act as a constraint upon our actions as well, the laws of morality, which determine those actions that are *legitimate*. These are the laws that are involved in legal thinking.

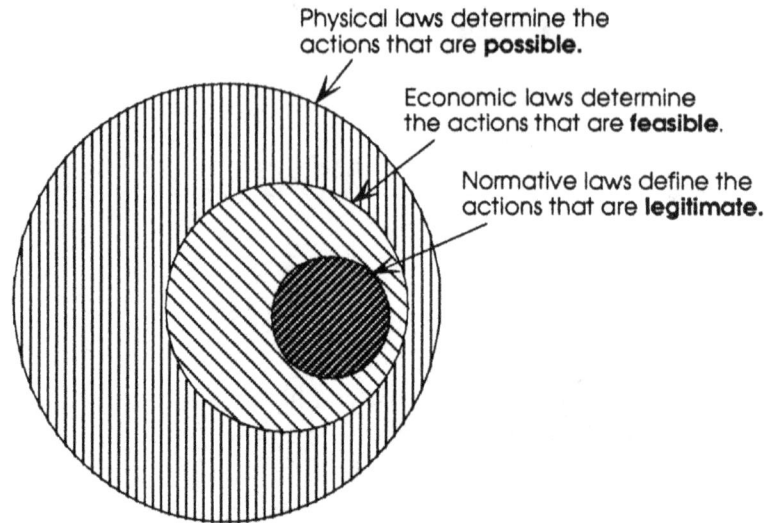

Figure 9.1   Limits upon the range of actions imposed by
             the laws of physics, economics, and morality.

Under normal conditions we choose our actions from the small set in Figure 9.1, from those actions that are not only possible and feasible, but also legitimate. There are occasions when we will attempt the impossible, or throw calculation to the wind and do things that are not economically feasible, or even things that are not legitimate. But normally we select our actions from the range of alternative actions that we have that conform to all three sets of laws.

Doing the right thing

When you decided to read this book, your first task was to get a copy of it. You could have bought it, borrowed it, or stolen it.

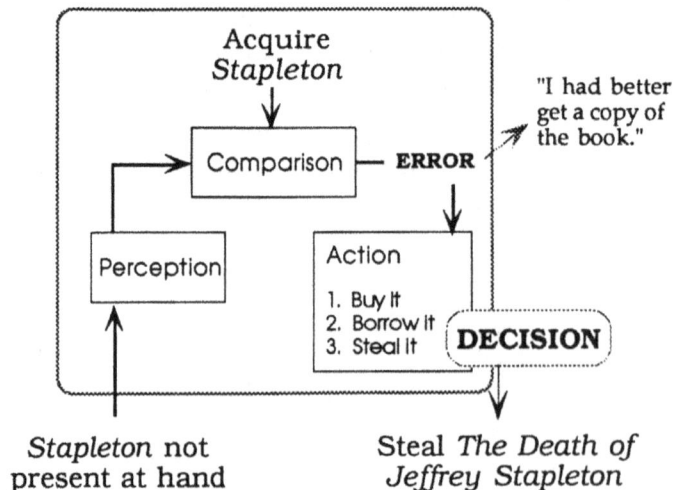

Figure 9.2   Deciding to acquire this book by stealing it.

You didn't steal the book. Why not? Stealing a copy was clearly a *possible* alternative. Perhaps you didn't steal it because that would not have been *feasible* to do so. That is, the cost of stealing it, when you took into account the possibility that you would be punished for your theft, was greater than the cost of buying it. If that was the case, I would guess that you do steal other things, for the present value of theft is strongly positive for any person with a modicum of cleverness.

But that was surely not the reason that you didn't steal this book. You did not even consider the possibility of stealing it. Why not? There is clearly at work in your mind some sort of selection process that excludes from those actions that are possible those which are wrong. That process acts as a constraint upon your pursuit of your desires in this way:

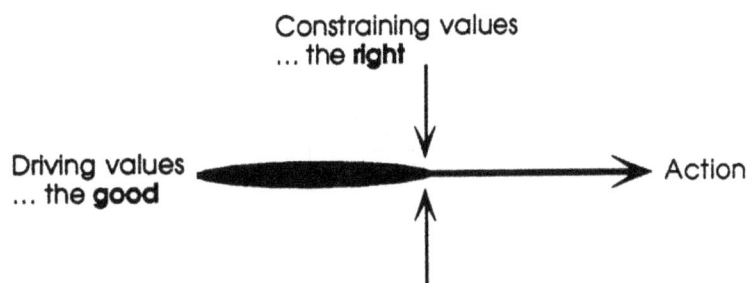

Figure 9.3   Normative values constrain the pursuit of the good.

Driving values underlie your pursuit of the good. They are the values—tastiness, warmth, friendship, intellectual stimulation, and so on—whose perception brings satisfaction. The pursuit of those values is constrained by another set of values, the "constraining values"—courage, honesty, courtesy, truthfulness, and so on. The constraining values do not generate behavior; one does not pursue truthfulness or honesty. They constrain actions that are in pursuit of driving values.

We pursue that which we anticipate will be *good* through actions that are within the limits of that which is *right*. As we saw in the last chapter, the control system model is adequate to describe our pursuit of the good. The values that drive our behavior are those which generate desired perceptions. But the model as presently developed is unable to account for the constraining values. They do not generate desired perceptions; we do not pursue them. They act only upon our choice of the actions that we will undertake to generate the desired perceptions. To account for them we will have to expand the model.

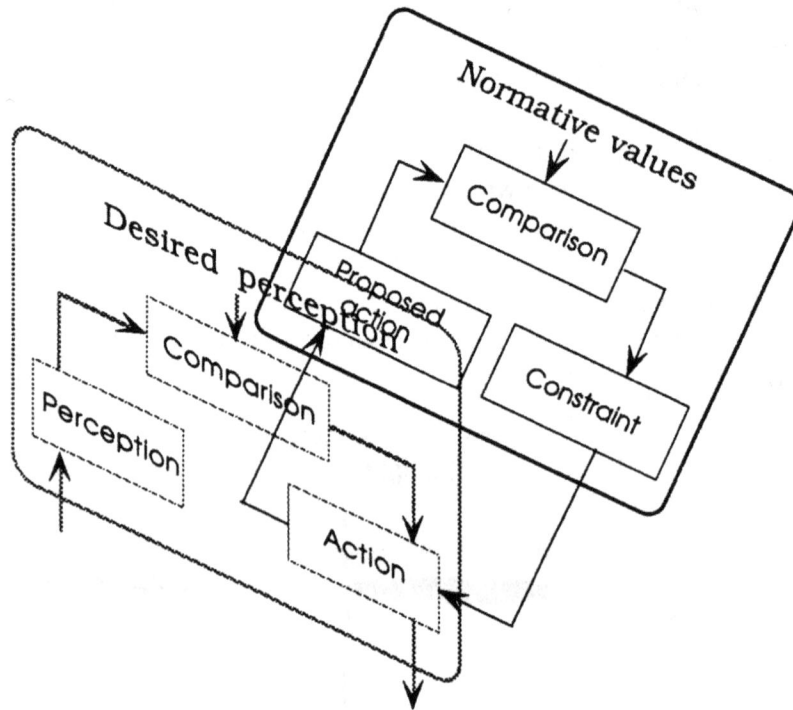

Figure 9.4   Normative values acting as constraints upon action.

The values that constrain our actions (which I will call "normative values") act as a different type of control system. They are a control system that acts upon the general system that controls our behavior. I have represented that difference in Figure 9.4 by putting the normative control system on a different plane from the system that controls our pursuit of the good. The normative control system evaluates our proposed actions for their conformity to our normative values. An action that violates the norm generates an error signal, requiring us to decide whether we will continue with the action anyway, or choose another action that does not generate a normative error.

As you well know, we can ignore the normative error signal and undertake an action that is wrong. But doing that exacts a cost on us, a cost in the form of the unresolved tension (sometimes referred to as "guilt") that the normative error signal generates. So strong is that tension that it may induce us to confess our error after the action and seek to redress it. Or we may simply repress the tension and let it exact its cost upon our self-concept and mental tranquility.

To continue with the illustration that we have been using, if you had seriously considered stealing a copy of this book in order to read it, that would (presumably) have generated a normative error signal, which we could represent in this way:

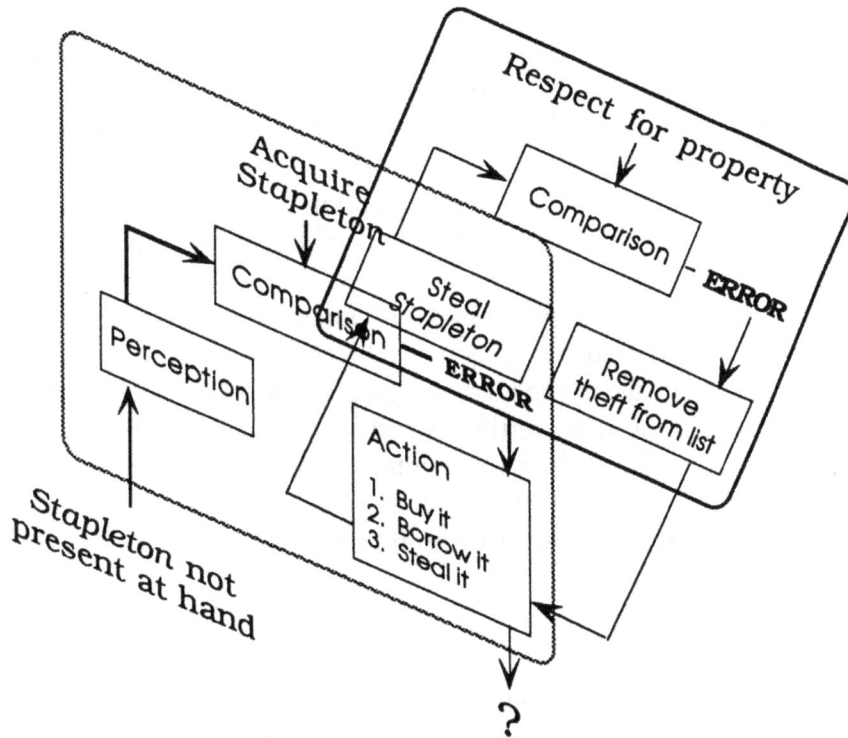

Figure 9.5   Normative analysis flagging a problem with
                 your decision to steal a copy of this book.

Here, an inner battle rages between the sense of the right and your pursuit of the good. Your desire to read this book generated an error signal that caused you look around for a copy of the book. When you found that you did not have it at hand, you had to develop a plan for acquiring it. One possible action was stealing it, but the inclusion of that possibility generated another error signal because stealing it would violate the norm that requires respect for another's property. That error generated a message that you should remove the possibility of stealing it from your list of possible actions. That message is the inner voice of what some characterize as "conscience."

I have pushed this illustration too far, for you never consciously considered stealing this book. That possibility was filtered out of your repertoire of actions long before it became conscious. But there have surely been instances, perhaps when you were a child, when the theft of something that you wanted was a lively possibility. In that case you consciously felt the inner battle between the good and the right.

The battle between the good and the right is not always won by the right. There are instances when we disregard the right or when the tension generated by the good is so great that it overwhelms the right. The latter situation is well illustrated by the case of <u>Ploof v. Putnam.</u> The Ploof family was out for a sail on a lake in their boat when a sudden storm of great violence blew up. We can easily imagine the tension in the skipper's mind as he contemplated the disaster that would follow if the boat was swamped. Casting about for a safe mooring, he spotted Putnam's dock. Putnam's dock was not a public facility, and we might imagine that Ploof would not even consider tying up to it under normal circumstances, any more than he would consider stealing this book if he had had the opportunity to read it. But the situation was extreme; his desired perception—a safe mooring—so strongly departed from his most likely future perceptions (i.e., sinking), that he disregarded the strictures of private property and tied up to Putnam's dock.

The story did not have a happy ending, for Putnam, in an excess of enthusiasm over the rights of property ownership, instructed his employee to sever Ploof's mooring lines, with great damage to the boat and great risk to Ploof's family. Putnam's actions were wrong, as the court certified when it awarded Ploof damages for his injuries. Norms of behavior, at least those enforced in law, are not absolute. They guide behavior, they discipline the pursuit of the good. They do not erect absolute barriers to any action, which means that humans must continually make difficult normative decisions.

Why follow norms?

It appears that there are people, called "sociopaths," in whom the normative control system is either dormant or wholly absent. The sociopath does not evaluate the moral legitimacy of his actions. That is not to say, however, that he is unaffected by legal norms. The strictures at work on the sociopath are solely physical and economic. If the law backs a norm with the use of coercion, the sociopath will take that coercion into account in planning his actions. He limits himself out of a *fear* of the costs that will attend the violation of legal norm.

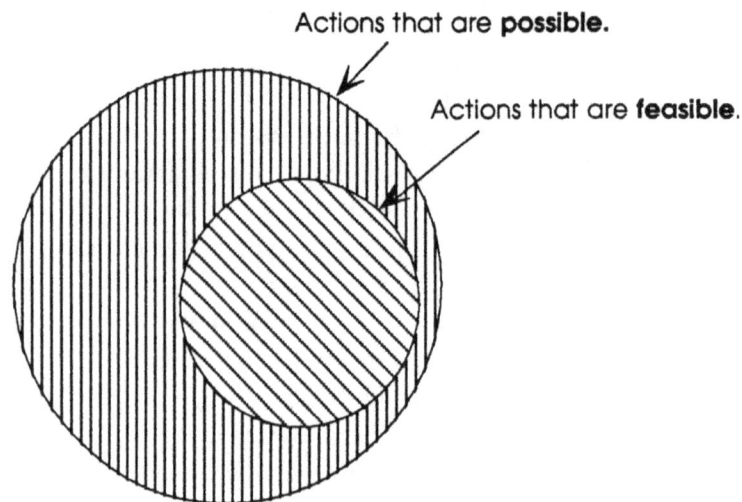

Figure 9.6   Limits upon the sociopath's actions include
physical and economic limits, but not normative limits.

The sociopath is "rational" in the sense that he takes the expected consequences of his actions into account in his planning. If the action will generate responses that may detract from his other aims, he will factor them into the calculus of his decision. A sociopath who desired to read this book, for example, might employ the following calculation:

LEDGER

COST OF BUYING BOOK		COST OF STEALING BOOK	
Time and effort needed to buy it	10	Time and effort needed to steal it	15
Dollar cost	50	Expected cost of the consequences, if caught (probability of being caught times cost imposed)	20
TOTAL COST	60		35

Figure 9.7   A sociopath's analysis of decision about acquiring this book.

The norm of property ownership makes itself felt only as it is backed by *enforcement*. The less likely he is to be caught and the lower the penalty for violating the norm, the less cost the sociopath must include in the ledger that governs the decision. To keep the sociopath in Figure 9.7 from stealing this book we would need to raise the combination of the penalty and the chance of getting caught, as he judged those costs, above 45 units to make its cost greater than the cost of buying the book. Even then, we might fail to turn the sociopath toward lawful action, for there is a perverse strain of motivation in the sociopath that generates a *positive* value from doing something illegal. By increasing our measures against shoplifting, we may increase the entertainment value that he enjoys by beating our efforts. That may well have been the situation with the car thief in Jeffrey's case, for he clearly did not steal the Newland car for financial advantage.

A law that was not enforced would be without effect on sociopaths. But it would not be without effect on most of us, for most of us take into account the legitimacy of our actions without reference to the consequences that would follow from them. Why do we do that?

The strongest case is the person who treats other people's error signals as if they were her own, a situation that I have referred to as "love." A person who loves another experiences that person's unhappiness as his own and undertakes actions that are justified only on the basis of the joint effect that they will have upon both the actor and the loved one. Consider the sociopath in Figure 9.6. Sociopaths can act out of love, so let's say that this sociopath takes into consideration the expected cost of his action not only upon himself but also upon his wife:

LEDGER

COST OF BUYING BOOK		COST OF STEALING BOOK	
Time and effort needed to buy it	10	Time and effort needed to steal it	15
Dollar cost	50	Expected cost of the consequences, if caught (probability of being caught times cost imposed): **to self**	20
		to wife	80
TOTAL COST	**6 0**		**1 1 5**

Figure 9.8   Cost analysis of sociopath's decision about acquiring this book, including its effect upon a loved one.

The sociopath's wife would take his being caught far harder than the sociopath—four times as hard, to be exact—and he knows that. He takes that into account in his calculations and, in our example. will now buy the book instead of stealing it. Sociopaths who are in love are clearly less of a danger to the rest of us than those who aren't, so we can generally applaud love when we see it.

It is interesting to note that love does not add anything basic to normative analysis beyond the calculations of the sociopath. It does induce the person who is in love to take another into account. but it does not trigger the normative process pictured in Figure 9.5. Both the sociopath and the person in love take into account only the present benefit of a course of action. I do not mean to demean love as a source of motivation, only to suggest that it is not sufficient either to explain how it is that normative thinking works or to explain how a society is organized.

The normative control system in Figure 9.5 does not act by changing the expected costs and benefits of an action. It acts by foreclosing possible actions from consideration, whether or not they are beneficial. It determines the legitimacy of an action independent of the consequences of that action. It is wrong to steal, even if one is confident that he can get away with it without penalty.

It is difficult for us to get our fingers on non-consequentialist reasoning. Most of our decisions are between courses of action that have different consequences. We weigh the consequences of each course against what we must give up in order to achieve them. That is not what we do when we decide not to undertake an action because it would be wrong to do so (unless we are sociopaths). We simply refuse to do that which is wrong. Why do we do that? Where do the norms that constrain our behavior come from? Why do we take them so seriously?

The answers to those questions are not at all clear. There is in fact great debate about them. It is clear that normative controls begin to develop before the child can articulate them. A child of three is well prepared to understand how to evaluate the proposition that a given action is *wrong* and to distinguish that from an action that is *dangerous,* like running in the street. Saying that an action is dangerous is making a statement about consequences: the action creates a risk of harm. Saying that an action is wrong is making a statement about its moral worth in the absence of any consequences. The child is able to understand both kinds of statements and to feel tension stemming from a wrong that he was in no danger of being punished for.

Control system theory throws no light on the source of normative thinking. [1] In what follows I will leave that question up in the air. Wherever they come from, normative values generate thinking that constrains our actions. To some extent those norms are learned. In addition to its other functions, law can function as a source of that learning.

The social dynamics of nonnative evaluation

The illustration that I have been using in this chapter—your decision not to steal this book—is probably not a good one, for it is likely that you did not consciously consider the possibility of stealing it. You long ago developed a habit of thought that prevented theft from becoming a possible action alternative. Let me change the illustration slightly to trigger the conscious operation of your normative system.

Let us say that the desire to read this book was "in the back of your mind." Perhaps someone mentioned it to you or it was assigned. It was not high enough in your hierarchy of desired perceptions to generate immediate action. But today you happened upon the book lying on a table where someone had left it. It caught your eye. Would you pick it up and read it? That would depend. would it not, on a lot of things, such as how well you knew the person who owned the book. how easy it would be to ask the person if you could take a look at it, and whether or not it was located in a place where the owner clearly intended others to pick it up (i.e., in a waiting room).

I have observed precisely that situation in a school cafeteria countless times. The eye of a student passing through the cafeteria falls upon a book or magazine lying on an unoccupied table, perhaps among a stack of other books. He changes position, crooking his neck to read as much as he can without touching the book. His desire gets the best of him and he reaches for the book. As he is about to touch it, his hand stops, pulls back, moves toward the book again—a visual manifestation of a conflict between the two control systems pictured in Figure 9.4. His desire to read the book and his normative sense that he should not take charge of another's book without permission fight for control of his actions. He looks around to see if he can spot the owner. Perhaps he sits down at the table, waiting for the owner. Perhaps he does look at the book. Perhaps he moves on.

Sitting down at the table to read the book is clearly not theft, for there is no intent to deprive the owner of its use. But would it be, nonetheless, inappropriate?

---

1   But see later literature discussing details of the hierarchical nature of Perceptual Control Theory, such as Forssell (2008) and Runkel (2003), which (at the highest levels) show Systems Concepts aggregating from groups of Principles while an individual grows up, and later, Principles being derived from Systems Concepts. By that time the individual may have forgotten how the Systems Concepts were derived.

Would it be an impermissible intrusion upon the owner's rights in the book? You and I might very well differ on that, for this illustration lies at the edge of our normative sense. I will tell you that I would (and have), in fact, take the book in hand if I were at the school where I teach, but not if I were at another school. Perhaps I am wrong in that. Perhaps the students who have kidded me about snooping in their reading material were trying to convey to me the sense that I had offended them, that I should add to the set of norms that guide my behavior the norm that other people's reading matter should be left alone, period.

Normative evaluation is not, of course, solely a personal matter. Each of us evaluates our own behavior in the way pictured in Figure 9.4. We evaluate the behavior of others in precisely the same way. Figure 9.9 represents the situation described above in which the owner of a book that I have helped myself to in the cafeteria comes upon me sitting at her table reading her book.

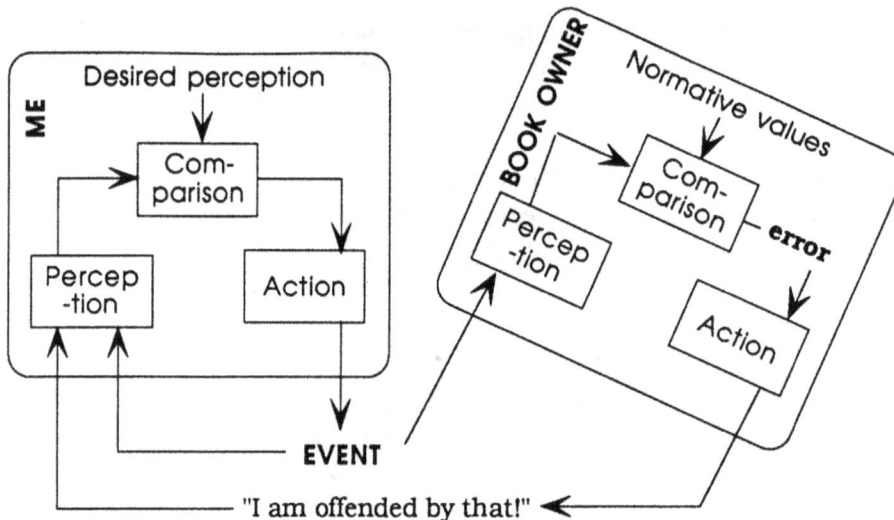

Figure 9.9   Normative evaluation exercised by one upon the actions of another.

My behavior generated an objective event, an empirically verifiable set of circumstances that she observed as she returned to her table with her lunch. She may in fact have confirmed her observation, turning to a friend and saying, "Check me if I am wrong, but I see Gibbons sitting at our table reading my book," though she would probably say that for effect, rather than for empirical verification.

She might say to me that, "I am offended by that!" I must say that no one has ever said that to me, but it may be that that is what they actually meant by their more jocular remonstrance. If that *is* what she meant, it is clear that her normative sense and my own are not in perfect correspondence. I would surely have asked her before I removed the book from her table. But I did not feel compelled to ask her permission to take a look at it.

Events like the one just described are *formative* (pardon the unfortunate similarity of that word to the similarly unfamiliar word "normative"). That is, the event tends to form or to reform one's sense of that which is legitimate. We absorb norms from others as we perceive their response to our actions. Those actions need not be actions like my reading of the student's book. They may simply be words, as when a group of people chew over a problem and discuss the rights and wrongs of it. Either way, the input from others shapes our sense of what is legitimate, or at least of what will be tolerated by others.

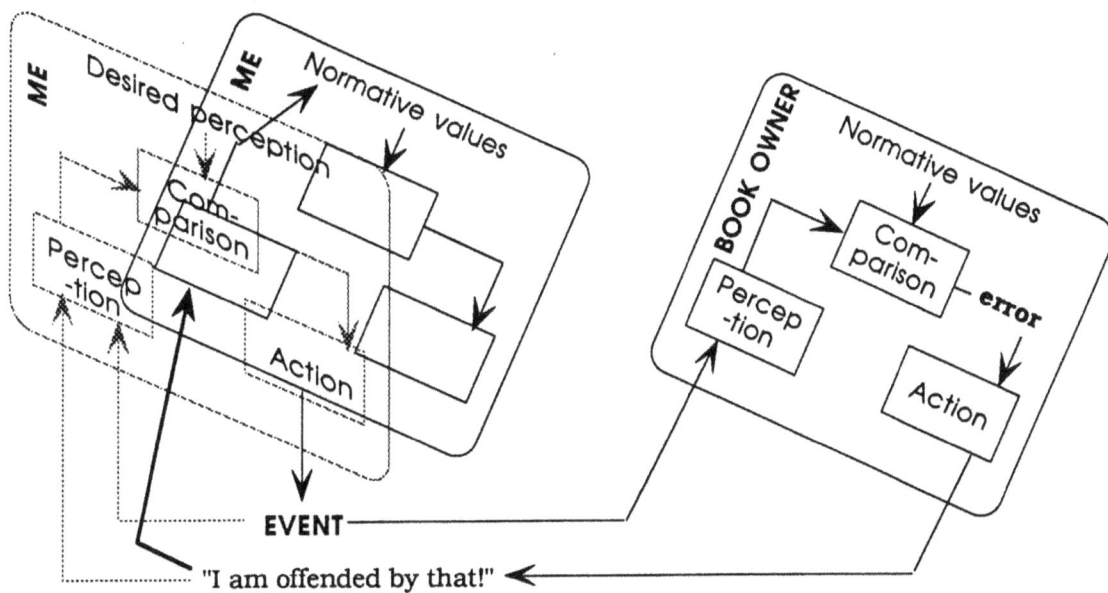

Figure 9.10   Reformation of one's values based on the actions of another.

Figure 9.10 represents the situation in which the response of another to one's actions is taken not simply as a response to that action but also calls into question the norm underlying it. In my case, that would happen if the student's indignant response to my action caused me to reflect upon what went wrong with my own normative evaluation of the situation. Her norm—that no one should touch her book without her permission—was clearly different from my own. Her response indicated that there was something wrong with my reference signal, with the norm that should have controlled my behavior. By calling it into question she suggests to me that my present normative sense should be changed. I may or may not do that, but I will at least remember in the future that picking up another's book without permission can cause trouble.

The control system model has now been developed to the point where we can use it to describe legal thought and action. Legal thought occurs in the context of a social relationship that is similar to that of the book owner in Figure 9.10. That is, it is a process by which one person evaluates the behavior of others according to normative standards. As we saw in Part I, legal thinking subjects the behavior of others to scrutiny, applying to them a set of norms that are in part formally legal (i.e., found within "the law") and in part personal. We now ask how that works.

CHAPTER TEN

A model of legal thought

Law is a social control system with teeth. John Newland will not be free to ignore a jury verdict that awards $800,000 to Jeffrey's estate. If he attempts to ignore it, people with guns will show up and force the sale of his farm. Because of these inescapable consequences, judges, jurors, and lawyers are not free to apply whatever normative standards they want, as they are free to do in their private lives.

Lawyers do the same kind of thinking that everyone else does, but they do it under a special set of constraints; the rules of law become rules of thought. The lawyer is herself a control system, but a control system that is part of the larger control system of law. As she attempts to control ("influence") her clients, other lawyers, witnesses, judges, and jurors to produce the end that she wants, she is limited by the rules of law. Those rules shape not only her action but her thinking as well. She is not, for example, free to argue that John Newland should have to pay money to Jeffrey's estate because he has a lot more money than it does. That argument is not permissible under American law and it will not even cross her mind as she evaluates Jeffrey's case.

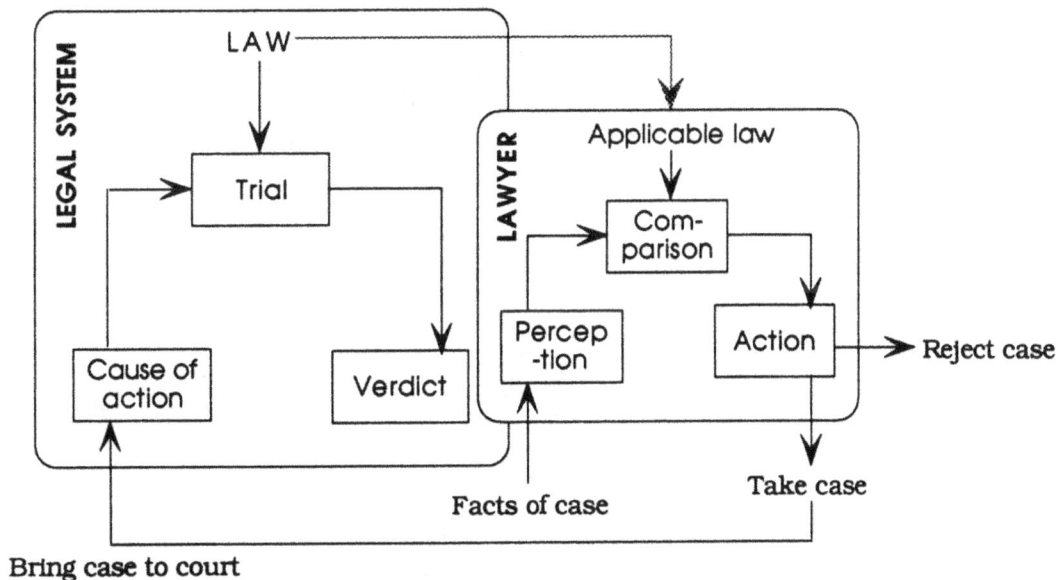

Figure 10.1   Our role in the Stapleton case, within the larger context of the legal system.

In Part I we evaluated the facts of Jeffrey's case within the context of the law. The law provides the standards against which the behavior of people is measured. Those standards are never wholly clear and sometimes in conflict. They require *interpretation* by the lawyer, who must modify them to make them relevant to the case at hand.

The lawyer in Figure 10.1 is not like a thermostat, which stupidly accepts any temperature that is set as the standard for the room. The lawyer plays an active role in interpreting the law applicable to the case. The law provides guidance, enough guidance to prevent us from asking in the Stapleton case, for example, about the religious or racial status of the people in the case. Justice is officially blinded to those qualities, and we were blinded as well.

The lawyer's first job is to decide whether or not to take the case. That is as far as we took the Stapleton case in Part I, for I decided not to take the case. My "action," in terms of Figure 10.1 was simply to write a letter to Margaret and Tom informing them that I would not accept the case.

Had we decided to take the case, we would have brought the case into the legal system by filing a complaint on behalf of Jeffrey's estate. If we had done that, we could apply the control system model to analyze the lawyer's function within the legal system, and the operation of the legal system itself. My aim in this book, however, is to explore legal thinking, not to describe the legal system, so we have enough before us in the Stapleton case to explain without getting into the legal system as a whole.

An overview of the model

In Figure 10.1 the lawyer applies the law to the perceived facts of a case to render a judgment about the legal liveliness of the case. That is a gross, or high level, description of what is going on in the lawyer's mind, far too gross to explain our thinking in *Stapleton*. To explain it we must look more closely at each of the three mental functions—"perception," "comparison," and "action"—performed by the lawyer. Each of those functions operates to answer a different set of questions:

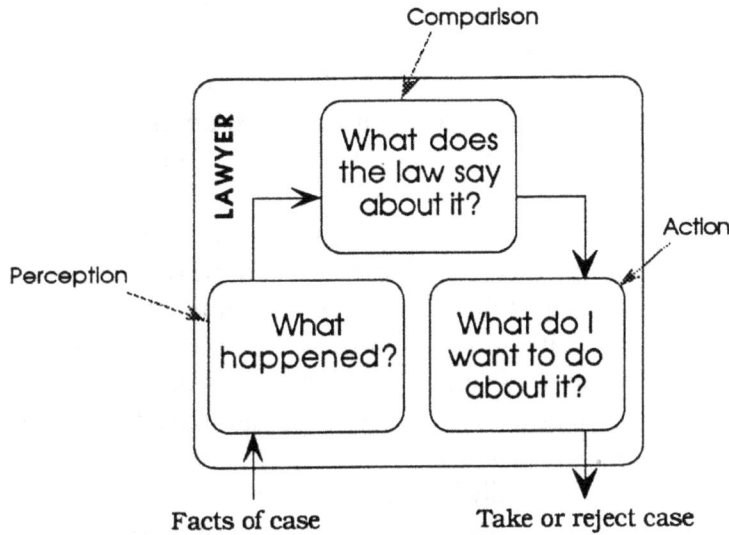

Figure 10.2   The function of each component of the lawyer's
thinking in the overall analysis of the case.

The function called "perception" refers to the process by which the lawyer determines what happened in the matter. This is the process that I referred to in Part I as solely *descriptive*, meaning that the lawyer is describing to her own satisfaction what happened. In the function called "comparison" the lawyer searches for a standard against which to evaluate what happened and applies the standard to her understanding of what happened. Finally, the lawyer decides on an "action," deciding what she wants to do about it, what further action she should take.

In terms of the Stapleton case, those three functions would look like this:

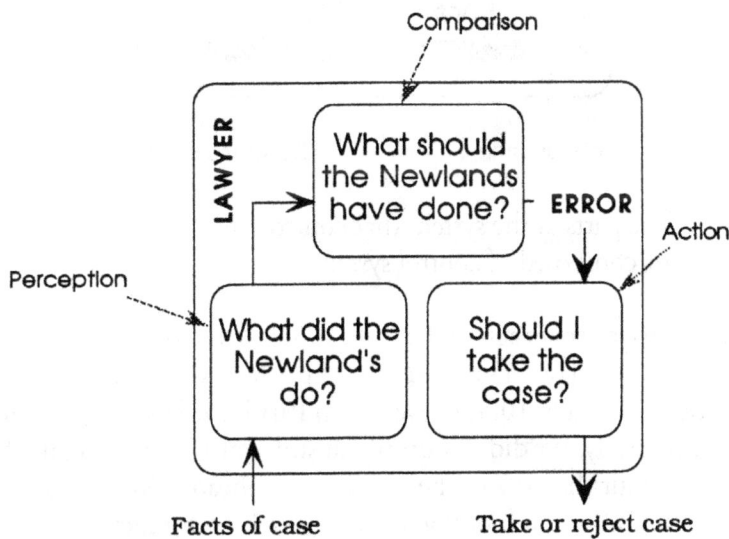

Figure 10.3   Our thinking in Stapleton in control system terms.

Our thinking generated an "error," a plausible interpretation of the behavior of the Newlands that departed from a plausible interpretation of the legal norms applicable to them. That error was not strong. It depended upon a somewhat tortured interpretation of the facts and upon the selection of a favorable set of legal norms. It would have been at least as easy for us to interpret the facts and law in a way that led us to conclude that the Newlands were faultless. The weakness of the error led me to conclude that I would take no further action in the case.

Figure 10.3 describes our thinking in *Stapleton,* but in terms that are too gross to be useful. For one thing, it is too stiff. It makes it look as though what we did was follow three mechanical steps. That may be *in effect* what we did, but it is definitely not what we did in *fact.* In fact, our thinking ranged around all three functions. We thought about the case against Margaret and rejected it. looked for further information about the accident, repeatedly looked for law to guide our thinking.

Figure 10.3 comes closer to describing our thinking if we regard each one of its three functions as itself a control system:

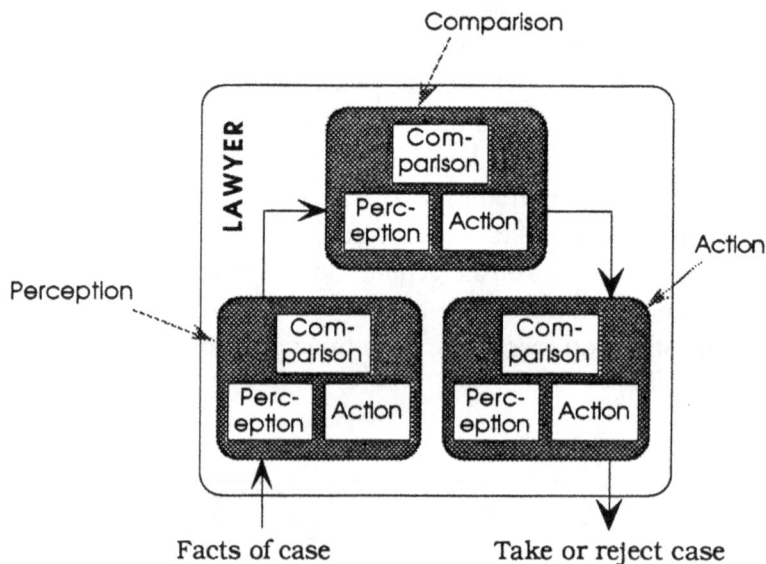

Figure 10.4   The parts of the system that control legal thought
are composed of control systems.

What does it mean to say that each of the three functions is itself composed of a control system? Consider the lawyer's assessment of the facts of a case, which is the box labeled "perception" in Figure 10.4. As we saw in Part I, the lawyer does not perceive the facts of a case passively. We did not simply sit still, waiting for Margaret Stapleton or someone else to pour the facts of the case into our heads. We evaluated the facts as they came in, then went out looking for more, looking for facts that filled in our picture of the case. That activity is guided by a control system—a "fact gathering and assessing control system," which I referred to in Part I as the "descriptive" process.

It was the same way with the law. There was no definitive source of law that we could mechanically apply to the facts. We had to make up the law that we applied to the case. We referred to our existing concepts of law and, when they proved inadequate, went looking for more law to build our concept of the law applicable to the case. That process was also guided by a control system, which I referred to in Part I as the "normative" process.

Notice that the model in Figure 10.4 generates a far more dynamic picture of our thinking than that in Figure 10.3, more in keeping with our actual experience of our thinking. There are four sources of tension (i.e., error signals) in that model: factual, generating a need for more information; normative, generating a need for a better grip upon the law; action, generating a need for a change in behavior; and the overall tension associated with the case as a whole. Each system generates tensions, which compete with each other for our conscious attention and lead to thinking that feels somewhat disordered as our minds race between factual questions, legal questions, and questions about why we are doing this in the first place.

In the model of legal thinking that follows I will describe our thinking in *Stapleton* in terms of the three processes in Figure 10.4 and the interactions between them. I will refer to the three general functions of legal thought with the terminology that we used in Part I:

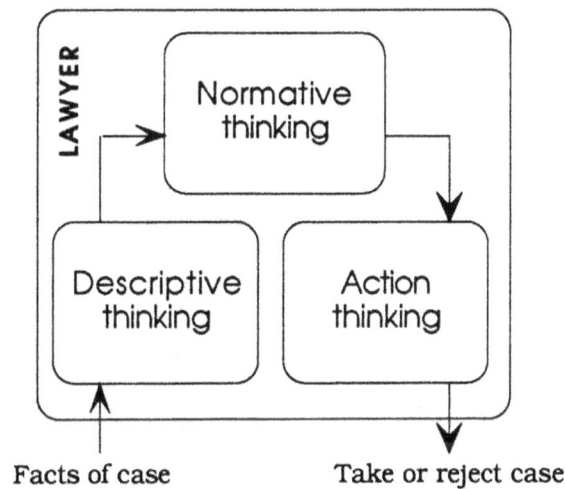

Figure 10.5   The terminology that will be used in this chapter.

I will take up each of these processes in turn. As we consider each part of the model, I will use little diagrams like the one below on the right to indicate which part of the model is under consideration. The little diagrams are shorthand versions of Figure 10.4.

Descriptive thinking

Descriptive thinking is that which addresses the question. What is? The environment provides us with data that we perceive, interpret, and build into a concept of what happened. Most of our thinking in Part I was of this type. Did Timothy Newland leave the keys in the car? Did the driver see Jeffrey and try to avoid him? Why was Jeffrey in the street? Each of those questions asks what happened. The answer to each built a description of the events surrounding Jeffrey's death.

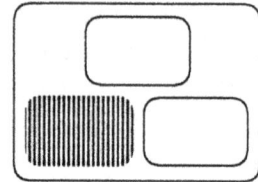

Descriptive thinking is an active process, a process by which we undertake actions —search for more facts—that we hope will build a more complete understanding of the event. Active processes are governed by control systems, systems that organize our thought and tell us what to do next. The control system that organizes descriptive thinking looks like this:

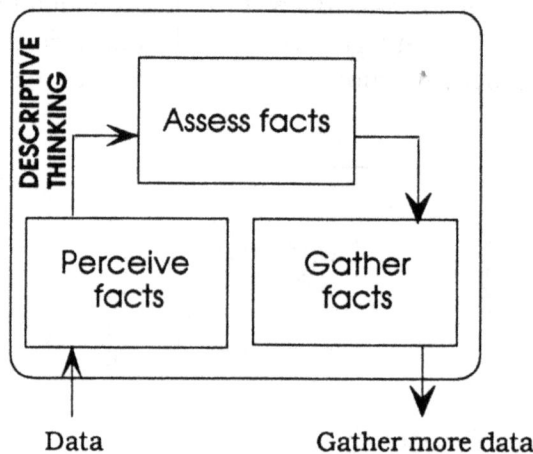

Figure 10.6   The components of descriptive thinking.

I will take up each of the three components of the descriptive process in turn.

1. Perceiving facts

This is hardly the place to come up with a control system theory of perception, and I am hardly the one to do it. But there are some general things that can be safely said about perception that are particularly relevant to legal thought.

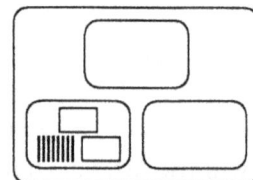

First, perception is a many-layered process. Consider again the example of making lemonade. When you drink lemonade it washes over your tongue and causes the taste receptors in your tongue to fire. Those taste receptors are of four types: receptors that perceive sweet, sour, salty, and bitter. There is no lemonade receptor in your tongue that fires off, telling you that you are drinking lemonade. Instead, the lemonade touches off receptors of all four types, roughly in proportion to the sweetness, sourness, saltiness, and bitterness of the lemonade.

Your nervous system must now subject those four types of signals to several layers of processing in order to produce what you consciously perceive to be lemonade.

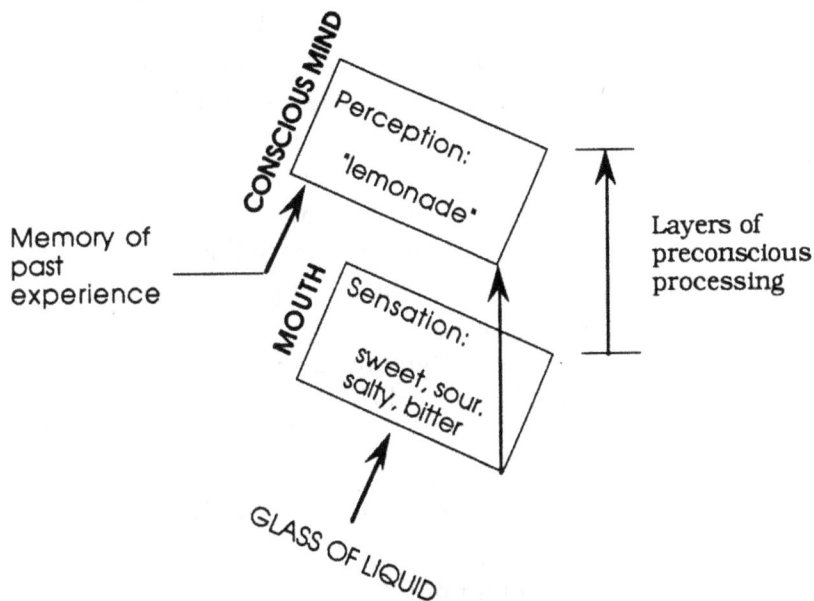

Figure 10.7   The perception that a glass of liquid contains lemonade requires many levels of processing of the basic sensory information.

You are normally completely unaware of all of that processing. All that you consciously perceive is drinking the liquid and tasting lemonade. Between the drinking and the tasting, however, the signals from your tongue were combined with other signals from your mouth about the wetness and texture of the drink, with your memories of prior drinking events, and with your expectations about what you were drinking to create your conscious perception. The drink eventually reached your consciousness, where you could attach a label ("This is lemonade.") to it.

The "facts" that lawyers take to be the bedrock of their thinking about a case are, in fact, batches of data that have already been subject to great mental processing by the time that they reach the level of consciousness where the lawyer can put a label on them. Even a "hard" fact, like the license number of the car that hit Jeffrey, had to be subjected to many levels of interpretation before you were conscious of it as "LK1072." Each of those levels of interpretation provides an opportunity to make a mistake.

Most of the data that lawyers deal with is verbal, either written or spoken. There is a special problem with verbal data: it has been processed by another person. If someone tells you, for example, that I am a "crook," what does that data mean? It clearly means that that person said those words. But does it mean that he meant them? Is he saying it just for effect, to ruin my reputation? As part of your processing of those words you will assess the likelihood that he is not being honest with you. By the time that you become conscious of the meaning of those words, there will be a set of inferences about the speaker's mental state and intentions attached to them.

Most of your processing of facts occurs in the background, that is, before it ever gets to consciousness. To illustrate that, let me ask you about how big you think Jeffrey Stapleton was when he was hit by the car. There is not a single word in this book about how big he was, but I will bet that you have at least a hazy mental picture of his size. I think of him as tall for his age (so that his hands are big enough to manage a full size keyboard), and slender, in keeping with the ascetic nature of the music that he plays. Your picture will differ from mine, depending in part upon differences between us in our prior experience with childhood piano players.

Unless you spent time consciously wondering what Jeffrey looked like, your image of Jeffrey was formed in the background, at the same preconscious levels that process sweet, sour, salty, and bitter into the taste of lemonade. That preconscious processing can get us, as lawyers, into a lot of trouble, for it can load up our interpretation of data with a lot of garbage. Unless we are careful, for instance, we can fill out our interpretation of Jeffrey with a load of stereotypical assumptions: skinny little ascetic kid, not very athletic, probably a daydreamer who paid little attention to what was going on around him, just the kind of kid to wander mindlessly into the path of an automobile.

If we allow that to happen, we will have solved our legal problem before we ever give it a chance. In forming our perception of Jeffrey we will see him as careless, so that by the time we get to the question of the impact with the car we will already have seen him as the cause of that impact. The word "scrutinize" is used a lot in law and that is appropriate, for the lawyer must scrutinize his every perception to ferret out unwarranted inferences that have crept into his perception of the facts of a case. What assumptions have I made about the parties to the case? What values have shaped my understanding of the people and organizations involved in it?

The second thing that can be said about our perception of the facts of a matter is that we treat as fact matter that is not empirically verifiable. The license number of the Newland car is verifiable, but Jeffrey's mental state at the time he ran into the street is not. Yet it is important to our understanding of the case to come up with a plausible reason why he ran into the street. Montefiori's story about the wind-blown newspaper provides us with a plausible description of the state of Jeffrey's mind that caused him to run into the street. That state of mind will become in our own minds a "fact" as we continue to think through the case.

The third thing about the lawyer's perception of the facts of a case is that it is highly *contingent*. The lawyer's understanding of a case is not composed of a set of facts about which he is absolutely certain. If we were to write a list of facts from the Stapleton case about which we were absolutely certain, given the information set out about the case in Part I, that list would be very short. Most of the key facts of that case—the role of the keys in motivating the thief; the mental state of the driver at the time of the accident: the meaning of the skid marks in the road—are highly problematic. Our understanding of that case is not a mosaic, a picture of the event composed of clear pieces that our minds have arranged into a whole. It is more like a network of alternative interpretations of the data that we have perceived about the case.

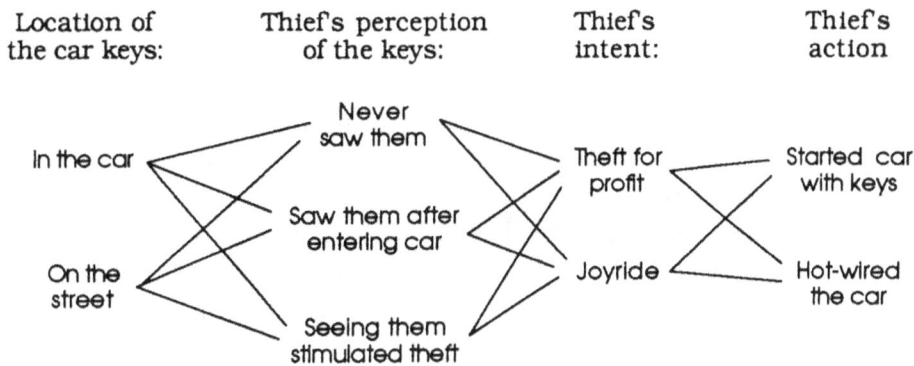

Location of   Thief's perception   Thief's   Thief's
the car keys: of the keys: intent: action

Never saw them

In the car

Theft for profit   Started car with keys

Saw them after entering car

On the street

Joyride   Hot-wired the car

Seeing them stimulated theft

Figure 10.8   The network of contingent interpretations that constitutes our descriptive understanding of Stapleton.

Each of the four "facts" in Figure 10.8 is important to our analysis of the Stapleton case. But the data in the case supports at least two plausible interpretations of each of those facts. Timothy Newland, for example, insisted that he took the keys out of the car, but confesses that they must have fallen onto the street through a hole in his pocket. But, given his past history, we must keep alive in our thinking the possibility that he left them in the car and is lying to cover that up.

The location of the keys matters in the case, for their location is critical to an assessment of the motivation of the car thief. If the thief saw the keys, and the sight of the keys motivated him to steal the car, Timothy could be said to have *caused*, to some extent, the theft of the car and the attendant tragedy. But that is not at all clear. There are other plausible scenarios, none of which can be definitively resolved from the data that we have.

Taken together, the plausible alternatives create a web, or network, of possibilities. It is that *entire web* of possibilities that constitutes our understanding of the facts of the case. Notice that there are 24 possible paths through the network in Figure 10.8. The thief, for example, could have been a professional who hot-wired the car.

Or he could have been a joyrider with no inkling of stealing the car until he saw the keys in the street.

Some of the 24 possible paths are not plausible. It is not plausible, for example, that the keys were in the street and the thief never saw them. We know that the keys were in the car when it was recovered after the accident. If the keys were on the street but the thief never saw them, the keys would not have been in the car when it was recovered. That knocks four possible paths out of the network, but it still leaves us with twenty paths that are plausible.

The ability to withhold judgment on the facts of a case, to accept the ambiguity in the data and to hold all of the plausible alternative interpretations of the data in mind, is crucial to legal thinking. The person who has difficulty dealing with ambiguity, who must resolve each and every factual question into a sharp picture of events, will not be an effective lawyer. She will reject lively cases because she fails to see a favorable interpretation of the facts: she will pursue dead cases because she has failed to take alternative interpretations of the data seriously. She will, in other words, fail to treat things as they actually are, which is deeply ambiguous and in need of constant reinterpretation.

This is not to say, of course, that lawyers revel in ambiguity. Like everyone else they seek to see things clearly, to generate a coherent understanding of events. To see how they do that, we must move to the next phase of the descriptive process.

2. Assessing facts

The heart of a control system lies in the process by which perceptions are compared against a standard to determine whether or not they measure up to it. At this point we have some grip upon the process by which facts are perceived. What are those facts evaluated against? What is the standard that we use to determine whether or not a factual interpretation is legitimate and to identify further data that we need clarify our picture of the event?

We have an illustration of that process close at hand, four paragraphs above. In that paragraph I argued that it was not plausible to think that the thief of the Newland car didn't see the keys *and* that the keys were in the street. If both of those possibilities were true, then a third fact—that the keys were in the car when it was recovered—could not be true. But we know that that was true, so it is not possible that both of those facts are true.

Those two possibilities do not *fit* with the rest of what we know. Put another way, if all three facts were true, the event would be *incoherent*. To explain how it could be that the keys were in the street, the thief never saw them there, but they wound up in the car, we would have to invent a magical creature, like a Gremlin,

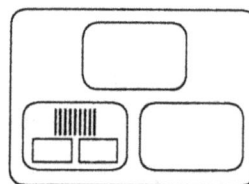

who, seeing the thief hot-wire the car, grabbed the keys from the street and tossed them into the car as it pulled away.

Our minds will not accept that kind of thinking, not, at any rate, unless all else fails. Our minds force facts to fit with our prior experience. In this case that prior experience includes the other facts of the case, including the fact that the keys were in the car when it was recovered, a fact that we have a great deal of confidence in.

Saying that we seek coherence is not enough, however, to explain what is going on in control system terms. A control system must have a *reference signal,* a standard against which to evaluate that which is perceived. That reference signal is, I propose, the sense of fairness that I described in Chapter 3.

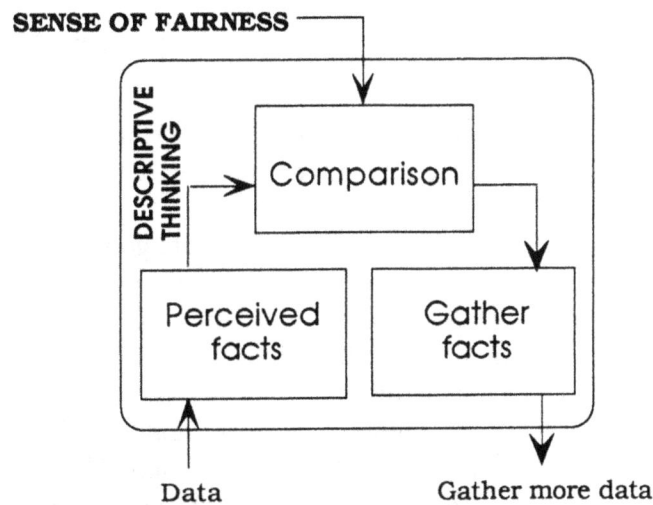

Figure 10.9   Factual assessment as a comparison between the
perceived facts of an event and the sense of fairness.

We evaluate our perceptions of the facts of an event against our sense of the fairness, or wholeness, of events. In Chapter 3 I illustrated the sense of fairness with a boat builder who, looking at the hull of a boat, spots a dent in its otherwise fair curvature. That dent violates his past experience of boat hulls, but it is important to note that he does not sense that violation by comparing the instant boat against his recollection of past hulls, one by one. Somehow, his prior experience of boat hulls has been melded into a sense of those hulls, into a sense of "hull fairness." It is that sense that is violated by the perception of the dent in the hull.

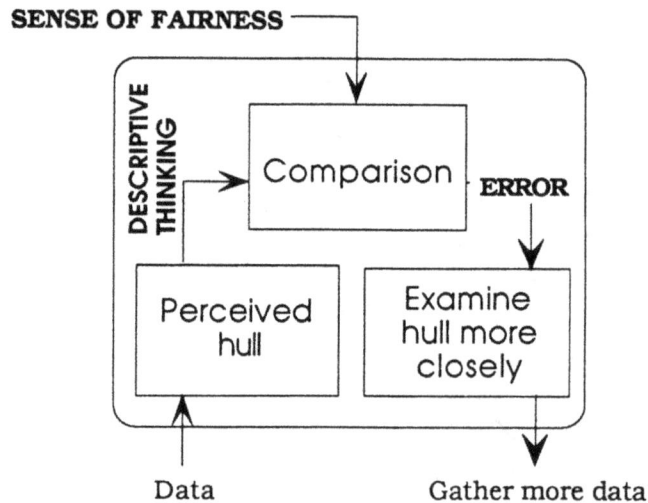

Figure 10.10   The boat builder's examination of the hull of the boat
generates an error between it and his sense of hull fairness.

That comparison generates an error signal—"What's going on with that dent?"—
that causes the boat builder to examine it more closely, gathering more data about
it. That examination may later reveal that the dent in the hull is, in fact, an error, or
that it conforms to ("fairs with") the boat designer's intention.

I do not mean to suggest by this that the sense of fairness consists of some set of
Platonic ideals containing the essential nature of things. The boat builder's sense of
hull shape is not an abstraction but rather an integration of his past experiences into
a dynamic sense of the way that things work. It is that sense, rather than the discrete
memories of past experience, that tests his present perceptions.

Notice that the test against the sense of fairness is not determinative. A perception that fails to fit it does not get thrown out. Instead, a perception that fails to fit
it generates an error signal, which creates a tension that demands resolution through
further thought or more data. That resolution may indeed show that the perception was accurate, as when the boat builder discovers that the hull conforms to the
designer's intentions. Only the most rigid thinker dismisses all perceptions that do
not fit with past experience. Our boat builder's sense of fairness is more fluid. His
sense of hull fairness will expand to incorporate the new design that he has perceived.

The boat builder has an advantage that the lawyer does not have. The perceptions
that he analyzes derive from a physical object, while the lawyer's perceptions generally

derive from accounts of past events. The boat builder can refer to the underlying reality any time he wants, testing and retesting his perceptions. The reality underlying the lawyer's problem is forever lost in the past. As she tries to build a coherent picture of what happened, she is awash in the inherent ambiguity of the data about the event and hamstrung by her inability to recreate it.

With the data itself in such a flux, how does the lawyer develop a coherent picture of events?

We can get some sense of that process by considering again the network of possibilities in Figure 10.8. Our prior analysis of the case has eliminated four possible pathways, leaving us with this:

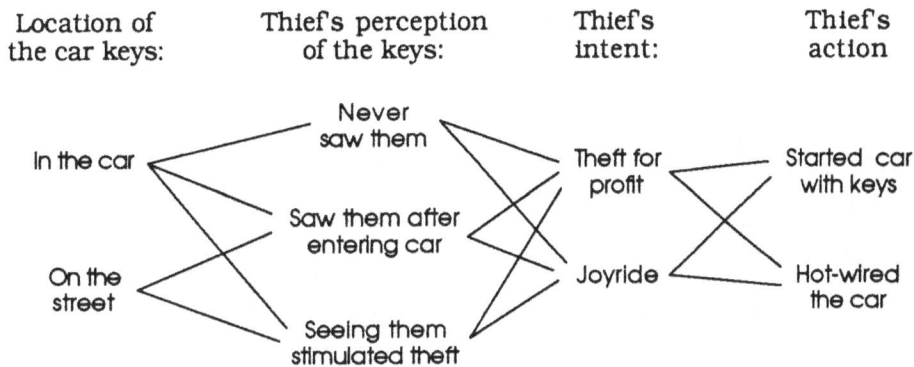

Figure 10.11   The network of possibilities remaining after removing the possibility that the keys were left on the street and the thief never saw them.

It is not plausible that the keys were left in the street and the thief never saw them. But that still leaves us with twenty possible scenarios, each of which has a very different impact upon the case against Timothy Newland. What do we do now? Just hope that the jury picks an interpretation of the facts that is favorable to Jeffrey? That would be like a boat builder who spots an unfairness in the hull, but crosses his fingers and hopes that it does not later sink at sea.

The twenty possible scenarios in Figure 10.11 are not equally plausible. It is not likely, for example, that the thief hot-wired the car, given that the keys were in the car when it was recovered. Nor is it likely that the car was stolen by a professional thief for profit. Nor is it likely that the keys were in the street and the thief saw them after getting into the car. Eliminating those possibilities leaves us with this:

Figure 10.12   The network of possibilities remaining after removing the alternatives that are not plausible.

That thinking reduces the number of plausible scenarios to four. But how were we able to eliminate them? How were we able to decide that the car was stolen by a joyrider? The alternative descriptions of the event simply did not fit with our experience and understanding of the way the world works. Professional car thieves do not steal cars like the Newland car. It is not *impossible* that that happened, it just *defies experience to* think that it did.

The five remaining scenarios are not equally plausible, either, but they are probably plausible enough so that we should not remove any of them from our thinking. Instead, we will weight them according to their likelihood:

Figure 10.13   Weighting the remaining scenarios according to their plausibility.

The thickness of the lines in Figure 10.13 indicates my judgment of the plausibility of each link in the scenario. If you asked me to tell you what I really think happened that day, I would tell you (following Figure 10.13) that I think that the keys did fall out of Timothy's pocket while he was crossing the street, that a kid on the sidewalk saw them fall, and, inspired by the ease of stealing the car, picked them up, put them into the ignition and took the car on a joyride. I am not certain that that is what happened, but it *fits* with the other things that I know about the case and with my understanding of human nature.

I have set out this evaluation of the facts in *Stapleton* at such length to describe what I mean by the process of evaluating the facts of a case. But my description of that process is clearly <u>not</u> the way it is actually is done in my head or in anyone else's head. We do not make an exhaustive list of every possible alternative and then think through each one. We might do that if we were preparing this case for trial and wanted to make sure that we had covered every possible interpretation of the facts of the case, but that is surely not the way that we evaluate facts in our minds.

What we do, as nearly as I can tell, is far more holistic. We absorb data and, as we do, build it into a story in our minds. Perhaps we fit it into a family of similar stories that we have created from past experience. But the new story will not fit exactly with our earlier stories. The new elements of the story will "stick out." just as the dent in the hull of the boat stuck out in the boat builder's mind. Some of those protuberances will be trivial, such as the names of the people in the story, and will simply be noted. We *expect* the names of the people in the new story to be different from past stories. But there are differences that we do not expect. They will have to be "faired" with our prior experience, their meaning evaluated in the light of our understanding of the world and ourselves.

In the mass of data and recollection that occurs when we perceive the facts of an event, our minds focus upon those elements that do not fit prior experience. That is what I mean by the "sense of fairness" in Figure 10.9. The elements that do not fit violate this sense, creating an error signal ("I don't understand that!" or "That couldn't be!"), and generating a feeling of tension that directs our attention and drives further inquiry. Notice in your own experience that the feeling that something does not make sense precedes your understanding of precisely why it doesn't make sense. The feeling causes us to search for what it is about it that causes that feeling.

Let me mention something that bothers me about the Stapleton case and has bothered me since I first read about it: Why is it that we know so little about the car thief? I can accept the proposition that the police could not find him. But did they try? If he was, in fact, a joyrider he must have left fingerprints on the car. Did the police lift the prints? Couldn't they find a match for them? And if he was a joyrider did the police not check out known joyriders in the town to see what they were up to that afternoon? The record of the case is silent on all of this. I have been a bit irked by the task of scratching around to come up with a case against Margaret and the Newlands when the absence of the obvious wrongdoer has not been fully explained. That is a lack of fairness in the case that has never been explained.

A violation of the sense of fairness identifies something that must be explained. That violation may be either descriptive (who was the thief?) or normative (was the thief driving responsibly at the time that he hit Jeffrey?). A violation that questions the meaning of a perception triggers a demand for an *explanation*. A violation that questions the *legitimacy* of something that has been perceived triggers a demand for a *justification*. Notice the odd similarity between the concept of "justification" and that of "fairness." To "justify" means to "bring into alignment with," as a printer justifies a line of text by making the left and right ends of the line true to the rest of the text. We "justify" an act normatively by showing that it is in alignment with the standards and norms that guide behavior. The act of justifying something is the act of "making it fair," making it conform to a prior standard or expectation, as when the boat builder justifies the dent in the hull by explaining it in terms of the designer's intention, or when we justify Margaret Stapleton's behavior by evaluating it under the standard in <u>Holodook v. Spencer.</u>

The dual nature of the sense of fairness—descriptive and normative—was brought to my mind one day by an event that occurred while I was driving. As I started into an intersection after waiting for the traffic signal to turn green, I spied a car coming into the intersection out of the right corner of my eye. I jammed on my brakes and he swerved around the front of my car; a very near miss. Both I and the passenger in my car uttered some kind of expletive at the same instant. I had imagined what would have happened if I had hit that car, seeing instantly in my mind's eye a vision of the accident report showing both cars smashed beyond recognition and lying upside down on the lawn across the street. In a few more seconds I could have fashioned a complete justification for my own behavior, showing that the fault was the other driver's, all the way down to the outline of a closing argument to the jury.

I turned to my passenger, assuming that the reason for his expletive was the same as my own, but found that his eyes were following the other car with wonder and admiration as it disappeared down the road to our left. The car, it seems, was a 1951 Henry J that was in mint condition. My friend was a classic car buff who had never seen the storied Henry J in the raw. While I was imagining the accident, he was wondering whether he could fit the Henry J into his already crowded garage. Both of us were doing exactly the same thing, but his interest in what he had perceived was descriptive, while mine was normative.

Unfairness, that which triggers a demand for explanation, lies in the senses of the beholder. It differs depending upon the interests (the "mind set"), attitudes, and experiences of the perceiver. The lawyer, the car collector, the accountant, doctor, and travel agent all perceiving the same data will pick out different unfairness in it. It is, perhaps, the curse of the lawyer that he is tuned to the normative dimensions of the story. The Super Bowl watchers in the story in Chapter 1 probably got more enjoyment out of the game than the lawyer who became concerned about the legitimacy of spearing. To them the event was the cause of amusement; to the lawyer it was a cause for concern. It was an act that violated her sense of fairness.

The perception of normative unfairness—that something that has occurred is "wrong"—triggers normative thinking:

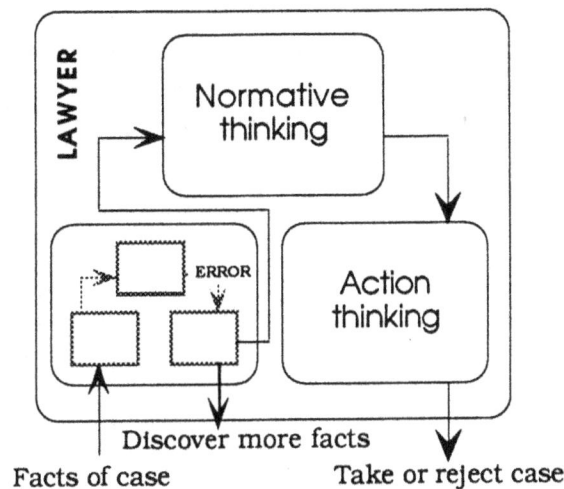

Figure 10.14   The perception of normative unfairness triggers normative thinking.

That is indicated in Figure 10.14 as the solid line emanating from the action box and connecting to normative thinking. The action triggered is subjecting the story perceived to normative analysis. The solid line pointing downward indicates that there is a descriptive error arising from the perception. The descriptive error will trigger more descriptive thinking, namely gathering more data and subjecting it to further analysis.

The fact that there are two arrows emanating from the action box in Figure 10.14 introduces a new idea into the model: that two things are going on in the mind at the same time—descriptive and normative thinking. This is called "parallelism" of thought.

Consider what parallelism means in terms of the automotive example above. Both my passenger and I perceived the same data—we both noticed the car coming from the right. In me, that perception generated both a descriptive error, which led me to hit the brakes to avoid the collision, and a normative error, which led me to think about who would have been at fault if an accident had happened. In my passenger, it generated only a descriptive error, one that led him to follow the Henry J with his eyes to gather more perceptions of it.

Parallel thought

Consider all that your mind is doing at this instant. It is keeping track of your body temperature and adjusting your body to adapt to subtle changes in room temperature. It is controlling your eye and hand muscles, monitoring your bodily functions, and making sense of these words. It is doing all of those things at the same time. That is parallelism.

To this point the model has involved no parallelism. As I have described it, the model makes it look as though you first perceive, then evaluate your perceptions, then do something if your perceptions create tensions. And so it is, but you do that on many levels at the same time. Thankfully, only two of those levels concern us here—the levels of descriptive and normative thought.

To convey the idea that descriptive and normative thinking are different types of thinking, I have treated them as separate control systems within the overall control system of legal thinking. To keep things clear, I will treat interactions between the three component control systems a bit differently from interactions within those control systems.

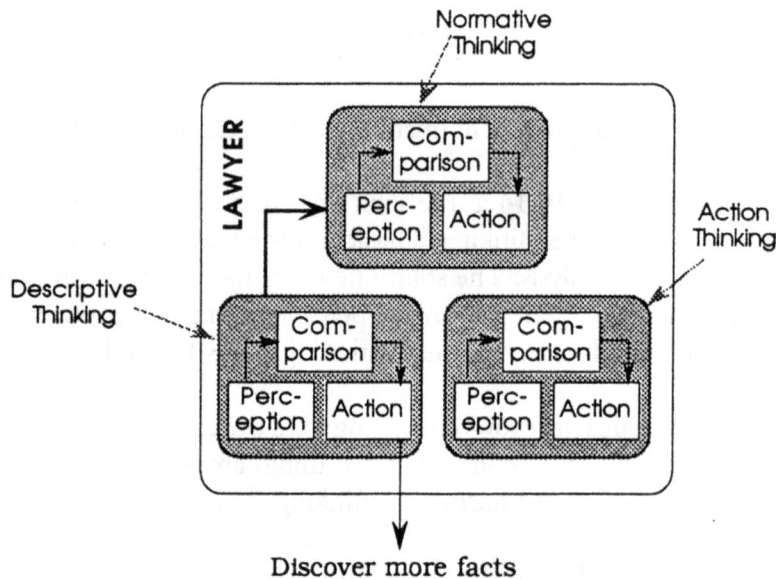

Figure 10.15   Interactions between the component systems
are shown by the darker arrows connecting them.

Figure 10.15 pictures exactly the same situation as Figure 10.14. That is, it pictures a situation in which a given perception triggers both further descriptive thought (indicated by the downward arrow labeled "Discover more facts") and normative thought (indicated by the arrow proceeding from the Descriptive Thinking system to the Normative Thinking system). Arrows that link the three systems are drawn as if they emanate from the system as a whole.

Where two arrows emanate from a system at the same time, as in Figure 10.15, two types of thinking are going on at the same time. There, Descriptive Thinking generated both a signal to gather more data and a signal to begin Normative Thinking about the facts that had been perceived. The perception of a normative unfairness, a potential wrong that must be explained, does two things at once. First, it directs the gathering of further facts to resolve the uncertainty in the situation. Second, it "turns on" normative thinking, triggering a search for applicable norms through which to evaluate the behavior.

Once triggered, normative and descriptive thinking interpenetrates itself. The two levels echo back and forth, as further factual information raises new normative questions and as normative thinking highlights certain facts as key to the evaluation of the situation. The continual interaction between the two levels of thought is obvious in our treatment of Jeffrey's case. New facts suggested new normative questions.

The difficulty with adding this dimension to the model is that it begins to make the model depart from our everyday experience of our own thinking. Our thinking does not seem, upon first reflection, to be parallel. It feels *sequential*—first we think about this, then we think about that. Thinking seems to have the same property as the words of this text: Each idea, like each word, follows one from the next in a linear stream.

The thing that is responsible for the feeling of sequentiality is *consciousness*. We consciously focus upon one thing at a time. Parallel thinking could overwhelm our ability to process information by overloading our ability to make decisions, which appears to be possible only one decision at a time. Consciousness screens that flood of thinking, presenting one after another of the questions that are on our minds for decision.

Consider what might be happening to you at this very minute. Your data acquisition control system is now in control of your consciousness: you are reading these words and consciously evaluating them. At the same time, however, your food acquisition control system may be trying to intrude itself into your consciousness. Your innards are sending error signals to your mind, and perhaps your memory is sending recollections of something truly inviting that is just waiting to be eaten. At some point the food acquisition system will win this competition. You will become aware of your desire for food, and you will consciously decide whether you should turn to that purpose, or stick with reading this book.

Consciousness is itself the best proof of the parallelism of thought. If there were not multiple processes at work in our minds, it would not be necessary to screen them before they were brought to mind. Consciousness is a traffic cop that orders the presentment of matters for decision.

"Go ahead, information acquisition system!"

Information acquisition system:	**Read On!**
Food acuisition system:	**Let's Eat!**
Warmth acquisition system:	**Turn up the heat!**

Figure 10.16   The Consciousness Cop controls the presentment of matter to conscious thought.

How that is done is not clear, but it appears to have something to do with the strength of the error signal emanating from each control system. In a replication of the squeaky wheel getting the oil, the control system presenting the greatest error signal gets the greatest attention, unless it is clear that nothing can be done about it. In that case, one can "put it out of mind," consciously suppressing it in favor of other concerns.

At any rate, we must recognize that at any instant in time there is a great deal going on at both the descriptive and normative levels of our thought as we think through a case. At any one time, only one level is in our consciousness. But the levels are interacting with each other at all times, so our conscious thought zooms from one level to the other, focusing now on this issue, now on that, all under the control of the error signals that each one generates, as they are modulated by the Consciousness Cop.

We will return to the process of detecting normative error when we take up normative thinking, but now we must complete the analysis of descriptive thinking by considering what happens when we detect a descriptive error in what we perceive.

3. Gathering facts

The feeling that there is something about a story that we do not understand is a tension that causes either a solely mental process—reevaluating our perceptions; seeking more subtle explanations—or behavior aimed at gathering more information.

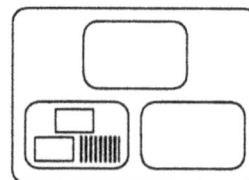

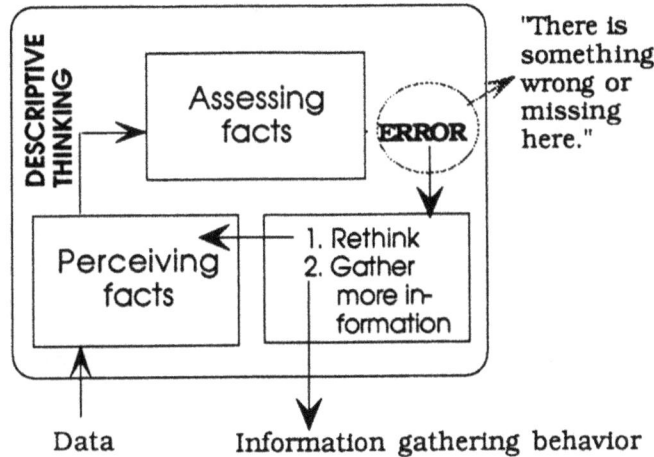

Figure 10.17   Tension generated by the assessment process causes us
to rethink our perceptions or to gather more information.

The information that we are after may be of two kinds: further data about the story or information that will expand our ability to understand what we have perceived. Further information, in other words, can enhance either our perception of the events of the story or our ability to analyze it. Both of these processes can be illustrated with our experience of *Stapleton*.

Consider our uncertainty about what motivated the theft of the car. If we could find the thief we could talk with him and, perhaps, get him to tell us what was going through his mind when he stole the car. Let us imagine that he told us that:

> I had it in for Tim Newland ever since he beat me out of a position on the track team. I stole his car a couple of times. The second time I stole it I wracked it up. I figured that that would really cook his goose.

> But then I saw him drive up on State Street that day. I got into his car and discovered that the idiot had left his keys in it again! This time I decided that I would drive his car to New York and leave it there. That would really fix him.

That information would allow us to completely collapse the network of possibilities that we have been dealing with on this subject.

Location of the car keys:	Thief's perception of the keys:	Thief's intent:	Thief's action
	Never saw them		
In the car		Theft for profit	Started car with keys
	Saw them after entering car		
On the street		Joyride; retribution	Hot-wired the car
	Seeing them stimulated theft		

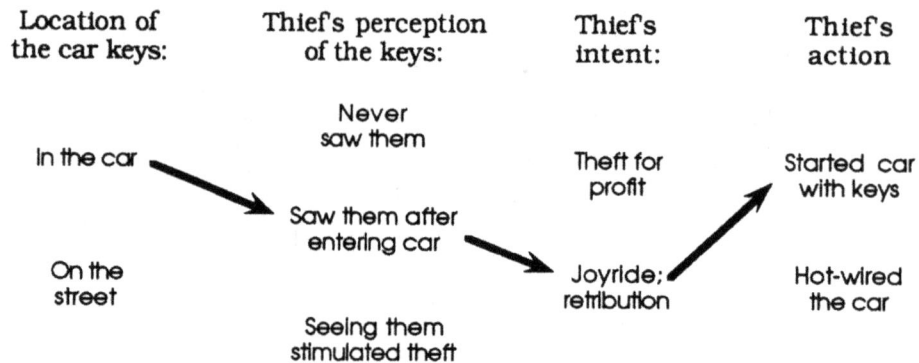

Figure 10.18   The thief's statement collapses the factual network.

Now we know what happened. Leaving the keys in the car played no role in its theft. Under my analysis in Part I, Timothy is completely off the hook. Leaving his keys in the car did not in any sense *cause* the harm to Jeffrey.

Additional information resolves ambiguity, collapsing the network of alternative possibilities in the story. Additional information can also allow us to evaluate the information that we have about the case; it can provide us with a richer framework for understanding it.

We gained this type of information from Officer McGinty, when she explained a bit about the accident reconstruction process that linked the Newland car to Jeffrey's death, and from Ron Fritzer, who gave us a framework for putting a dollar value on the earnings that Jeffrey could have anticipated. Jeffrey's case did not raise particularly difficult technical issues, so we felt that those explanations gave us a sound basis for understanding the case. In a more complex case, such as an airplane crash, we would have had to rely upon the analysis provided by an expert unless we felt that the case was important enough for us to take time off to get a degree in aeronautical engineering.

Explaining what causes lawyers to seek more information about a case, however, does not fully explain information gathering behavior. Any case, even one as simple as Stapleton raises literally countless descriptive questions. How does the lawyer know which of them to pursue? Why didn't we concern ourselves with Jeffrey's size, visual acuity, performance of arpeggios, or gait? That information might well be relevant to Jeffrey's doctor, optometrist, piano teacher, or shoe salesperson. But it was not relevant to us. How did we know that?

The answer to that question lies in the normative layer of the lawyer's thought process. The legal rules applicable to the case determine the facts that must be present if the law is to be invoked on Jeffrey's behalf. Those rules direct the lawyer's attention, as we saw in Chapter 5 as we began to build the case against the Newlands. The general rule of law provided us with a series of elements that we would have to prove to establish the case. Our understanding of the case to that point allowed us to assess the strength of the case relative to each of those elements.

Element:	Tension level:
(1) A person ...	0
(2) ... who creates a risk of injury to another ...	100%
(3) ... if that risk results in injury ...	30%
(4) ... so long as the person knew or should have known of the risk created ...	51%
(5) ... unless it would be unreasonable for the person to avoid the risk.	40%

Figure 10.19   The elements of the case against the Newlands and the tensions associated with each element from Figure 5.3.

Learning Jeffrey's size would have been useless because it would not have reduced our tension (that is, "shed any light") upon any element of the case. Learning why the thief stole the car, by contrast, would shed light on element 2, for it would enable us to assess whether Timothy induced in any way the action of the thief. The value of that information would have been considerable, given that it is an essential element of the case and our uncertainty about it is complete. The lawyer who is unclear about the law, or who chooses the wrong law to guide her understanding of the case, will spend a great deal of time gathering irrelevant information.

Figure 10.19 doesn't provide us with a full account of the lawyer's decision about what information to gather, for it does not tell us what information the lawyer will go after first. Under Figure 10.19 the obvious thing for the lawyer to do is to seek information about the element that generates the greatest tension. But that would violate some fundamental laws of economics, and we saw in Figure 9.1 that normative laws are contained within the realm of economic laws.

Economics would suggest that the lawyer would seek that information which would result in the *greatest likely reduction in tension*. This is a variation on the "greatest bang for the buck" test of economics. The lawyer will consider not simply which issue is the most burning, but also the cost of attaining information about each element, and the probability that the information, if attained, will result in an actual reduction in tension.

Following that analysis we would predict that the lawyer faced with the case in Figure 10.19 would spend precisely no time gathering information proving that Jeffrey was a person. That element is crucial to the case, but it is already shown to a certainty in the information the lawyer possesses. We must accept the fact, of course, that some lawyers are procrastinators who will diddle around with points that are already established, but we would expect another law of economics, the law of competition, to make short work of them.

From the remaining elements the lawyer will pursue information about the one that will take the least time and effort to resolve. You will recall that when we went through this phase of the analysis in Part I we pursued element 5. We made a quick telephone call to John Newland to determine why it was that he sent Timothy to the store. It turned out that Tim went to the store to pick up the daily newspaper, which suggested that it would not have been unreasonable for John to have kept Tim at home, thereby avoiding the theft of the car. We got a quick reduction in the tension on element 5 from 40% to 5%.

There is no need to go further into the economics underlying the lawyer's choice of what information to pursue. Those laws are well understood, and at any rate you surely act under them, whether you understand them or not.

Was the car actually stolen?

You can get a sense of the process described above in operation if you ask yourself why it is that you think that the Newland car was stolen, as Timothy said it was. That question should produce an error signal in your understanding of *Stapleton*. Precisely what is it that leads you to think that Timothy was not the driver of the car when it hit Jeffrey? We slid over that question in Part I. Apparently Officer McGinty never considered it, for there is nothing in any of her statements to suggest the possibility. Timothy and John, of course, deny it, saying that the car was stolen. But a great deal of our remaining tension about the case is resolved by the conclusion that Timothy was at the wheel of the car. The missing driver, the mysterious lack of information about the investigation of the car, the muddle about the location of the car keys, all would fall into place if we discovered that Timothy was at the wheel. What information that we received in Part I would have to be false if Timothy were the driver of the car?

Did this possibility occur to you as you read Part I? If so, did you pursue it as the facts of the case unfolded? If you did, you undoubtedly subjected the information that I provided you to far greater scrutiny than I did as I unfolded the analysis. Or did you simply accept my analysis of the facts as you read along? That is called "being led down the garden path" and is a great danger in legal thinking.

If you were aware of the possibility that Tim was the driver, that created a network of possibilities in your mind similar to the one in Figure 10.8. If you let that possibility dissolve with the passage of the discussion, a discussion that never addressed the question, you lost your grip on what might be the crucial inference in the case without subjecting it to full analysis. If you failed to see the possibility at all, you should be thankful that Margaret did not, in fact, approach you with this case. At the very minimum it is the lawyer's duty to spot cases which are likely winners, which this case is, if Tim was at the wheel of the car. Was he?

Normative thinking

Normative thinking is fundamentally different from descriptive thinking. Its job is to provide a standard against which the story generated by descriptive thinking can be justified. The legal standard that it generates will have teeth, for, if the facts of the situation violate the standard, consequences will follow.

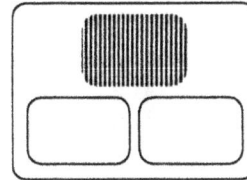

Descriptive thinking rides upon a substrate of empirical reality; if you felt that Margaret ran over her own child after stealing the Newland car, that feeling would so run afoul of empirically observable facts that it would be unlikely that anyone else would feel the same way. Normative thinking, by contrast, is not grounded upon an empirical reality. If you feel that it is wrong to work for pay on the Sabbath, no one can demonstrate that that feeling is in error.

What is normative thinking based upon? That question, which is crucial to law, is not very important in private life. Most people simply have their beliefs. They may change them, but they rarely ask where, in a mental sense, they come from. Why not work on Sunday? There is a Commandment that says that the Sabbath must be kept holy. Why follow that Commandment? Because you must. What makes Sunday the "Sabbath"? Who knows?

There is a tendency to ignore questions about the grounding of norms in law, as well, for law provides an easy dodge: You are not allowed to mail a parcel containing an alcoholic beverage because it says right here in Section 124.42 of the United States Postal Service Domestic Mail Manual that no package will be accepted if it contains an alcoholic beverage." Behavior is wrong if there is a law that says it is. Thinking of this type does not require the kind of normative thinking that we undertook in Part I. It is simply a different sort of descriptive thinking.

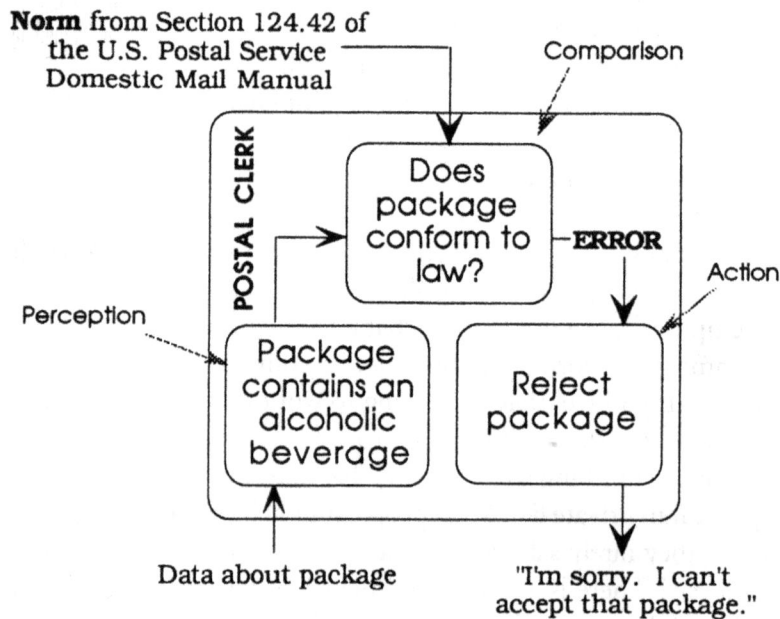

Figure 10.20   The mechanical application of a legal norm to a situation.

The postal clerk's only job is to identify the applicable norm and apply it to the facts of the case. No interpretation is required. The clerk simply acts as an extension of the Postal Service's institutional control system. Were we interested in the reason for the rule we would have to go higher in the organization to those who formulate its regulations.

Mechanical law is possible only in the most limited situations. Even the postal regulation against mailing alcoholic beverages gets muddy if you try to mail a mouthwash containing alcohol. The mouthwash is not really a beverage, but it can be consumed. To determine whether or not it is banned the clerk must interpret the regulation in the light of the presumed purpose of the Postal Service. That requires a different style of thought from sheerly descriptive thinking, for it is rooted in the *purpose* of the regulation, not in any objectively verifiable circumstances.

The normative thinking that we employed in Part I required considerable interpretation, if not outright invention, on our part. That activity suggests the presence of a control system, a system that generates norms that the lawyer will apply to the facts determined by descriptive thinking. The lawyer plays a *formative* role in fashioning those norms. While it is very easy for each one of us to do that, it is not at all obvious how it is done.

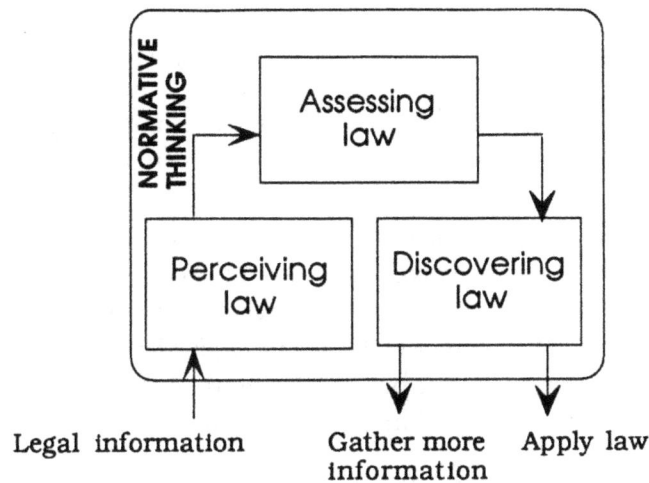

Figure 10.21   The components of normative thinking.

Normative thinking generates a legal norm that is applied to the set of facts, unless the tension resulting from the error signal caused by assessing the norm is too great. If it is, the lawyer will search for more legal information and continue the process of devising a norm applicable to the case. The tension associated with the norm is, in my experience, rarely zero—the lawyer cannot be *certain* that the legal standard that he decides to apply to a case is correct.

1. Perceiving law

The task of perceiving the law that is relevant to a given situation is remarkably complex. I don't mean to give a full account of it here, but simply to point out some of the reasons for that complexity.

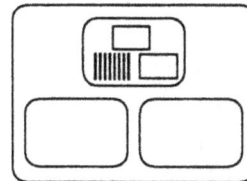

The task doesn't get much simpler than that done by the postal clerk in the example above. She asked what was in the package that was handed to her and was told, "Six bottles of mouthwash." Her past experience told her that mouthwash contained alcohol, which triggered a recollection that there were regulations about alcoholic beverages. Perhaps she remembered the regulation, perhaps she had to look it up. In either case the ambiguity of the stated rule struck her: "Is mouthwash an 'intoxicating beverage' because it can be consumed like a beverage and contains alcohol?"

That question can legitimately be answered (there is always the chance that the clerk will answer it arbitrarily) only with a sense of the *purpose* for the rule. Is the purpose of the rule to cut down on alcohol consumption? or to prevent the mails from being contaminated by broken containers that contain alcohol? or to keep people from avoiding taxes on alcoholic beverages? If it is the first or third purpose, mouthwash would not be considered an "intoxicating beverage," but, if it is the second, it would.

It is impossible to understand what a law means without understanding its purpose. Without understanding what the law means it is impossible to apply it to an ambiguous situation, and almost all factual situations are ambiguous. Consider the apparently clear rule that a driver must bring his car to a stop at a stop sign. What constitutes a "stop?" Must the forward motion of the car come to a complete halt? For how long? And what constitutes stopping "at the stop sign?" Must the forward end of the car be precisely perpendicular to the sign? How far beyond or short of the sign may the front of the car be before the stop is no longer "at the sign?" If you have already come to a full stop behind a car stopped for the sign, must you pull up to the sign and stop again?

There is a purpose implicit in the stop sign rule that guides our interpretation of it. If the driver's vision is obscured by trees close to an intersection, a "stop" might be a period long enough for the driver to check carefully for traffic in both directions without any motion from the car. If the intersection is wide open, a reduction in the speed of the car to five miles an hour might be a satisfactory "stop." In either case, the purpose of the law is to lower the risk of collision at a dangerous intersection to the level of risk at intersections in general. That purpose will guide the enforcement of the rule by the police officer, unless she is in a bad mood or suffering from an empty, mechanical understanding of law.

The need to interpret rules of law in the light of their purpose begins to explain why the lawyers in the law firm that I worked for spent so little time reading rules of law. They had been practicing law long enough to build a holistic concept of the areas of law in which they practiced. They could "feel" the law; they could "just tell" when a given set of facts violated the law, just as the police officer can "just tell" when a driver's action at a stop sign fails to rise to the level of a full stop. That feeling is the lawyer's stock in trade.

The lawyers in my firm did keep themselves up to date on changes in the law. They read new cases, statutes, and regulations that applied to their areas of practice. They did not, however, become filing cabinets of law. They integrated the new laws into their general concept of law. Few of them could give me the specific citation to the law applicable to a given case, but they knew when there was a specific rule applicable to the case and they could usually point me in the right direction to find it. Most of the specific rules of law had been subsumed into their general feeling for the law.

In Figure 5.1, I set out the perception of law that guided my analysis of the case against the Newlands:

A person who creates a risk of injury to another is liable in damages if that risk results in injury, so long as the person knew or should have known of the risk created, unless it would be unreasonable for the person to avoid the risk.

Figure 10.22   The general principle of liability for injury, from Figure 5.1.

That statement is a pallid representation of my own understanding of the applicable law. It is the best that I can do, but it fails completely to convey my feeling for what is going on in this area of law. It contains many huge concepts, like the concept of a "person," which are themselves the names for countless experiences, insights, and interpretations that my mind has made of law. You might have gotten a sense of some of what I understand those words to mean from the way that I applied that principle to the Newlands in that chapter. But words convey far too little information to allow you to *adopt* my concept of law. A concept of law is something that each person must build for himself or herself.

Principles of law like the one in Figure 10.23 have some of the properties of the lawyer's concept of law. The principle integrates countless lower level rules into a statement that guides analysis. When the facts of a case raise normative questions under the principle (e.g., would it have been unreasonable for John Newland to keep Timothy at home?), the principle can be unbundled into norms that are applicable to the case, as shown in Figures 3.5 and 3.6. Those norms describe what should have happened in the case. They can then be applied to the facts of the case to determine whether or not there is a potential violation.

2. Assessing law

Rare is the case that the lawyer can evaluate with confidence on the basis of his existing concepts of law. The key to the last sentence are the words "with confidence," for the lawyer and the non-lawyer alike can in fact resolve any normative question without further research. I have heard people who had no experience with governing a state, raising children, or teaching third grade, hold forth at considerable length with their critique of what a governor, a parent, or a teacher was doing wrong. In private life our normative conclusions are usually without consequence; we indulge ourselves, treating others to our grand assessment of the moral worth of whatever is under discussion.

The lawyer may do that in her private life as well, but as a lawyer consequences follow from her normative analysis as a case. Those consequences require the lawyer to constantly assess whether her perception of the applicable norms is justified.

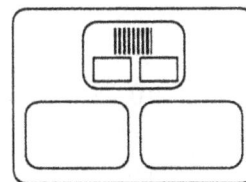

Recall how that happened in Part I. We called into question the legitimacy of Margaret Stapleton's behavior, wondering whether she supervised Jeffrey as well as she should have. At the time that I raised that question I was well equipped to answer it without reference to any cases. The general principle of liability in Figure 10.22 covers her situation. Under that principle we would wonder whether or not Margaret had "created the risk of injury" to Jeffrey by her lack of supervision. I would answer that question in the negative by referring, as I did, to my own mother's supervision of me as a child.

I find it no more difficult to answer normative questions than anyone else. What I, and other lawyers, find difficult is to accept our own assessment as a sufficient guide to the case. My assessment killed any prospect of a case by Jeffrey's estate against his mother. That is not an idle speculation; consequences follow from it. What if my assessment is wrong? What if mothers *should* keep their children out of the way of known dangers? Why should I be comfortable with my own normative standard?

Those questions are signs of tension, signs that all does not rest comfortably with my assessment of the case. Tension is the smoke that warns of the fire of an underlying error signal.

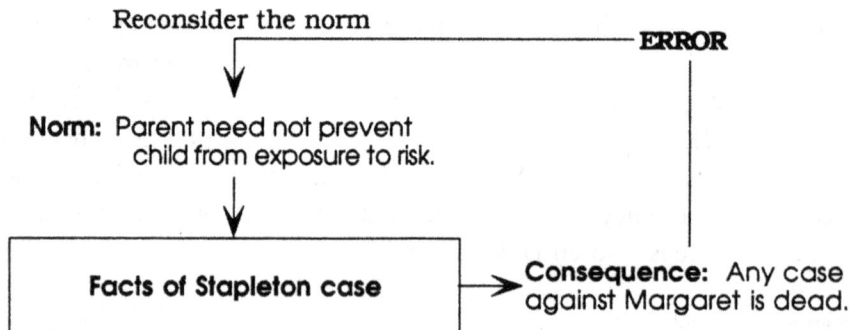

Figure 10.23   Reconsidering a norm because of its effect upon the case.

It is the lawyer's sense of responsibility for his normative judgments that largely accounts for the difference between lawyers and non-lawyers. The lawyer does not cast off normative judgments casually. He reflects upon the fairness of his interpretation of the facts and the norms that guide his analysis. Where, as in Figure 10.23, grave consequences follow the application of a norm to the case, he reconsiders the norm in question. In *Stapleton,* that led us to look for law on the subject of parental responsibility. We found, if you will recall, that parents may indeed be sued by their children, but only under the California rule may a court review the parent's supervision of the child. Under the New York rule the norm is the same as the one that I applied in Figure 10.23; the parent is free to expose the child to known risks without being second-guessed by a court.

What are we to do in such a situation? Here is what that we face in control system terms:

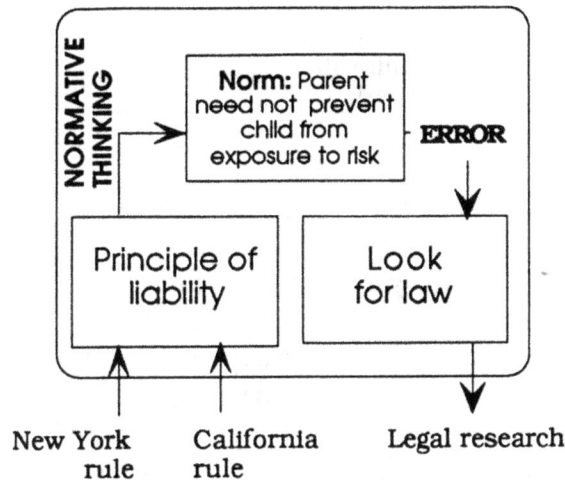

Figure 10.24   Rethinking a norm by looking for case law on it.

Notice that the error in this case does not stem from a conclusion that the norm is wrong: It stems instead from the fear that the norm may not be right, that there may be another arguable interpretation of the principle of liability. And so there is, for our action—doing legal research—turned up the California rule. We now have two interpretations of the proper norm that are at direct loggerheads.

What are we to do? Neither of those rules is *authoritative. That* is, neither of them has been adopted as the controlling law of the state that we are in. We are not forced by the authority of law to apply either of them. How should be proceed? One approach would be that of maximum conservatism: since a case would lie against Margaret Stapleton under the California view, bring suit against her and argue for the adoption of that rule. But that ignores the fact that the lawyer is himself a moral actor, capable of evaluating the legitimacy of a proposed norm of law. The lawyer will assess the two views under the control of his own sense of justice:

SENSE OF JUSTICE

NORMATIVE THINKING

Comparison

New York
rule versus
California
rule

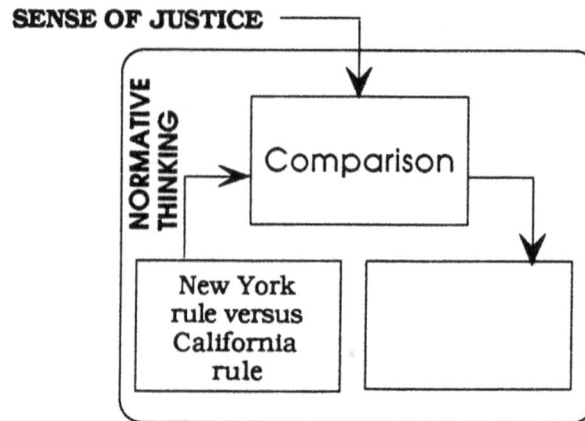

Figure 10.25   Assessing the legitimacy of a legal norm.

The lawyer evaluates a norm against his own sense of legal right and wrong. The purpose of that assessment is not to decide which of two rules is *right*. The lawyer is not in a position of authority in the legal system. A judge may decide authoritatively which rule is right, but the lawyer may not. The purpose of this assessment is to determine what each norm *means*. The lawyer may well apply a norm that he thinks is wrong, bringing action in a case that he thinks the law should not entertain. But after his assessment of the norm he will understand the weaknesses of the rule; he will be able to identify the ways in which it will cause concern to the judge and jury and head off those concerns by introducing additional facts into the case or by effective argumentation.

Some non-lawyers are troubled by the lawyer's ability to argue strongly for positions that he does not sincerely hold. But that ability is. in fact, an integral part of the American legal system. It is not the lawyer's role in that system to decide what norms the law should apply. It is the lawyer's job to present the court with plausible interpretations that it may select from. The lawyer must make his own assessment of the legitimacy of a proposed norm, for that is the only way that he can understand it, but it is not true that a norm that fails his own test of justness is therefore wrong.

In my discussion of the case against Margaret I concluded that the California rule did not pass muster with my own sense of justice. I found it intolerable that parents would be second-guessed by a jury for their day-to-day raising of their children simply because it didn't work out right. But that was not to say that I would have turned down the case against Margaret if it had looked like a good one under the California rule. If it had, I would either have taken the case, accepting the inevitable tension that would have followed if I had argued for the court to adopt a norm that I thought was wrong, or referred the case to another lawyer who had different sensibilities.

The sense of justice

The lawyer's sense of justice provides the fulcrum for her evaluation of the meaning of a legal norm. In control system terms, it is the reference signal—the standard— against which law is compared to determine its legitimacy. That it exists is subjectively obvious; each one of us can feel it at work in our own minds. But it has proved to be extremely difficult to describe in words.

Consider the case of a young woman whose contraceptive device was lost in her baggage by the airline on her trip to Florida. The airline returned her baggage to her the day after her arrival, but it was too late because the night before she had slept with a man she met that night, without the protection of her contraceptive. She wanted to know whether she could sue the airline to make it support the child who would be born, if that union had made her pregnant. *Should* she be able to win child support from the airline?

I will bet that you had an answer to that question almost before you finished reading it. And I will bet that your answer had precisely nothing to do with your knowledge of the law that applies to the problem. Further, I will bet that you are comfortable with your answer, that hardly anything that I could say will shake you from it. It would be wrong to force the airline to support the child (I have yet to find anyone who feels differently).

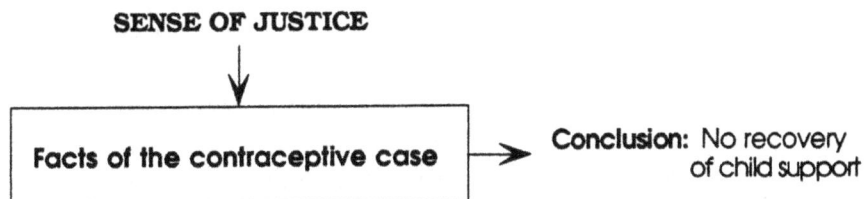

SENSE OF JUSTICE

↓

```
┌─────────────────────────────────┐      Conclusion: No recovery
│  Facts of the contraceptive case │  →              of child support
└─────────────────────────────────┘
```

Figure 10.26   Your resolution of the case was guided by your sense of justice.

You did not think your way through that case to evaluate it. You *felt* your way through it. It would be ... what? ... ridiculous to make the airline pay? Absurd? Outrageous? The answer is so obvious that it is not necessary to put words to it. Which is fortunate, for it is not all that easy to put words to your conclusion. It is always difficult to put words to a feeling. Why is it, precisely, that you like (or dislike) lemonade? What is it, precisely, that wrong with this sentence is?

Your sense of right and wrong is a sufficient guide to your own behavior, but it is not a sufficient guide to legal behavior. In law, your feeling-based conclusion must be backed by reasons. Why is that? The answer is not obvious.

Reasons cannot describe *how* you reached your conclusion in the contraceptive case. Let me try to do it. I concluded that the woman should not receive child support because she was aware of the risk posed by intercourse without a contraceptive, but she willingly subjected herself to that risk anyway, in the face of the fact that she had available many alternative means of contraception. She brought the child upon herself. A person should not recover from another for an ill that is self-inflicted.

Those reasons do not describe *how* I reached my decision in the case. The reasons are stated in words. There were no words going through my mind when I resolved the case. The words are an after-the-fact fabrication that does not begin to convey my emotional state as I thought about the case. I could add some words to the reason to attempt to describe my mental state—it would "shock my conscience" to allow her to recover from the airline—but they would hardly add anything to my reasons.

There is a radical discontinuity between the mental process that we use to reach a normative conclusion and the reasons that we adduce to support the conclusion. Why, then, does law place such heavy weight upon reasons? We don't trust feelings, or the sense of right and wrong that gives rise to those feelings. They vary from person to person, from time to time, and from culture to culture. By forcing a decision maker to adduce reasons, the legal system places a constraint upon feelings. Feeling may guide each person's normative judgments, but forcing the person to adduce reasons allows us to spot really screwy judgments and weed them out.

Reasons do more than that: they shape our feelings. Reasons are *formative*. Our sense of justice is not static, any more than our sense of taste, or rhythm, or smell, or fairness is static. Tastes are modified by experience. Listening to African music reshapes our sense of rhythm. Reflecting upon reasons reshapes our sense of justice. Two hundred years ago many Americans entertained the feeling that slavery was justified. Today, none do. The reasons adduced against slavery were an important part of reshaping that sensibility.

The formative effect of reasons is what makes normative thinking into a control system, for it is the consideration of those reasons that controls the lawyer's initial sense of justice. We have seen that it is entirely possible for us to resolve a normative question with reliance simply upon our sense of right and wrong. That is probably what you did with the case of the woman whose luggage was lost by the airline.

You did not pause to consult the law before you resolved it. And, when you had resolved it, you did not check your resolution with the law on the subject. You simply relied upon your sense of right and wrong as a guide.

The lawyer may do that as well, at least in a simple case. But the lawyer has less faith in the naked sense of justice. The lawyer will look for ways in which his sense of justice may mislead him. He will consult the law when he feels that he may be biased on a matter, or when its resolution is not clear, or when he feels that social history may have generated a legal standard about which he is not aware.

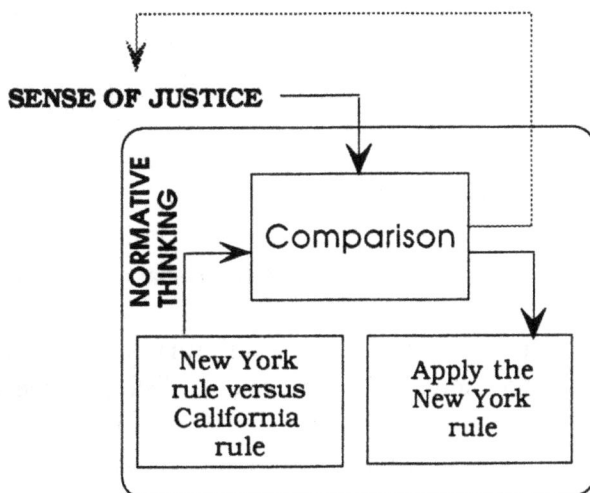

Figure 10.27   The lawyer's sense of justice is shaped by
his understanding of the reasons for law.

In Jeffrey's case I decided to apply the New York rule, but my reading of the California court's opinion in <u>Gibson v. Gibson</u> was not without effect. It showed me that there is a problem with the New York rule: That rule shields a parent from ever having to explain her behavior in supervising her child. People who are shielded from view tend to become irresponsible. That concern will modify my sense of parental responsibility. In the future I will not be so quick to dismiss a case by a child against a parent.

The interaction between the law and the lawyer's sense of justice is what accounts for some of the special character of the lawyer. Lawyers are troubled by things that non-lawyers find obvious. They look for the other side of a case that seems open and shut. They represent reprehensible people, according them a level of respect that baffles non-lawyers. They will bring an action, for example, on behalf of a burglar who was killed when the owner of the home he was burgling shot him to death. The lawyer wants to know whether the homeowner was acting out of fear or out of vindictive reprisal for an indignity. The former is justified, the latter isn't, regardless of how great an indignity one feels from the burglar's actions.

The importance of reasons in law is what bothered me about the California rule of negligent parental supervision. Under the California rule, you will recall, the court allows the jury to inspect the facts of a case to determine whether or not the parent's behavior conforms to what an "ordinarily reasonable and prudent parent" would have done under the circumstances. Those words are not illuminating. They will not shape the jury's sense of justice. The jurors will apply whatever intuitive sense of proper behavior they had when they walked into the court. Worse, the jury is not required to adduce any reasons to back its decision. Its judgment will not be *formative.* Its reasons will not enter into the flow of ideas that guide and develop the understanding of future parents as they raise their children. The only message that will reach parents will be that they had better watch out because they can be sued by their children.

The law can, however, go too far with reasons. Their importance can intimidate the uninitiated, making law seem like the arcane preserve of the lawyers, rather than the institution where the dictates of the sense of justice are played out. In American law, the centrality of the jury and the voter is an crucial antidote to the professionalization of law.

Reasons can also mask dishonesty. The California judge who ruled against the Gibson could have been motivated by a personal dislike of the way they raised their children, which he masked with an apparently dispassionate exercise of legal reasoning. Reasons can create a smokescreen that only the most deft and dedicated can penetrate.

The greatest risk, however, is that reasons are not symmetrical. Some things are easier to explain than others. The positions that are easier to explain will prosper at the expense of those that are more difficult. This factor generally favors measures proposing social controls over those favoring liberty. Should law, for example, leave parents alone to raise their children as they will? If we do, very specific evils will befall children from parental abuse and neglect. If we don't, if we subject parents to judicial scrutiny, what will happen? They won't like it, but that is not a reason not to do it. It is very difficult to identify the effects of social controls and to remove them when they are not justified.

Each lawyer reaches some balance between confidence in his own sense of justice and in the need to consider reasons for conclusions that violate it. Some lawyers are innately rebellious in the face of authority. They regard reasons critically, trusting their own sense of justice in the face of overwhelming law to the contrary. Others have little confidence in their own sensibilities, accepting whatever legal schema is presented by authority and adapting their own sense of justice to the prevailing view. These lawyers have high prospects in areas of positive law, for they are able to internalize a statutory or regulatory scheme as if it were their own guiding principles.

3. Discovering law

An error signal generated by the lawyer's assessment of the law generates further effort on the lawyer's part to develop the norms that guide the case. That effort may be solely internal, as the lawyer rethinks the law and searches for related legal ideas that may shed some light on the problem. The effort may be external, involving legal research to generate more legal information to expand the lawyer's knowledge.

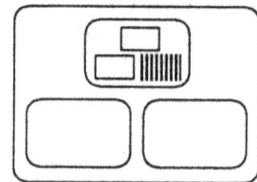

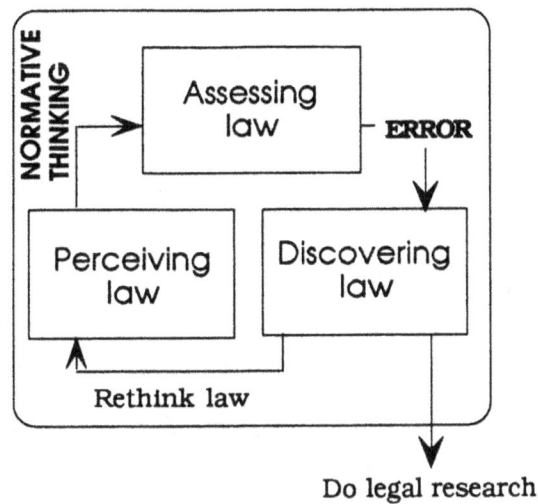

Figure 10.28   An error in the understanding of law will lead
the lawyer to do legal research or to rethink the law.

The error associated with the norm under consideration will generate a tension associated with that norm in the lawyer's mind, a feeling that, "I'm not comfortable with this rule." Rarely, however, does the lawyer draw a complete blank. The lawyer's understanding of the law will generally provide a norm which, though problematic, is *plausible*. The lawyer will note the tension associated with the norm and proceed to subject it to scrutiny, but the lawyer will not wait until the norm is run to earth before trying it out on the *facts* of the case.

That is another illustration of parallel thinking. The lawyer's mind will continue to scrutinize the law applicable to the case, while at the same time using his present concept of the applicable law to evaluate the facts of the case as he understands them. His thinking will proceed on all of the levels—descriptive, normative, and the overall analysis of the case—simultaneously.

Action thinking

The analysis of a case is an iterative process in the lawyer's mind. Even as the first inkling that a factual scenario raises a normative question dawns on the lawyer, the lawyer will begin to apply to it normative standards that experience has indicated may be relevant. At first, the normative standard may be no more than the lawyer's naked sense of justice. The sense of justice, illuminated by his understanding of law, will begin to direct the lawyer's search for the facts of the case. Further facts will, in turn, trigger different normative concepts.

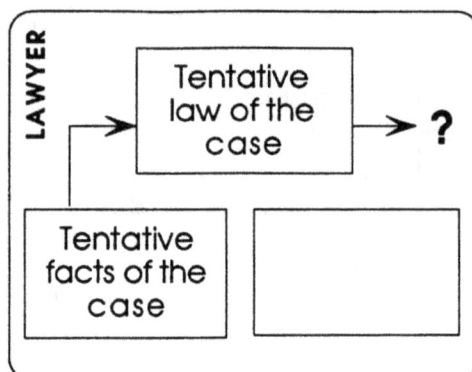

Figure 10.29   The lawyer will subject the facts of the case to normative evaluation long before all tension has been removed from the facts and law.

Figure 10.29 pictures the overall system of the lawyer's thought. Descriptive thinking has generated at least a sketchy picture of what happened and normative thinking has provided some tentative idea of the legal norms that apply to those facts. Both facts and law are so sketchy that it is difficult for the lawyer to tell at this stage of the case whether or not an actionable wrong has been done, which is suggested by the question mark.

As thinking on the case progresses, the facts and the norms that apply to the facts will get clearer. The lawyer, at least one who is in the position that we were in the *Stapleton* case of advising a client about whether or not Jeffrey's estate could bring suit, is looking for an error. Notice, however, that this error is different from the types of error that occur in the component systems. The error generated in descriptive thinking tells the lawyer what it is about the situation as she understands it that doesn't make sense, while the error signal in normative thinking tells the lawyer that she is unsure of what legal standards to apply.

On the overall level, by contrast, the error signal concerns the substance of the case itself. When the lawyer applies the law, however tentative, to the facts, however tentative, an error indicates that what happened in the story is not what should have happened according to the legal standard. This type of error, unlike the others, is *actionable* in a court of law. It was this type of error that we were looking for in the *Stapleton* case.

By the end of Chapter 5 we had developed a sense that there *was* a plausible case to be made for error on the part of Tim and John Newland. That did not end our analysis, however. We had to decide whether or not we would do anything about it, whether or not we would take action. That decision calls for yet another kind of thought: thought that determines action.

In Chapter 6 we had to decide whether or not we would take Jeffrey's case. By that point we had a fair grip on the merits of it. We were at the point in Figure 10.29 indicated by the question mark. We had developed a plausible sense of the facts of the case, though there was considerable tension left in them, many loose ends. And we had applied a legal standard to the case. It appeared that there was a plausible case to be made against the Newlands. We had to decide whether or not we would take the case, representing Jeffrey Stapleton's estate in a suit against the Newlands.

That introduced a new set of considerations, personal considerations, into our thinking: What would be in it for us? How would taking the case serve our own purposes?

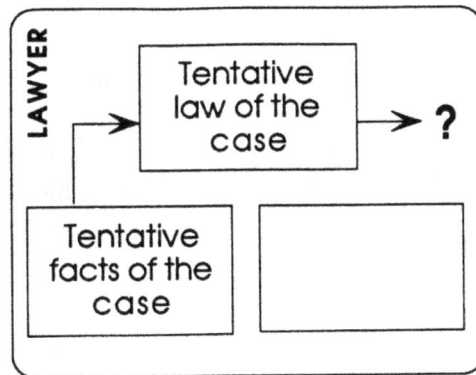

Figure 10.30   When we had gotten a grip on Jeffrey's case, we considered the possibility of bringing action on his behalf.

This question involved us in a way that the prior questions did not. We are not legal slaves who, in the presence of an arguable injustice, must act to redress it. We are beings with our own purposes who are free to decide whether or not we will bring suit. How do we make that decision? It was made under a control system that determines our actions:

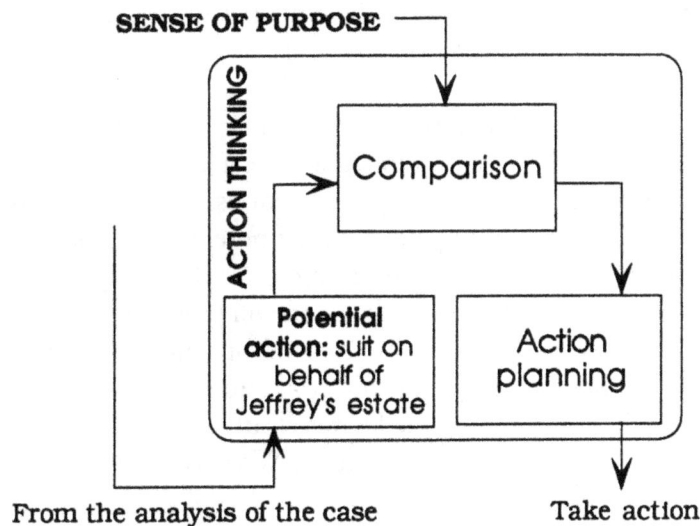

Figure 10.31   In making our decision in Stapleton we compared the proposed action against our sense of our own purpose.

1. Perceiving potential actions

The potential action on behalf of Jeffrey's estate constitutes the "perception" component of action thinking. It takes its place alongside a great many other potential actions in our inventory of things that we've thought about doing but have not yet decided to do.

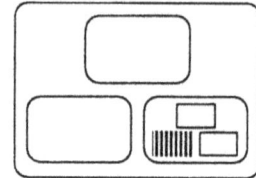

Each component of legal thinking—descriptive thinking, normative thinking, and action thinking—is a general capability of mind. It does not exist simply to serve legal thought. The descriptive thinking involved in legal analysis is, for example, exactly the same as the descriptive thinking that we employ in figuring out any other event in life. So too with action thinking, which means that the potential actions generated by our legal thought must compete with all of the other actions that we may undertake.

The lawyer will have set aside in his mind a block of time that he devotes to legal actions—while he is "at work." That means that the potential action on Jeffrey's behalf only competes against the other *legal* actions that the lawyer is considering, not against everything else in the lawyer's life. But, even then, non-legal actions may still intrude. This is particularly troublesome if the lawyer is experiencing personal problems, like a divorce, which create error signals that simply must be addressed with action.

At any instant in time only one, or at most a few, potential actions are in consciousness. You can confirm that by pausing to reflect upon the number of potential actions that lurk in your mind. With a little effort you should be able to retrieve dozens of errands that need doing, calls that you should make, projects that you are in the middle of. Retrieving them brings them to consciousness (it tells the Consciousness Cop to give you a list of the potential actions that are awaiting your attention). But consciousness can deal with only one at a time. Trying to deal with more than one brings confusion.

To decide on a potential action, you must bring it to consciousness. But consciousness acts sequentially, one decision at a time. That presents a question about how you make a choice between competing actions. The obvious thing for your mind to do is to consciously compare all of the potential actions with each other, then assess how likely it is that you will succeed on each, finally assess the extent to which the perceptions generated by each action will produce the values you desire.

That would, however, require that *consciousness* operate in parallel, for consciousness would have to hold hundreds of things in attention at once, and make tens of thousands of calculations on them. That is clearly not what is going on, at least not in the consciousness that we are aware of. What is going on as we evaluate a potential action?

2. Evaluating potential actions

Consider what was going on in Chapter 6. There, we focused upon Jeffrey's case to the exclusion of other matters that were awaiting out attention. We considered what taking the case might do for us: we considered, in other words, the perceptions that taking the case might generate for us. One set of perceptions was financial: Taking the case could generate substantial income.

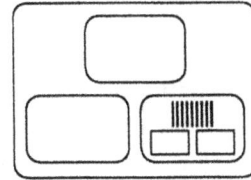

The significance of that perception—the imagined perception of endorsing a check for $200,000 or so—does not lie in the dollars directly, but rather in what those dollars would mean to us. They mean the continued prosperity of the firm, or the purchase of a high tech computer system for the firm. or perhaps a year-end bonus that could send our children to college. That meaning is not, however, a list of the things that we could do with the money. It is rather a *sense* of the significance of the money, a feeling of what it might mean in our lives.

"Senses" are the way that we integrate experience into understanding. The sense of fairness, for example, integrated our experience of the world in a way that allowed us to form *expectations* about the way the world works. A new perception of the world was compared against the sense of what we expected in order to identify those discontinuities ("unfairnesses") in it that required further consideration. Similarly, a potential action and the perceptions that we imagine it will produce, are compared against our sense of *purpose:* Does the potential action fit our purposes? It is a sense of our direction, an overall sense of the perceptions that we desire for the future, against which we compare the contribution that the potential action that is under consideration might make.

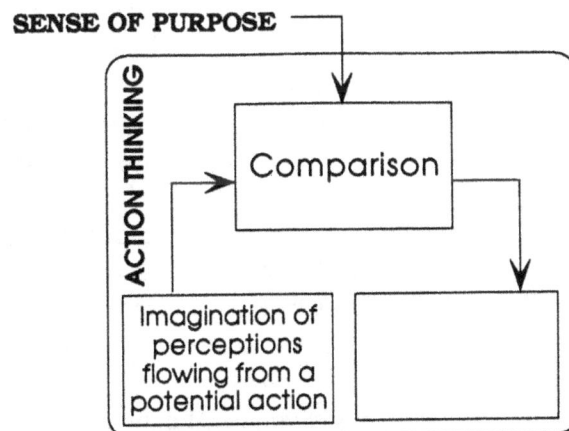

Figure 10.32   Potential actions are evaluated by comparing the perceptions that we imagine will flow from them against our sense of purpose.

Individuals differ greatly in their sense of purpose. Some are unable to deal with risk; they cannot seriously consider any action that may fail to deliver what they want. For them, the great likelihood that Jeffrey's case would generate no revenue simply eliminates it from consideration. They need to sense a flow of perceptions that will surely come about. They are ideally suited to be employees.

Others cannot deal with time delay; a desired perception must happen immediately or it is without value. For them, the long delay between the time that we accepted Jeffrey's case and the time we could expect some money from it would be intolerable. Lawyers who are of this sort are happy handling cases in Traffic Court, for there you get a client at 9:00 AM and are paid for your work a few minutes or hours later.

People decide on actions according to the way they "feel." That suggests that people are not "rational," at least not in any simple sense. They usually cannot support their decisions with reasons beyond the conclusory, "I just wanted to do it." or words to that effect. They rarely undertake an action whose objectifiable present value in dollar terms is the highest of all of the potential actions that they could take. And they often regret the decisions they've made.

If we conceive of rationality, however, as a deeper integration of reason and emotion, it is not clear that any action, even one for which the person is utterly unable to adduce a reason, is "irrational." There is no objective meaning to the individual's sense of purpose. It is not possible to represent it in an objective way that would allow us to determine that a person's action does not fit with his overall perception of his own purpose. We accept each person's autonomy simply because we have no choice but to do so. We cannot extirpate their sense of purpose, modify it, and reinstall it into the person. We must simply stand back from it and watch it roll on, influencing it where we can.

That was particularly obvious in Chapter 6, for I would not take Jeffrey's case whatever the expected dollar payoff was. Why is that? Part of it is that I don't like the argument that I would have had to make about the law in order to make a compelling case against the Newlands. I can imagine the feelings of unease that I would experience as I made it. It doesn't comport with my sense of justice, and my sense of justice is wrapped up in my sense of purpose. To me there doesn't seem to be much point in being a lawyer unless what I do is at least arguably consistent with justice.

You may well feel differently about the case. You may have a different sense of justice, a different understanding of law. Or your sense of justice may not be wrapped into your sense of purpose. In the extreme case, your sense of your purpose in law may simply be to generate the revenues to pay for the other actions that you would like to pursue. In that case I would expect you to take the case if doing so would not displace another case that had a higher expected return.

But there is more to my decision than my unease about the law that I would have to argue. I have represented clients who I thought were wrong, and I have not felt bad about it when I won on their behalf. My unease about filing suit against the Newlands has something to do with the devastating impact that it would have upon their lives, an impact that is, in my judgment, out of all proportion to their actions. I can easily imagine the perceptions that I would be flooded with as I handled Jeffrey's case, fought it through to a judgment, then levied on their farm to collect on the judgment. I do not like the prospect of those perceptions.

There is probably much more to it than that, but I am unable to attach words to it. I am quite confident, however, that the potential action in the Stapleton case is not in keeping with my own sense of purpose:

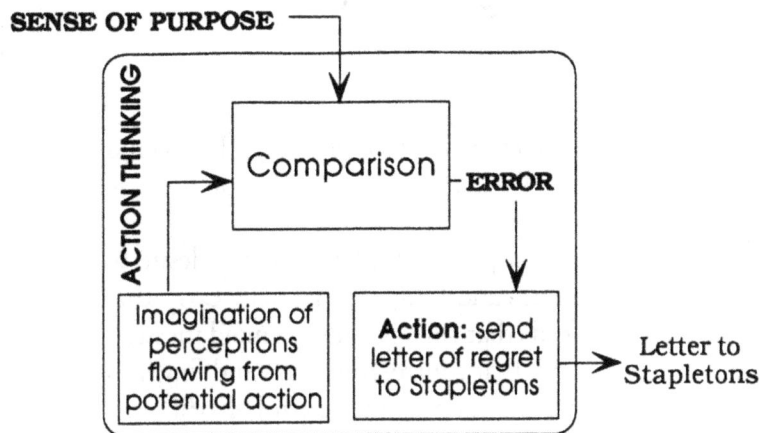

Figure 10.33   Filing action against the Newlands did not fit with my sense of purpose: that error generated my decision to turn down the case.

3. Taking action

My decision to reject the case resulted in very little action—writing a letter to the Stapleton notifying them of my decision. Even that act is, however, highly complex. Consider what is involved in it. At the lowest level, that action simply amounts to movements of my muscles as I insert paper into my printer, type the message, stuff the envelope and mail it.

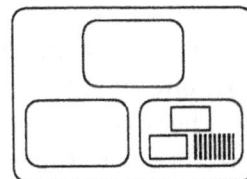

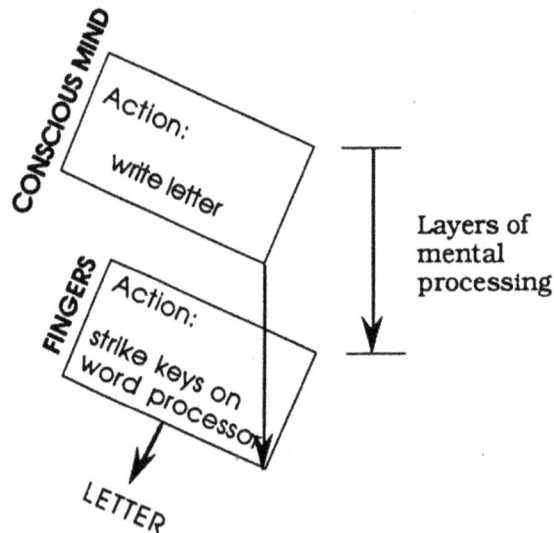

Figure 10.34   There are many levels of processing between the conscious level of writing a letter and the physical movements that carry it out.

There are many levels of processing between the desire to write the letter and the movement of my fingers and body that actually carry that desire into action. I must generate a set of words that conveys my intended message, then translate those words into muscular signals that control my hands and fingers to produce the correct characters. Each level of action is under the control of a different control system. The control systems are nested under the overall purpose that drives the action, though that need not concern us here.

What does concern us, however, is the complexity of the actions required in the practice of law. From the base necessities of operating a personal computer, to the great complexity of arguing a case before a trial court, the practice of law requires an enormous inventory of skills. No one is equally good at all of those skills. The lawyer's actions, indeed the lawyer's perception of himself, will be influenced by his repertoire of skills.

That did not come out in our assessment of the *Stapleton* case, but it should have. The fact of the matter is that I am not much of a trial lawyer. I have done it, but I am not very good at it. It calls for a variety of capabilities that I have no gift for. One of them is simply dealing with the barrage of nonsensical procedures that the lawyer who will represent the defendant is likely to let loose on their behalf. There will be endless questions to answer, pointless telephone calls to return, interminable motions that are without legal significance, but kill you if you ignore them. Defense lawyers are paid by the hour. It makes sense for them to turn the case into a procedural nightmare. They get paid for every one and they wear down the lawyer for the plaintiff. I am too easily worn down.

It may well be, then, that the most important single fact in the Newland case for me was the fact that the Newlands are not covered by insurance. If there is to be any recovery against them, it will be out of the proceeds of their farm. They are going to do everything in their power to avoid that, which means that this case will go to trial. Which means that I will have to put up with endless nonsense. Were I more clever at dealing with defense lawyers this might not loom as a problem. But I am not. I just don't have the skills for it. I had better include in my letter a recommendation that Margaret consult another lawyer, one with a set of skills more in tune with the case.

Legal thinking as a whole

I have modeled legal thinking as a three part control system, each part of which is itself composed of a three part control system. We must consider the system as a whole, lest our sense of it be confused by the focus on each part.

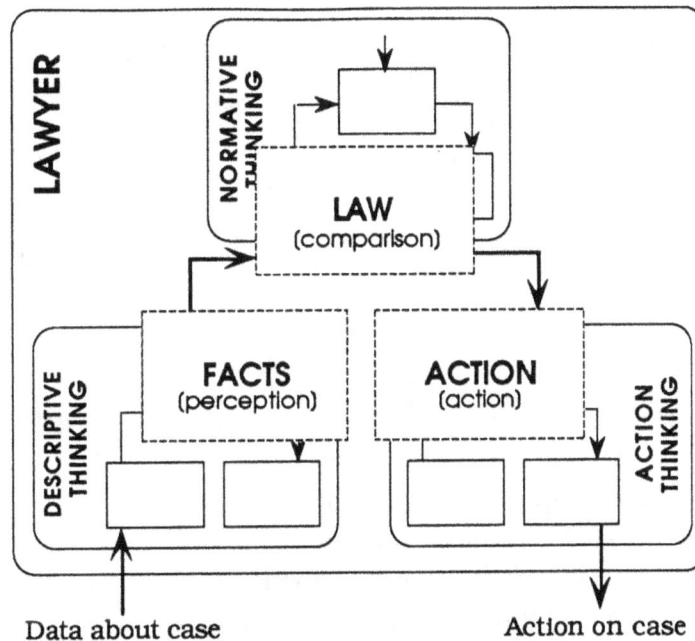

Figure 10.35   The overall model, showing the systems
that underlie the behavior of lawyers.

The descriptive, normative, and action thinking employed by the lawyer is not at all singular to law. They are processes that everyone employs and that the lawyer employs for purposes other than the practice of law. The singular component of legal thinking is, not surprisingly, the Law. The lawyer's judgment about the law applicable to the case is the reference signal by which the facts are evaluated.

The thing that makes that reference signal singular to lawyers is not its normative nature. Every person generates norms to evaluate his or her own behavior and the behavior of others. In daily life, however, we are not *responsible* for our norms. We are fully entitled to judge others according to any standard that we want. That is not true for the lawyer. The lawyer who sues someone for violating God's law against worshiping graven icons will quickly find that the legal system will not tolerate the case.

Only in the simplest case will the law provide a clear standard to apply to the facts. The lawyer will need to interpret the law against his own sense of its purpose. That will often generate two or more plausible standards, both of which must be applied to the case. That situation can be pictured this way:

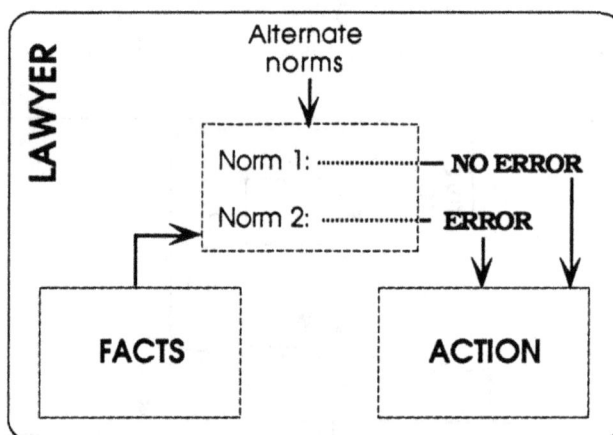

Figure 10.36   Evaluation of the facts under alternative
norms produces contingent thinking.

Evaluating the facts of the case under the two interpretations of the applicable norm produces different results. The facts of the case conform to the first norm ("no error"), but not to the second ("error"). In such a situation the lawyer must ask whether or not it is possible that a court adopt the second norm. If it is, the lawyer's thinking must become *contingent*. The lawyer must keep both interpretations alive in her mind as she continues to think through the case.

Figure 10.36 just begins to suggest the actual complexity of what is happening in the lawyer's mind. Every law has multiple elements (recall Figure 5.3). each of which may have two or more interpretations. Facts are ambiguous as well, as we have seen (Figure 10.8), each elemental fact having two or more possible interpretations. Multiplying the number of plausible factual interpretations in a case by the number of normative interpretations results in an unimaginably complex logical structure, even for as simple a case as *Stapleton*. Our minds, which would boggle at the task of diagramming that logical structure, have little trouble dealing with it. Why?

Part of the answer lies in the mind's use of feeling and emotion. The feeling of tension guides us through the case with little conscious intervention. The next thing to think about in a case simply "comes to mind." Rarely do we have to consciously list the elements of a case and think about each one in turn. Instead, the tension associated with each element and interpretation of the case arranges them for our consideration. Elements with negligible tension *become* settled, not bothering our consciousness for attention. Factual or legal elements that are under high tension compete for our attention. Our attention to a case follows no particular order; the Consciousness Cop does not have a little logical map of the case which he goes through in an orderly way. Our minds jump here and there as the emotional force of the elements of the case vie for attention.

Most legal thinking, like any other thinking. happens in the background. To illustrate that, consider this new statement about the Stapleton case: Mr. Montefiori has twice been convicted of the sexual abuse of minor children. What does that do to your thinking about the case? Do you have to retrieve all of the facts of the case and think through the implications of the new fact on each one? I doubt it. Instead, that fact will race through the mental structures that you have created for the case, raising some tensions and lowering others.

Could it be that Montefiori lured Timothy across the street and to his death? that his story about the newspaper was nonsense? If so, that would explain why Officer McGinty did not report seeing newspaper all over the street around the scene of the accident (has that loose end to the story been bothering you?). And it would explain why Montefiori made such an effort to avoid the police investigation. The new fact changes the tensions of the elements of the case and creates new errors, errors that demand further thought and investigation. All with virtually no conscious effort.

The other thing that makes it possible for us to solve problems whose logical complexity would quickly boggle us is that our minds are massively parallel. They do many, many things at once. All four of the control systems in Figure 10.35 operate at the same time. We evaluate the new information about Montefiori on a factual level (does it fair with the other things that we know about the case and about human nature?), normative level (what law would apply to Montefiori's behavior?), action level (how do we find out more about him?), and legal level (does it feel like there might be a case against him?) all at once. Within a few seconds of hearing that statement an experienced lawyer would have Montefiori fully penciled into the case, with a complete plan for gathering more information that was ready to go into action. That is massive parallelism. It allows us to make short work of cases that would defy logical solution.

The emotional basis of thought means, however, that no human judgment can ever be logically *proved*. We can use logic to test our inferences and conclusions, but that test can only demonstrate that we are <u>wrong</u>. We cannot use logic to show that we are right. Rightness is forever based upon our own judgment, our feeling for that which is and that which should be.

Senses

This model of legal thought places central weight upon three things that I have called "senses"—the sense of fairness, sense of justice, and sense of personal purpose. Those senses provide the fulcrum for the control system. They set the standard against which all is evaluated.

It is not a good idea to explain that which is mysterious (our thinking) in terms of things that are even more mysterious (senses) if that can be avoided. What are we to make of senses?

We use the term in three different ways. First, we use it to refer to the five ways in which we extract data from our environment (e.g., touch, smell, taste, sight, hearing). Second. we use the word to refer to ideas that guide our mind. We say that a person has a "sense of decency" if he treats others with respect, or a "sense of perspective" if all of the buildings in a drawing that he has made look like they are all sitting on the same plane. Third, we say that we have "made sense of something if we feel that we understand it.

The commonality in these three uses of the word seems to be that there is something that we perceive but cannot put words to (e.g., the smell of a lilac, the feeling of socially appropriate behavior, the meaning of a concept) that nonetheless plays a guiding role in our thinking. We are guided by our sense of touch when we grope around in the dark. We are guided by our sense of decency when we deal with others. And we are guided by the meaning that we make of that which we perceive.

In all three cases the "sense of ..." is a feeling that guides thought and behavior. That is precisely the role that senses have been given in the model. They are the integration of ideas and feelings into a single entity which generates the signals that guide thought and behavior. They are the root of individual autonomy, for they are something that each person must build for himself or herself. And they are immune to direct manipulation by others.

The dependence of this model of thought upon senses cannot be logically justified. It is justified, if at all, only by direct reference to your own experience of yourself. If, as you reflect upon your own thought, you cannot feel your senses of yourself and the world guiding your thought and behavior, this model will have little effect upon your perception of your own thought. In that case. I would be highly interested in your observations about what your mind (or my mind!) was doing in the Stapleton case.

CHAPTER ELEVEN

What makes law organic?

We are now in a position to address a question remaining from Part I: What makes law organic? In Chapter 5 I made some weight of the distinction between positive law and organic law, between "leg-" and "yewo-." In Chapter 8 I drew a parallel between the individual's pursuit of the good through individual action and a nation's pursuit of the good through the medium of positive law. In Chapter 9 I argued that the individual's pursuit of the good is constrained by another set of values, the "right." Here, I will make the parallel argument about positive law: It is constrained by organic law.

To begin, we must ask what sense it makes to speak of a social system as being "organic" at all. To say that a social system is "organic" is to say that it is in some important way similar to a living organism. How could that be?

It is easy to see law as a positive control system, like a thermostat: some person or group of people set the desired standard and the system swings into action to bring about the desired standard. There are many areas of law that are difficult to understand in any other way. Tax law is, quite obviously, simply a system by which government brings about a desired perception (i.e., a given level of revenue) by legal action (i.e., tax law and its enforcement). Similarly, traffic law is a system that sets a standard speed on highways and attempts to bring it into effect through enforcement.

Yet neither tax law nor traffic law can be understood in a vacuum. Both exist to serve larger purposes. When we inquire into the larger purposes that they serve, the sense that law is positive—that it is simply a system that aims to produce specific social outcomes—becomes untenable.

Consider the tax law. Its purpose is to finance government. Desired tax revenues follow from desired governmental expenditures. But whose desires are we talking about that establish these "desired governmental expenditures?" Organizations do not have desires. The desires that animate government must be furnished by a person or group of people. Tax law, then, is part of a hierarchy of purposes similar to the hierarchy pictured in Figure 8.5.

Set desired level of government services ("politics")
  ⮡ Pay for costs of government
       ⮡ Raise tax revenues through tax law
            ⮡ Collect taxes from Citizen X
                 ⮡ Shut down Citizen X's business

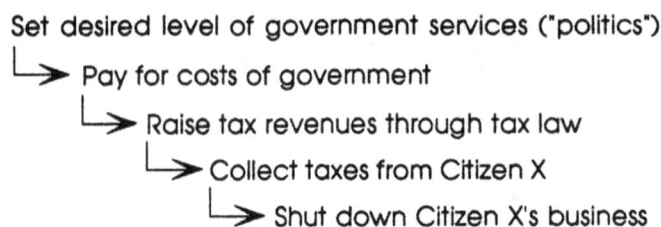

Figure 11.1   The hierarchy of purposes underlying tax law.

When the Internal Revenue Service puts a padlock on the door of a citizen's business in order to make him serious about paying his taxes, that action should be traceable back to the purpose of government itself. It should not be that the purpose that animated the action resides solely in the mind of the IRS official who installed the padlock. That official must justify her behavior in terms of the purpose of the system as a whole.

Tax law serves desires that were put there by humans, whose desires in some fashion determined the size of government. When we ask how human desires combine to direct government, the simple view of law as a positive control system becomes hopelessly weak. It is not possible to identify whose desires control government, or how they do it. There is some kind of mess going on there that we call "politics" that generates a public budget. The most we can say is that there is some kind of process that integrates human desires into a set of desired perceptions that shape government, and that positive law follows from that in an attempt to produce those desires.

But positive law is not free to roam as it will, to produce whatever desires that those who control government desire. It is constrained in two ways. First, it is constrained as to its inputs, as to whose desires are to be taken into account as public desires are formulated. Those constraints are the rules of democracy. Second, it is constrained in its *actions,* in what it may do. The desires generated by the democratic process are themselves constrained by individual rights. If everyone in the state where I reside voted to ban the publication of this book, that action, while commendably democratic, would be void as an infringement upon my right of freedom of speech.

The significance of these constraints is that there is in public institutions a similar relationship between the pursuit of the good and the constraints imposed by the right as there is in individual life:

Constraining values
... the **organic law**

Driving values
... the **positive law**

Action

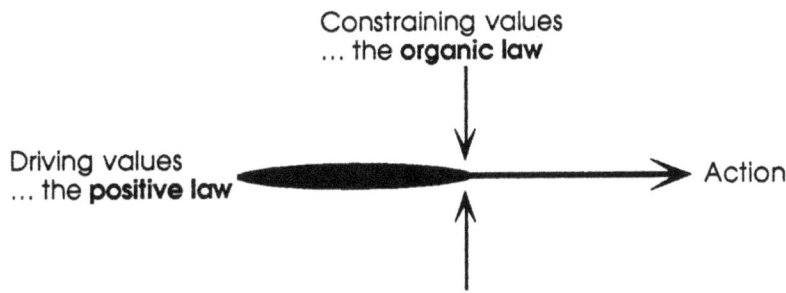

Figure 11.2   The relationship between the positive law and the organic law
in public institutions is similar to the relationship between
the *good* and the *right* in human thought (Figure 9.3).

Individuals and organizations both pursue a vision of desired ends, subject to the constraint of values that define what actions are permissible. This begins to give us a grip upon what is meant by "organic" law, for we have here a parallel between an organism, the human being, and a social institution.

The parallel is far deeper: The laws that constrain the state derive from the same source as the norms that constrain the individual, from the individual sense of justice. Further, the individual sense of justice is implicit in the nature of human beings as purposive control systems. Further still, normative control on behavior is essential to the survival of any purposive control system, human or animal.

Those are lusty propositions. I will take them up in reverse order. First, consider the proposition that normative controls are essential to the survival of any purposive control system. Those who study the behavior of vertebrates have long recognized that the behavior of every vertebrate is internally constrained: Lions may fight with each other to get what they want, but rarely does that fight result in death. Something turns off the animal's aggressive behavior before it causes the death of its competitor. In animals that have great offensive power, like male lions, aggressive behavior is turned off before contact is made with another male lion. Two male lions competing for the attention of a female will go through an involved aggressive ritual, growling and striking at each other, but the ritual will break off before blows are struck. The victorious lion, aggressions aroused to the breaking point, will let the loser off without a blow, coming down from his aggressive high to a calm indifference when he perceives that the other lion has yielded.

The brain processes that account for this behavior are called "inhibitory" processes. Aggressive behavior is driven by "excitatory" processes, neural processes that prepare the animal for a fight. They are modulated by the inhibitory processes, neural signals that constrain the operation of the excitatory signals and turn them off when the situation no longer requires aggression. The relationship between excitatory and inhibitory processes is similar to the relationship between the human's pursuit of the good under constraint by the right.

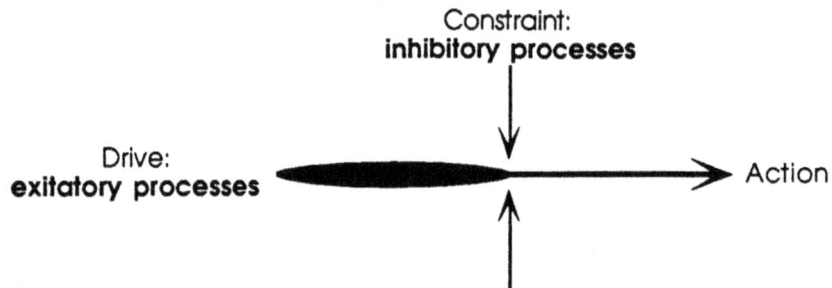

Figure 11.3   Exitatory neural processes are constrained by inhibitory processes.

The lion's desire (speaking anthropomorphically) for a mate is pursued through excitatory processes, which rise in intensity at the perception of a competitor. At the same time, inhibitory processes go to work, shaping the lion's behavior. He does not wildly attack the competitor but goes into an elaborate ritual. When the lion perceives that the inhibitory processes of its competitor have overcome its exitatory processes, so that it either flees or adopts a posture of submission, the lion's own inhibitory processes take over and the competition is at an end.

It is a stretch to call these inhibitory processes "normative," for they appear to operate autonomically within the animal. They operate at neural levels in both humans and animals that are not consciously perceived. We know that to be true from self-reflection, for we have the same excitatory and inhibitory processes as the lion. Certain perceptions automatically trigger the "fight" response in us, and just as automatically modulate and turn it off when it is no longer appropriate.

Humans have a layer of constraints upon behavior—normative constraints—that animals do not have, at least as far as we have been able to determine. Normative processes in humans are heavily emotional; we "feel" a wrong long before we can articulate what it is about it that makes it wrong. But they can be modified cognitively; they can be changed by experience. That fact is both a blessing and a curse. It is a curse because it can be used by others to eliminate constraints that are innately present. Humans can be taught to ignore the implicit impulse against killing others in order that they might kill in a good cause. Humans are the only animals that will systematically exterminate members of their own species.

But the ability to modify the inhibitory process by the creation of norms to guide behavior is essential to the emergence of civilization. Civilization requires a population density and level of interpersonal interaction that would not be possible with unmodified excitatory and inhibitory processes. It is difficult even with them, for activities like riding in elevators or walking among crowds triggers some deep excitatory impulses.

Law is one of the social institutions that shapes the individual's inhibitory processes.

Like social norms, mores, taboos. and belief systems, law modifies the individual sense of appropriate behavior.

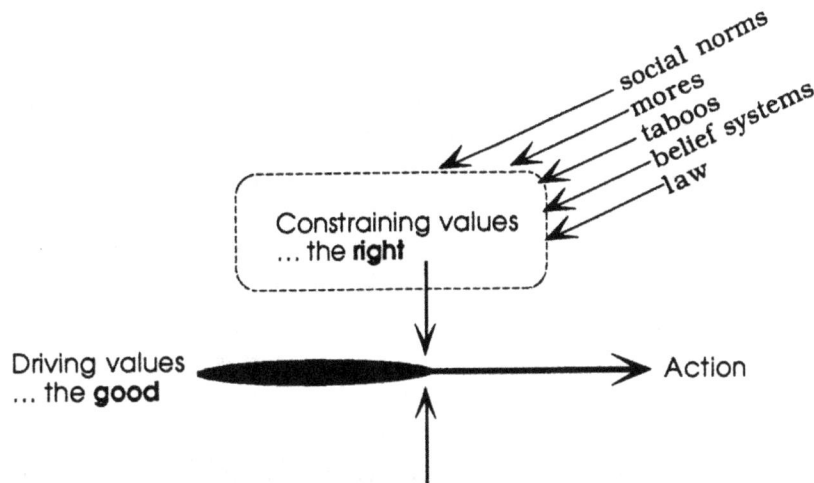

Figure 11.4   Social norms, mores, taboos, and law modify
the individual's sense of the right.

When it operates in this way, law is *formative*: It forms, or reforms, the neural controls that the person applies to the pursuit of desired perceptions. Most people most of the time conform to law not because they fear the consequences of violating it but because it would be wrong, even unthinkable, not to do so. As we have seen, it never occurred to you to steal this book.

Law also operates by inducing in the person a *fear of the consequences*. There are surely people who would pursue their own ends at the expense of others were it not for the danger that such behavior would bring swift reprisal from law. But fear is a very poor constrainer. It is expensive and highly subject to the individual's taste for negative reinforcement. In order to extinguish behavior through negative reinforcement, the negative reinforcement must be swift, sure, and often. The kind of negative reinforcement that law can bring to bear is effective only upon people who don't need it.

The nice thing about enforcing law through fear of the consequences is that it allows law to be arbitrary. The law need not make any sense to the person: it need only be remembered. I have no idea what makes it wrong to ship alcoholic beverages by mail, but I do know that if I try to do it my package will not get through. If I find, however, that my packages containing alcoholic beverages are sneaking though, I will have no compunctions about mailing them. Section 124.42 of the Domestic Mail Manual has had no formative effect upon me. It *feels* like a naked prohibition, not like one that is based upon a wrong.

For law to be formative it must be understood, accepted, and internalized. The person must accept it as a norm that guides her own behavior, along with the countless norms that are her own. That places an enormous limit upon law, for its edicts must speak in terms that are available to the person. That means that they must fit with the person's existing sense of the right, that there must be few enough of them that their number not overwhelm the person's cognitive abilities, and that they be conveyed in terms that the person can assimilate.

Notice that those three requirements are precisely the opposite of what is required of good positive law. Positive law exists because it is *different* from what people would expect. It exists to conform individual behavior to institutional mandates. Positive law requires a body of highly articulated rules; the Domestic Mail Manual is huge. Since its edicts are not intuitive, they must be spelled out in rules that are never explicit enough. And positive law need not be conveyed in terms that people can assimilate. They need only *follow* the rule, not understand or internalize it. Positive laws must have teeth, so that people understand the consequences of a violation.

Organic law, by contrast, is conveyed in a small number of general principles of the, "It would be wrong to ...." rather than, "Thou shalt not ...." variety. There is no need to describe the penalties that will follow from a violation of principle, for they do not operate by inducing a fear for the consequences. They shape the person's understanding of himself in interaction with others.

The requirements of formative law make it unattractive to despots. They don't want to hear about "rights." They don't want to be limited by principles that fit with the person's sense of justice. They do not like the idea of "yewo-," that each person is entitled to that which is due him. The idea of "that which is due" raises all kinds of questions that the despot would rather not answer. Despots like the idea of "leg-"—that which is written down in lists.

The requirements of formative law make law "organic" in the sense that it must fit with the individual's normative sense. That is the point of the control system model set out in Chapter 10. To apply law to himself or to others the person must understand it. According to the model, understanding law requires that the person evaluate it against his own sense of justice. A law that doesn't fit is a law that is in need of challenge.

This process places an odd duality of requirements upon the judges, jurors, and lawyers. On one hand, it requires of them a confidence in themselves, in their own sense of justice. It requires the courage to demand justification and the refusal to accept the naked threat of force. On the other hand, however, it requires humility. It requires that they be suspicious of their own senses. It is not enough that an action or a rule of law "outrage the conscience," for the conscience that is outraged may be one that has not been fully formed, or has been misformed. The person must be open to illumination, to the subtle nuances of right and wrong lurking in the distasteful. The California rule of parental negligence, while obscure, may be right.

Courage and humility do not go easily together. The person who questions authority too frequently possesses an arrogant faith in his own intuition. Just as bad, the person of humility is too frequently passive in the face of authority. An excess of courage or of humility sends law to tyranny, either to the tyranny of the petit despot or the tyranny of the unquestionable state. The balance between the two is not stable. Justice will always be an impulse that requires struggle.

Useful Websites

www.biologyoflaw.org

The author's website, where, among other things, you will find:

Gibbons, Hugh (1984) *Justifying Law: An Explanation of the Deep Structure of American Law*, Law and Philosophy, Vol. 3, No. 2, pp. 165-279.

Gibbons, Hugh (2001) *Rights and Wrongs: The Tangled Twins of American Law.* Multimedia Program on CD-ROM, here converted to a series of video files.

Gibbons, Hugh (2002) *The Biological Basis of Human Rights*, Presented at the 4th Annual Scholarship Conference of the Society for Evolutionary Analysis in Law, Tallahassee, Florida, April 19-20, 2002. Published in Boston University Public Interest Law Journal, Vol 13, Number 1 (Fall 2003).

www.iapct.org

Website for The International Association for PCT, aka the Control Systems Group, a loosely knit group centered on the creator of PCT, William T. (Bill) Powers.

www.livingcontrolsystems.com

The publisher's website features books and introductions to PCT, plus tutorials and simulation programs you can run on Windows.

www.pctweb.org

This well developed website is maintained by Dr Warren Mansell from the University of Manchester as an international resource for the dissemination of PCT.

www.pctresources.com

Website featuring Control Systems Group archives.

www.mindreadings.com

Rick Marken's website features books, articles and demonstrations you run using your Internet browser.

Recommended Reading

The range of applications and body of literature that has developed around Perceptual Control Theory is significant. These pages hold an overview of this literature.

Books in order by author and publication date, except for Cziko.

Publishers
Benchmark: Bloomfield, NJ: Benchmark Publications.
LCSP: Menlo Park CA: Living Control Systems Publishing.
Kiddy World: Arnhem, The Netherlands: Kiddy World Promotions B.V.
MIT: Cambridge MA: MIT Press.
New View: Chapel Hill, N.C.: New View Publications.
Routledge: Routledge / Taylor & Francis.

Books by LCSP can be downloaded at the publisher's website.

Carey, Timothy A. (2006). *The Method of Levels:
How to do Psychotherapy Without Getting in the Way.* LCSP.

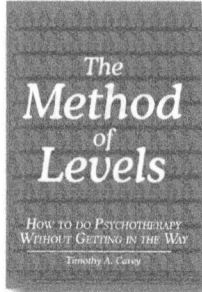

Tim Carey is the peerless expert on and practitioner of the Method Of Levels (MOL), based on the hierarchical structure of PCT. While working for Scotland's National Health Service he used this approach exclusively with his primary care patients. Some of his colleagues learned MOL from Tim and used it too. MOL achieved a new level of service efficiency as evidenced by the fact that the waiting list went from 15 months when he arrived to less than one month five years later.

Carey, Timothy A. (2008). *Hold That Thought! Two Steps to Effective Counseling
and Psychotherapy With the Method of Levels.* New View.

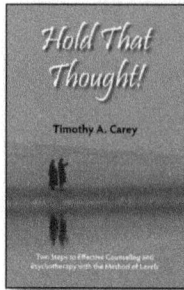

Believing that people with psychological problems get themselves better, Carey introduces readers to the Method of Levels, an approach to psychotherapy based on PCT.

Carey's lighthearted style does not obscure his message: that people can change only themselves, and do not need prescriptive solutions from psychotherapists. With lots of examples, Carey shows readers how to find a new perspective on their conflict and ultimately resolve it.

Carey, Timothy A. (2012). *Control in the Classroom:
An Adventure in Learning and Achievement* LCSP.

This new book is a great addition to the educational literature. It introduces educators to the most important and revolutionary new development in psychology in decades, PCT. And it does this in an easy, accessible style. It has something for everyone in education, from pre-school teachers to secondary teachers, as well as their students. Even college instructors and educational policy makers can find much of value in this slim volume. ... Read this book! You'll be glad you did.

— Hugh G. Petrie

Forssell, Dag (2008). *Management and Leadership: Insight for Effective Practice.* LCSP.

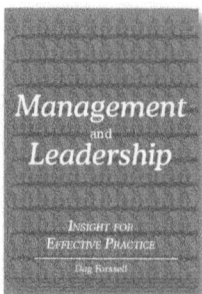

When i first learned of PCT [back in 1998], I read everything I could get my hands on and your articles, for me, most clearly explained PCT. Somehow, your unique use of language, (perhaps it's more humanizing?) allowed me to understand it better, whereas much that was written (that seems to be changing) is so technical. The result being, if one has not mastered PCT language one becomes lost—at least for a time. Your explanations revealed PCT almost immediately for me.

— David Hubbard, LMHC

Mansell, Warren, Carey, Timothy A., and Tai, Sara (Dec. 2012).
   A Transdiagnostic Approach to CBT using Method of Levels Therapy. Routledge.

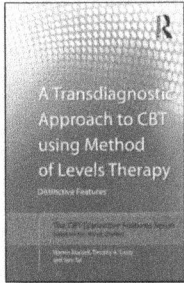

This innovative volume will be essential reading for freshly minted as well as experienced Cognitive Behavior Therapists (CBT) who wish to work using a transdiagnostic approach. Its core principles also apply to counselling, psychotherapy and a range of helping professions. Its accessible explanation of Perceptual Control Theory and its application to real world problems also makes a useful resource for undergraduates, graduates and researchers in psychology.

Cziko, Gary (1995). *Without Miracles: Universal Selection Theory and the Second Darwinian Revolution.* MIT.

Cziko, Gary (2000). *The Things We Do: Using the Lessons of Bernard and Darwin to Understand the What, How, and Why of Our Behavior.* MIT.

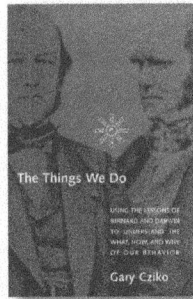

The inside flap of *The Things We Do* (Complete)

The remarkable achievements that modern science has made in physics, chemistry, biology, medicine, and engineering contrast sharply with our limited knowledge of the human mind and behavior. A major reason for this slow progress, claims Gary Cziko, is that with few exceptions, behavioral and cognitive scientists continue to apply a Newtonian-inspired view of animate behavior as an organisms output determined by environmental input. This one-way cause-effect approach ignores the important findings of two major nineteenth-century biologists, French psychologist Claude Bernard and English naturalist Charles Darwin.

Approaching living organisms as purposeful systems that behave in order to control their perceptions of the external environment provides a new perspective for understanding what, how, and why living beings, including humans, do what they do.

Cziko examines in particular perceptual control theory, which has its roots in Bernard's work on the self-regulating nature of living organisms and in the work of engineers who developed the field of cybernetics during and after World War II. He also shows how our evolutionary past together with Darwinian processes currently occurring within our bodies, such as the evolution of new brain connections, provides insights into the immediate and ultimate causes of behavior.

Writing in an accessible style, Cziko shows how the lessons of Bernard and Darwin, updated with the best of current scientific knowledge, can provide solutions to certain long-standing theoretical and practical problems in behavioral science and enable us to develop new methods and topics for research.

Gary Cziko is Professor and AT&T Technology Fellow in the Department of Educational Psychology at the University of Illinois, Urbana-Champaign. He is the author of *Without Miracles* (MIT Press, 1995).

Marken, Richard S., *Mind Readings* and *More Mind Readings: Studies of Purpose.*
New View (1992) & (2002).

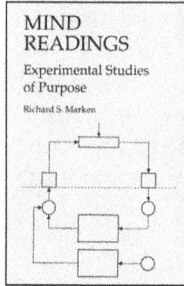

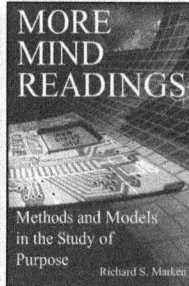

[These are books] that can show a willing psychologist how to do a new kind of research. The theme that runs through all these papers is modeling, the ultimate way of finding out what a theory really means. Richard Marken is a skilled modeler, as will be seen. ... He finds the essence of a problem and an elegantly simple way to cast it in the form of a demonstration or an experiment.

— William T. Powers

Petrie Hugh G. (1981, 2011). *The Dilemma ef Enquiry and Learning.* LCSP.

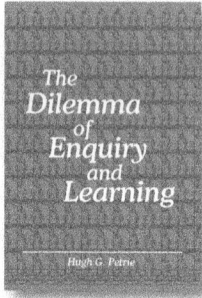

I think that this book will be 'compulsory reading' in graduate schools of education around the country, and that it will arouse a vigorous and healthy controversy by shaking people out of unexamined assumptions and compelling them to rethink stale issues in fresh terms.

— Stephen Toulmin

Petrie Hugh G. (2012). *Ways of Learning and Knowing.* LCSP.

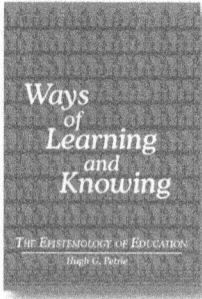

For most of his career, Hugh was way ahead of his time. His papers in this volume still are. The role of the evolutionary process of blind variation and selective retention in all knowledge processes and the understanding of behavior as the control of perception are still mostly unknown in mainstream educational research, theory and philosophy. These perspectives, combined with Hugh's analytical skills and accessible writing, lead to some radical (and radically useful) implications for our understanding of the process of knowledge growth and the practice of education.

— Gary Cziko

Powers, William T. (1973). *Behavior: The Control of Perception*
Second edition (2005). Revised and expanded. Benchmark.

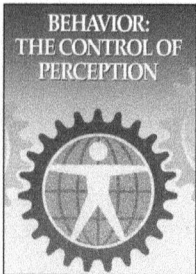

Powers' manuscript, *Behavior: The Control of Perception*, is among the most exciting I have read in some time. The problems are of vast importance, and not only to psychologists; the achieved synthesis is thoroughly original; and the presentation is often convincing and almost invariably suggestive. I shall be watching with interest what happens to research in the directions to which Powers points.

— Thomas S. Kuhn

Powers, William T. *Living Control Systems I & II: Selected Papers of*
William T. Powers. Benchmark (1989) & (1992).

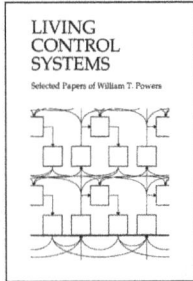

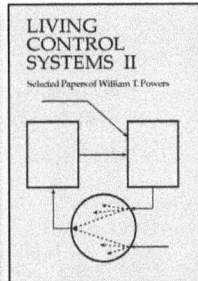

Some of the best science is done by people who refuse to take the obvious for granted. Copernicus didn't take the sun's daily trek across the sky for granted, and Einstein didn't take the regular tick of time for granted, and William T. Powers didn't take the appearance of behavior for granted.

— Richard S. Marken

Powers, William T. (1998). *Making Sense of Behavior:*
The Meaning of Control. Benchmark.

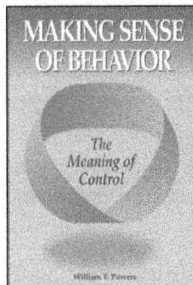

This is the first book on PCT written for "the rest of us." Powers describes in a relaxed, easy-to-read style the fundamentals of this revolutionary theory of the behavior of living organisms—in particular, human beings.

This book is for anyone interested in how our systems work and how people interact and why. For researchers new to PCT, a comprehensive reference points to further studies, demonstrations and applications.

Powers, William T. (2008). *Living control systems III: The Fact of Control.* Benchmark.

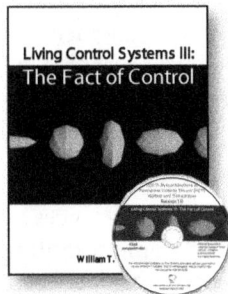

... A unique feature of the book is the accompanying computer programs where Powers 'puts his models where his mouth is,' graphically demonstrating how negative feedback control systems can account for a wide range of goal-oriented behavior. This book is required reading (and computing) for anyone seeking a deep understanding of the behavior of living organisms.

— Gary Cziko

Powers, William T. (Creator). (2016 version).
Perceptual Control Theory; An Overview of the Third Grand Theory
in Psychology—Introductions, Readings, and Resources. LCSP.

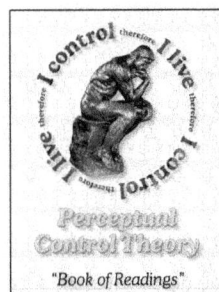

This *"Book of Readingss"* provides a sampling of the literature on Perceptual Control Theory, the science and applications to date.

34 papers cover subjects such as Science, Origin, Comparisons, Demonstrations, Therapy, and Dogma.

Chapters and samples from 24 books on PCT.

Free PDF file at the LCSP website along with all other books published by LCSP.

Powers, William T. and Runkel, Philip J. (2011)
   Dialogue Concerning the Two Chief Approaches to a Science of Life:
   Word Pictures and Correlations versus Working Models. LCSP.

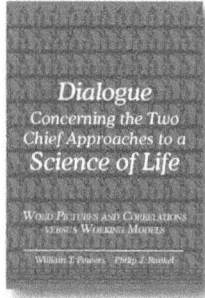

This book holds more than 500 pages of tightly focused, original correspondence between two lucid gentlemen—the creator of PCT, William T. (Bill) Powers, and Philip J. (Phil) Runkel. The significance of the correspondence lies in the subject matter, Perceptual Control Theory (PCT).

The preface and Part II provide
—a brief introduction to PCT (p. 509)
—notes regarding PCT and scientific revolutions
—a guide to resources for your study of PCT

From *Dialogue* / Comments on this volume — the letters and the emerging science

[This volume] provides an outstanding case study of how science develops when real scientists are involved. There are suggestions, descriptions of experiments, computer modeling, explorations of consequences, criticisms, false starts, new breakthroughs, and throughout it all the sense that this is real science in the making. ... It is a must read for anyone who is interested in bringing psychology out of the dark ages and in observing how two outstanding scientists make science really work.

> Hugh Petrie, Ph.D. (Philosophy) Professor Emeritus and Dean,
> Graduate School of Education, State University of New York at Buffalo

Bill Powers is one of the clearest and most original thinkers in the history of psychology. For decades he has explored with persistence and ingenuity the profound implications of the simple idea that biological organisms are control systems. His background in engineering allowed him to avoid many of the traps that have victimized even the best psychologists of the past. I believe his contributions will stand the test of time.

> Henry Yin, Ph.D. (Cognitive Neuroscience)
> Professor of Psychology & Neuroscience, Duke University, NC

Bill Powers' work in the 20th century will prove to be as important for the life sciences as Charles Darwin's work in the 19th century. By the time this notion has become common knowledge, historians of science will be very happy with this correspondence between two giants.

> Frans X. Plooij, Ph.D. (Behavioral Biology) Director,
> International Research-institute on Infant Studies, Arnhem, The Netherlands

... When I discovered PCT in the late 1990s, I saw immediately a theory that could bridge the gaps between cognition, behaviour, and motivation by considering them as integral components of a single unit—the negative feedback loop. When I read Powers (1973) further, I realised that these units could be configured in such a way as to model learning, memory, planning and mental imagery. I was 'sold', and since this time I have endeavoured to test and apply PCT within my research and clinical work. It is often difficult for therapists to grasp the notion that there can be a precise, empirical and quantitative model of purposive, humanistic psychology—but here it is.

> Warren Mansell, Ph.D. (Clinical Psychology) Reader, Chartered Clinical Psychologist,
> Accredited Cognitive Behavioural Therapist, University of Manchester, UK

Roy, Shelley A.W. (2008). *A People Primer: The Nature of Living Systems.* New View.

What a blast of a book! Shelley Roy obviously has a deep and clear understanding of Perceptual Control Theory, and her style of presentation shows respect for the intelligence of the reader while at the same time making sure that her message gets across. Shelley successfully suppresses the writer's ego and never condescends—a very nice combination.

— William T. Powers

Runkel, Philip J. (1990). *Casting Nets and Testing Specimens.*
Second edition (2007). Revised and updated. LCSP.

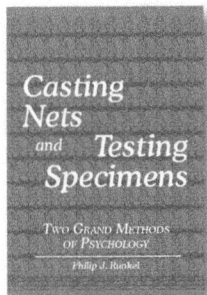

A major contribution to the study and practice of socio-psychological research. Runkel's prescriptions understood and followed would revolutionize the behavioral sciences. ... Runkel shows what statistical studies of groups of people, which he calls the method of relative frequencies or "casting nets" can do and what it cannot do: tell anything specific about the nature of individuals. Runkel shows how the scientific study of the individual can get done, what he calls "the method of specimens."

— Bruce I. Kodish

Runkel, Philip J. (2003). *People as Living Things:*
The Psychology of Perceptual Control. LCSP.

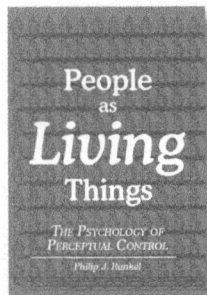

Runkel has written a book ... which is at one and the same time: a text book for graduate and undergraduate psychology; an introduction to perceptual control theory (PCT) for the general reader; a paean to William Powers and his achievement—PCT; a memoir about his (Runkel's) exposure to PCT; and an integration of the research and theoretical work on PCT for those familiar with the theory. In my opinion, he succeeds in all these tasks....

— Len Lansky's complete review: tinyurl.com/lansky-runkel

van de Rijt, Hetty, and Plooij, Frans (2010). *The Wonder Weeks:*
How to stimulate your baby's mental development and help him turn his 10
predictable, great, fussy phases into magical leaps forward. Kiddy World.

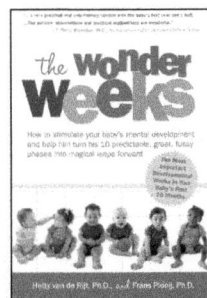

The Dutch title for *The Wonder Weeks, Oei, ik groei!,* can be translated as Wow, I am growing! Since the original Dutch version was published in 1992, it has sold more than 550,000 copies—in a country of 17 million, one 20th that of the U.S.

This book shows how and when the levels of perception outlined by Hierarchical PCT develop in human infants. The English edition enjoys excellent reviews at Amazon and numerous comments by mommy-bloggers, saying that the predictions about the timing and nature of infant mental development in the first 20 months are right on.

Twijnstra, Margreet H. and Plooij, Frans X. (2011)
   Oei ik Groei! Voor Managers Spring door je mentale blokkades Kosmos

Dutch title translated: (Title relates to *The Wonder Weeks*, prior page).

Wow, I am growing! For Managers
Jump through your mental blocks

This work features interviews by organizational consultant Margreet H. Twijnstra with 15 top managers who tell of crises in their lives. Frans X. Plooij provides an overview of PCT and explains what is going on during the crisis periods in terms of reorganization, a concept that is integral to Perceptual Control Theory.

Papers recommended – download and enjoy!
These and many more at www.livingcontrolsystems.com

Powers, William T. (2009).   *PCT in 11 Steps.*

Powers, William T. (2009).   *Reorganization and MOL.*

Powers, William T. (2007).   *On Emotions and PCT: A Brief Overview*

Soldani, James (1989).   *Effective Personnel Management:*
      An Application of Control Theory.

Soldani, James (2010).   *How I Applied PCT to Get Results.*

Forssell, Dag (2013).   *The Experimental Method is Crippling Psychology.*

www.ingramcontent.com/pod-product-compliance
Lightning Source LLC
Chambersburg PA
CBHW080403270326
41927CB00015B/3328